THE MISSILE NEXT DOOR

THE
Missile
Next Door

The Minuteman in the

American Heartland

GRETCHEN HEEFNER

HARVARD UNIVERSITY PRESS
Cambridge, Massachusetts
London, England
2012

Library of Congress Cataloging-in-Publication Data

Heefner, Gretchen.

The missile next door : the Minuteman in the American heartland /
Gretchen Heefner.

p.   cm.

Includes bibliographical references and index.

ISBN 978-0-674-05911-5 (alk. paper)

1. Minuteman (Missile)   2. Intercontinental ballistic missile bases—United
States—History.   3. Cold War—Social aspects—West (U.S.)   4. West
(U.S.)—History, Military.   5. Great Plains—History, Military.   I. Title.

UG1312.I2H43   2012

358.1'75482097309045—dc23   2012003666

For my parents
and
of course
for
Brian

Contents

Introduction

A Strange New Landscape

On August 4, 1996, Paul Jensen did something he never thought he would do. He blew up a piece of his ranch land—the same land that his grandfather had homesteaded nearly 100 years earlier. It was a clear, crisp morning when he pushed the button that set off a large underground explosion. A few hundred yards away a plume of concrete dust spread into the air with a poof and then fell back to earth. The handful of men standing with Jensen cheered and applauded.[1]

Technically Jensen was not detonating anything on *his* land. More than thirty years earlier his father had signed that particular plot over to the U.S. government in perpetuity, for national defense. From 1963 to 1994 a Minuteman intercontinental ballistic missile (ICBM) was implanted there, buried some three stories belowground in a silo, a concrete shell hardened to protect it from a potential nuclear attack. The small plot of land required for the missile—just 2 acres— was protected from the world with an 8-foot-tall chain-link fence. Inside the fence the land was barely distinguishable from the surrounding plains—a few antennas, level ground, and a concrete silo lid were the only markers of Armageddon. If the Soviets wanted to pick a fight (something this missile was supposed to ensure they did not do), they would have something coming to them. Actually they would have a lot coming to them. Between 1961 and 1967 the U.S. Air Force buried 1,000 Minuteman missiles across tens of thousands of square miles of the Great Plains. For three decades those missiles remained underground, cloistered on constant alert, capable of delivering their payload—a 1.2-megaton nuclear warhead—to target in less than 30 minutes.

This is how some Americans lived the Cold War. Never before had the military permanently implanted its weapons amidst the population and expected life to go on as usual. People living in the missile fields were to pretend that they did not notice the chain-link fences, the high-frequency antennas, or the lumbering Air Force trucks. With a few exceptions, they were not asked to move or relocate. On the contrary, they were told that living a half mile from a missile silo was no big deal, that their cattle could graze on pastures nearby, that they could get close to the fence. One of the missile silos was a few hundred yards from a school.

During that time Jensen drove by that 2-acre plot of land in the middle of his ranch, stopping at times to think about the missile buried there. Often he stopped just to wonder about the runoff that seemed to bleach the color out of the grass and soil—dead spots spilling out from under the edges of a government-issued chain-link fence.

For Jensen, blowing up the silo brought satisfaction—getting rid of the scar on the land, having a full ranch back, saying good-bye to the military, going back to the way things used to be.

Of course, the way things used to be was a long time off now. Much had changed since the day in 1961 when someone from the Pentagon came and told Paul's father, Leonel, that his land had been selected to house a nuclear missile. For one, the Cold War was over, which was why the missile could come out. The international struggle that had for decades cleaved the world into two spheres had crumbled along with the Union of Soviet Socialist Republics. In those years, South Dakota lost nearly 30 percent of its rural population, a sign of a collapsing farm economy. Paul Jensen was one of them: he had moved from the family ranch house, opting instead to live in Rapid City for the economic and social opportunities there. After nearly a century in the family, the ranch was now run by farmhands.

It may have seemed particularly peculiar, then, that blowing up a missile silo was so anticlimactic. A poof of smoke and the ground caved in. An outsider would not notice the difference. The wind did not stop its relentless howl to note the passing of an era. Indeed, if one were looking for continuity across the decades, something steady amidst all the change, perhaps it could be found in this land, the rolling prairie of western South Dakota—the short, tight grasses that fell and rose, interrupted only occasionally with river breaks, prairie dog towns, and exceedingly scarce and gnarled trees. The weather and the rain changed the contours of the plains, pushing and pulling and moving the heavy claylike soil. But such minute detail could not surmount the overwhelming feeling of sameness that confronted most outsiders when they entered this particular place.

It was, in fact, a sameness that was hardly broken by the presence of the Minutemen. Despite the vastness of the missile program, very few people outside of the missile fields knew much about it; certainly, few people knew where the silos were, and even the people who did know generally chose not to think about them. The Minutemen were hidden in plain sight—implanted in out-of-the-way places whose vast desolation seemed to swallow up the meaning of the weaponry. Perhaps, then, an unremarkable end to Jensen's Minuteman silo was appropriate.

We are still meant to overlook the plains, to continue past those silences and let the remnants of concrete missile silos leach into the ground. But there is a story buried there, too, a story that belies the myth that nothing happened here during the Cold War. In a literal sense the Cold War was never fought—there was no thermonuclear war. There are no Cold War battlefields in the United States. We are told that Cold War tensions were released instead through so-called proxy wars—tragedies in Korea, Vietnam, Angola, Afghanistan, and elsewhere—allowing the Cold War to leave its mark on distant lands, providing most Americans with a comfortable detachment from the meaning of this conflict.

But scattered here and there across the Great Plains are scars: an imploded missile silo in Chugwater, Wyoming; the charred remnants of a chain-link fence near Newell, South Dakota; the extant and fully operational missile silo in Great Falls, Montana. Here are the leftovers of deterrence, the residue of the Cold War, uncomfortable reminders of what the government asked and in some cases still asks of the population and what was taken away. And within these leftovers is the story. It is a story of how Americans came to live with the Cold War, how they came to accept the tenets of nuclear deterrence and to live, in some cases, literally next door to nuclear weapons.

This is also a story that risks disappearing into its own "success." After all, the Cold War is history. The missiles, we are told, served their purpose: there was no global war. As Jensen's story suggests, many of the Minutemen have been deactivated, taken from the ground, and dismantled. We are told that nuclear deterrence is no longer our bulwark against global conflict. We have stepped back from the precipice. Our children no longer wake from nightmares about thermonuclear war. Our contemporary nuclear fear, a dirty bomb or rogue nuke, is of a different variety, less cataclysmic. The massive armaments of deterrence do not make sense in the age of global terror. Not even the people of South Dakota who lived for so long with the Minutemen seem to want to tell the missiles' stories. But these silences and spaces are as misleading as the quiet that fell over the missile fields during the Cold War.

In fact, of the 1,000 Minuteman missiles deployed in the 1960s, nearly half of them remain. Those are 450 ICBMs still capable of reaching targets around the world as quickly as you could have a pizza delivered to your door. This represents countless megatons of thermonuclear material—enough to turn the world into what journalist Jonathan Schell once warned would be a "republic of insects and grass."[2] This means that thousands of Americans still live next door to Armageddon. We still require billions of dollars to staff and maintain those concrete holes in the ground.

The Minutemen were initially designed in the late 1950s in the service of nuclear deterrence: the idea that the United States had to amass enough nuclear warheads to ensure that the Soviets would never launch a first strike. "Deterrence is simple if extraneous frills are eliminated," President Eisenhower was reminded by a scientific adviser in 1958. "It is not a selective attack on military bases. It is crude mass devastation and mass murder."[3]

Each slender Minuteman missile was built to rest for long periods in an underground silo, covered with a concrete blast door. Ten missiles were linked to one centrally located launch center, also underground, where two missile officers sat, twenty-four hours a day, ready to launch their missiles. Each missile had to be at least three miles from the next—which is why the missile fields were spread out across tens of thousands of square miles. The logic was that in order to "neutralize" all 1,000 Minutemen, the Soviets would have to lob no less than 1,000 of their own missiles at the United States. As one critic charged, the heartland would thus serve as a giant "sacrificial sponge." Many area landowners thought of the silos as giant red bull's-eyes, their ranches always in the crosshairs of a Soviet missile.

This book explores this hidden landscape of nuclear deterrence and its ongoing legacy. It is the first recounting of how and why nuclear Minuteman missiles were placed in people's backyards, and how they treated those missiles once they were there. This story takes place on multiple levels, from strategic decision makers in the White House and Air Force down to rural ranchers in places like western South Dakota. Tying these threads together sheds light on critical questions of the Cold War: How were people convinced to live for so long next door to nuclear weapons? Did anyone protest? Who decided where they would go? Why did this country build so many? If the Cold War is over, why do we still have them today? Are the decommissioned sites contaminated? What else would people be willing to live with in the name of national security?

The Missile Next Door is concerned with the intimate and surprising ways the modern national security state transformed politics and society in the United States. The Cold War demanded unparalleled levels of peacetime military spending and organization. The federal government expanded with the creation of the Central Intelligence Agency, the National Security Council, a unified armed services, and a permanent Department of Defense. Defense spending ballooned, equaling 10 percent of the nation's economy in the 1950s.[4] In turn, many Americans came to understand the federal government—"the state"—not just in terms of the social programs and policies historians have examined, but also through the defense bureaucracy. This was most obvious for the men and women who served in the military, but the vast network of defense installations also created new dependencies and relationships. Communities and regions across the country became tied to Pentagon funds, leading to what anthropologist Catherine Lutz has called "the military normal."[5]

The stakes in understanding the role of the national security state—not only how it took shape, but also how it became so ordinary—are considerable. Decades after the fall of the Berlin Wall, more than 20 percent of the nation's budget goes to the Department of Defense, a figure that underreports the actual dollars spent on defense-related items.[6] That is as much as is spent on Social Security each year and exceeds the rest of all discretionary spending combined—for sectors such as education, transportation, diplomacy, and energy. Defense spending plays an enormously important role in the national economy, directly or indirectly affecting the lives of nearly all Americans. You may not work for a defense contractor, but you probably use their products or live in a district where defense spending is important.

We have yet to come to terms with the centrality of the Cold War defense establishment in modern American history. I suspect this is partly because of historical myopia; it is hard to study things one lived through. Moreover, examining a gradual systemic process is less striking than exploring moments of great social or cultural change. But the barriers are more than historiographic; they are also practical. It is simply difficult to study the military and defense bureaucracy. For one thing, the documentary record is often concealed behind walls of classification. Only people with security clearance can easily access the complete record. Moreover, there seems to be an invisible line of decorum that is threatened when investigating the nation's defenses. Is it unpatriotic to question missile programs? The latter issue highlights an important facet of the national security state: its very normalness renders it illegible. Most Americans accept the premise that national security is an important and necessary function of the government, and as a result they are often reluctant to ask difficult questions about the form and function of that project. Politically, of course, questioning national security can be deadly. During the Cold War, Red-baiting was a powerful tactic for defeating opponents. The necessity to be seen as tough on Communism led to some of the nation's most cataclysmic experiences, such as the war in Vietnam. Today the tactics aren't as crude, but national security and the so-called War on Terror evoke a similar devotion. Being tough on terror is a prerequisite for national power.

Scholars across disciplines have made important contributions to understanding this phenomenon.[7] *The Missile Next Door* is unique in using the early development and deployment of a weapon to examine the surprisingly intimate and subtle ways defense dependency took hold; how the national security apparatus was explained and justified, despite its seeming contradictions; and how Americans integrated it into their daily lives with remarkable alacrity. To that end,

I make three broad and overlapping arguments. First, local response to the national security state matters.[8] Strategic decision making is generally assumed to be above everyday politics. In the case of the Minuteman missiles the line was not always so straight. To be sure, most Americans embraced the missiles, just as they embraced new Cold War defense imperatives. In the rural West, where the missiles were deployed, defense requirements clashed with long-cherished ideas about property, land ownership, and citizenship. Even before the Cold War, rural Westerners had a long and often contentious relationship with the federal government, but these new connections would upend the tenuous balance achieved over decades of compromise and accommodation. Tracing local reaction from the 1950s through the 1990s demonstrates how Americans have contested and shaped the national security state in both practical and ideological terms.

That the rural West has long been considered a "flyover zone" is, of course, precisely why missiles were deployed there. But despite, or perhaps because of, such monikers, the region matters. It matters because its sparse population, active political participation, and iconic status as home of the rugged Western individual make it a fitting place to explore a critical transformation of the American state. As historian David M. Kennedy asserts, it is "time to revisit the Rural West."[9] In the Cold War missile fields the heritage of agrarian populism collided with national security imperatives in unexpected ways. In the early years of deployment, for example, some South Dakotans protested what the missiles would do to their property and livelihoods. Later, protest was taken into the missile fields, where people scaled fences to decry the national security state itself. All the while, others supported the arming of the heartland and sought more ways to link their fortunes to the national security bureaucracy. Missile-field residents were changed by the Minutemen—sometimes in radical ways—and their new strategies for dealing with the government have intriguing implications for "Populist" politics on the left and right even into in the twenty-first century.[10]

But this is much more than the story of how Paul Jensen and his neighbors coped with the constant reminder of Armageddon; it is also a look at how Americans in general confronted the brave new world of instant thermonuclear war and how the government persuaded them that a strategy with the potential for global genocide was an acceptable means of keeping the peace. Widespread public acquiescence was needed to bury 1,000 ICBMs in the heartland. Throughout the decades of the Cold War, public support for nuclear deterrence and its instruments had to be continually cultivated and bolstered. It took work to make Minutemen acceptable and invisible across the plains.[11] The second theme in *The Missile Next Door* is thus that the Minuteman system was much more than a weapon built for military capabilities and needs; it was also designed to help Americans embrace the arms race as a legitimate means of waging war. Beginning in the late 1950s and continuing until the end of the Cold War in the 1990s, the U.S. Air Force and its corporate partners went to great lengths to sell the Minuteman program to the public. This was not only a pragmatic quest to gain appropriations for the ICBM, but also a concerted effort to persuade Americans that while the meaning of war had changed, Minutemen would ensure that their own lives would not have to.

Finally, tracing the Minuteman system provides a distinctive lens on the creation and maintenance of what President Eisenhower would call the military-industrial complex. Scholars have examined important facets of this process—namely, how the military-industrial complex became important to certain industries and politicians and ultimately helped perpetuate the Cold War—but little has been written about how American citizens came to link their own lives to the maintenance of conflict, often in very direct ways.[12] The deployment of weapons and the gradual insinuation of military installations into local economies was an important, if poorly understood, component of this larger process. The massive Cold War budget created defense dependencies around the country, whereby citizens living near military installations became addicted to Pentagon funds. In the missile fields this relationship became macabre: much was done to keep nuclear missiles in the ground and, even more surprisingly, to acquire more of them. For many communities, such as those in western South Dakota, the Minutemen were more product than bomb.

Despite the rationales given for the missiles and the palliatives provided to worried residents, the government was, in effect, asking landowners to make their property, their homes, and their families into potential ground zeros. A Soviet weapon always targeted the missile silos. This was not quite war, just the preparation for one. And the Minutemen, while not quite soldiers, were certainly front-line warriors. It was a condition that blurred the lines between peacetime and war, that confused the balance between military and society. If the Minuteman missiles were the new technological warriors of the age, what were residents to make of the Third Amendment, which guaranteed that they would not have to quarter soldiers in a time of peace?[13]

This was one of the faces of American militarism. The United States did not become militarized in the classic formulation—a society built on and maintained by war and war making, reveling in its martial heritage and led by a military—but it did become armed in its own peculiar way. The Cold War forced Americans into asking uncomfortable questions about their own role in the world and raised doubts about long-held ideas regarding the place of the military in society and government. Would the United States have to become an armed society, a "garrison state," as President Eisenhower frequently warned? Did countering the Soviet threat constantly looming over Europe and the world necessarily mean that Americans would have to accept a state of permanent war? These were questions of great significance in the decades following World War II.

A strong national aversion to militarism and war shaped and drove the form and function of the Cold War defense establishment.[14] Private corporate partners such as Boeing, Thiokol, and General Motors carried out many of the tasks of research, development, and increasingly even operations. This approach mitigated some of the most obvious pitfalls of militarism, diffusing power between the state and private entities. But still the military-industrial complex created a unique form of economic and political militarism that placed high value on the potential bounty of weapons production and deployment.[15] The Minutemen were a case in point. By the mid-1960s hundreds of companies, communities, and individuals owed their livelihoods to this system.

The missile fields—the arming of the heartland—provided the ultimate escape hatch for ideological tensions about the role of the armed services in society. By isolating militarization in high-tech weapons and burying the weapons in out-of-the-way places, much of the country could have its massive deterrent without having to think of the consequences. Deterrence, after all, was a strategy that was meant to be forgotten. It would not do for Americans to dwell on its implications or assumptions; those were absurd enough for the people who knew about such things. Leave it to the "thermonuclear Jesuits" at the RAND Corporation to play war games and "think the unthinkable."[16] Science and technology were on the case. And the Minuteman system was created to fit perfectly into this calculation. The missiles were only slightly less visible than the place they inhabited—places like Fergus, Montana; Starkweather, North Dakota; and Prairie City, Missouri.

The Cold War and nuclear deterrence thus required uneven sacrifice. Landowners in the missile fields, like the Jensens in South Dakota, would have very intimate connections with the operation of American nuclear strategy. For the rest of the country it was a comfortably detached way of fighting the Cold War. In the end, as the Minuteman system shows, the Cold War militarized certain sections of the country so that others could be spared.

The Minuteman missile fields were not alone in this new land-scape. Many Americans who lived through the Cold War recall un-conventional military installations in their own backyards. In the 1950s and 1960s the Army deployed batteries of Nike antiaircraft missiles to protect urban areas from a Soviet air attack. Missiles sud-denly appeared on the Marin headlands in San Francisco, in Chi-cago's Lincoln Park, and at Fort Tilden in Queens, New York. Some of these small weapons carried nuclear warheads.[17] Yet the geogra-phy of nuclear America was disproportionately in the American West, creating what Valerie Kuletz has called the "geography of sac-rifice." Beginning with the first nuclear test site at Alamogordo, New Mexico, and eventually encompassing tens of thousands of square miles, the American West became "the largest peacetime milita-rized zone on earth."[18] The military had long been important to the region, of course, extending back to much-fabled frontier outposts and the Indian Wars. The Cold War amplified and transformed the scope and meaning of this relationship.[19] This was a nuclear geogra-phy marked by restricted spaces as much as by defense installations. Huge swaths of the land were made off-limits to even those who called it home. In general, not only were Cold War land require-ments far greater than those of traditional bases, but their purpose was far less understood as well. While the Minuteman missile fields were a part of this broader nuclear geography, they were also quite distinct. The missile fields were to be *living* militarized zones, con-trary to places such as the Nevada Test Site, which was closed to public view.

This strange new landscape of deterrence was not accidental. On the contrary, a handful of men in starched shirts, wielding pens and maps and grids, ultimately determined where, exactly, the United States would place and protect its weapons of mass destruction. Throughout the 1950s, decisions about nuclear weapons were increas-ingly made by a network of strategic thinkers, "defense intellectuals," as author Fred Kaplan has called them, who had a disproportionate influence on the nation's strategic posture.[20] Darkly depicted in the now-classic films *Dr. Strangelove* and *Fail-Safe*, these strategists were instrumental in creating a language and logic of thermonuclear warfare. They wrote reports, played war games, and spent afternoons crafting spreadsheets of nuclear Armageddon. They coined new terms, devised strategies, and imagined vast new weapon systems— Titans, Minutemen, the MX, B-1 bombers, nuclear submarines, Star Wars.

It is tempting to think that the Minuteman missiles were somehow an inevitable extension of the atomic bomb and the theory of deterrence. But the rapid pace and mind-boggling size of the arms race was not predetermined by the discovery of fission. Politics, men, and strategic planning determined them. The Minutemen were the result of a particular path taken, of choices made, of biases left unquestioned, and of a healthy dose of groupthink.

This book is skeptical of many of those choices.[21] The standard story of the making of the ICBM is that a small group of energetic and visionary men created the U.S. missile force—bucking bureaucracy and using good old-fashioned American ingenuity. This story is misleading. It is true that these men (and they were nearly all men) worked doggedly and often against the suggestions of their president and superiors. But by wrapping their story in the tropes of American individualism and hard work, a larger point is lost: just because these men believed in the absolute power of these missiles, that did not mean that the missiles were absolutely necessary. To be sure, the nation's nuclear arsenal worked in that nuclear war was avoided. Yet there is no evidence that the United States needed so many missiles. More damning is the fact that the United States, in deciding to pursue the Minuteman program, accelerated the arms race. Before Minuteman, the United States had missile superiority; after Minuteman deployment the United States had overkill.

Because so few people stopped to ask critical questions while the missiles were being developed and deployed, the country continues to live with this legacy. It's a legacy measured not only in the acres of land used, but also in the follow-on weapons built and proposed to enhance and protect the Minutemen, in the hours spent manning the sites, and in the hundreds of millions of tax dollars spent on missile silos rather than on other things. The tragedy lies in the fact that this trade-off was not necessary to wage—or even to win—the Cold War.

While decision makers were generally comfortably removed from the day-to-day implications of their strategizing, such theories fit less easily with life on the plains. And so it was there, on the ground in the missile fields, that the abstraction of nuclear deterrence found its way into everyday life. In the end, the arming of the Great Plains was the result of careful bargains struck between the American people, not just those in the missile fields, and the new national security state. It was a trade-off that declared certain areas to be more expendable than others; it is a trade-off that continues today. This is the story of how that happened and how for a long time almost no one seemed to notice. It is no less than the story of how some Americans were enlisted to fight the Cold War.

1

Ace in the Hole

At 5:00 AM on September 17, 1960, three U.S. Air Force trucks pulled up to the Bay Bridge Toll Plaza. It was still dark, though in a few hours the sun would burn off the fog that habitually clung to San Francisco. That Saturday would be an ideal day: crisp blue skies, highs around 70 degrees. It was a good day to build a missile.[1]

The trucks, loaded with 10-foot-wide Titan missile cylinders, rumbled across Market Street and came to rest on Grove Street, in front of San Francisco's Civic Auditorium. The night before, just a block away, *Tosca* had opened the season at the War Memorial Opera House. It was "the leading tribal rite" of fall, declared the *San Francisco Chronicle*, which also carried a brief story about the Titan's arrival. If opening night at the opera was the event of the season for San Francisco's elite, then the fourteenth annual Air Force Association Convention served a similar purpose for the nation's aerospace enthusiasts. Convention organizers predicted that for five days the Bay Area would become the "aerospace center of the world." So for the rest of the week there would be plenty of time to see a missile on the way to the opera.[2]

By Thursday, in addition to the Titan missile, millions of dollars' worth of military hardware had been deposited near city hall. Much of the material was on exhibit inside the civic center auditorium as part of the *Aerospace Panorama*, though a handful of weapons remained outside, "contributing to the city's skyline." The display was "dazzling," providing the public with a glimpse of the instruments of the newly arrived space age. There was a Bell X-1B rocket plane and North American Aviation's Hound Dog air-launched standoff missile. The Titan stood nine stories tall. The Thor-Able missile promised a trip to the moon. Alluding to contemporary fears about Soviet military superiority and the much-hyped "missile gap," reviewers noted that "the Russians may have outstripped us in the missiles but not in displaying them to the public."[3]

The real coup of the convention, however, was the unveiling of the Air Force's newest intercontinental ballistic missile (ICBM): the Minuteman. Descriptions of the weapon had been circulating since 1958, when the Pentagon funded Minutemen for development, but Thursday, September 22, 1960, would be the *"first time anywhere"* that the missile would be seen by the public, according to the Air Force Association press release. General Thomas D. White, the Air Force chief of staff, flew in for the occasion. San Francisco mayor George Christopher expressed his delight that the city could host such an important moment. Both shared the podium with NBC producer Roy Neal, who introduced the new missile. At precisely 7:00 PM White pushed a button and said "Off we go . . . ," and the gleaming dummy missile rose to a vertical static display, where it would remain through the weekend. Floodlights bathed the scene. An Air Force band played. "It was truly a heart warming sight," the convention newsletter, *The Booster*, gushed. "The big bird appears ready to defend City Hall and Old Glory, which truly in a short time it will be doing." Once fully erect the missile stood 60 feet tall.[4]

Here was the country's "ace in the hole," literally and figuratively. The Minuteman was presented as the ultimate deterrent force; it was the nuclear weapon that would keep the peace. It was also the first rocket that could be stored underground—in a hole. This was because the Minuteman was powered by solid fuels, rather than the liquid fuels that propelled the other big rockets, Titan and Atlas. Solid fuels are far more stable, making underground storage and launch possible. Air Force planners noted two major benefits to this approach. First, the Soviets would have a harder time eliminating underground weapons in the event of war. The missiles were built to be relatively invulnerable. In addition, the Minuteman could be fired remotely and instantaneously, vaulting out of its underground silo and capable of covering more than 6,000 miles in less than 30 minutes. Enough, the savvy listener would have realized, to reach the other side of the world.[5]

Push-button war, long the stuff of science fiction, had arrived. And the Air Force would not miss a chance to herald its importance. Indeed, White understood the power of image. He knew that making the Air Force the nation's preeminent deterrent force depended on the good graces of the American public. "It is only through public support that [the Air Force] gets resources," he had reminded the airmen assembled for the annual Air Force Commanders conference earlier that year. White found the topic "sufficiently important" to devote an entire session to telling his commanders how to be public relations agents. When speaking with the press, he warned, "don't try to be funny," "don't gild the lily," "don't be evasive or criticize the newspaper profession," and "don't play favorites." The stakes were considerable. In White's estimation, the Navy "out sells us." More damning still, "even the Army has seen the light." As a result those two services were basking in positive attention.[6]

By sharing the podium with the Minuteman missile in San Francisco, White was thus sending a strong signal about the importance of this new weapon. He had long been an advocate for missiles. The chief of staff had little patience for those airmen who refused to see the future. And missiles, he knew, were the future.[7]

But the questions remained: Would the American people accept the strange new requirements of this type of war? Would they allow the deployment of nuclear weapons across the country? Even strategist Herman Kahn, known for obtuse and fantastical thinking about nuclear weapons and strategy, understood this anomaly. "If somebody ten years ago had said that in the mid-'60s we would be living with thousands of nuclear missiles poised on either side," he wrote in 1961, "we would have said 'You're crazy. It's too dangerous.'" Yet in 1960 this is precisely what the U.S. Air Force had planned. And White knew it. Clearly this was going to be a complicated "sell."[8]

The Minuteman was not the first weapon featured in advertisements, magazine stories, and publicity tours. But promotion for these missiles was exceptional—and revealing—in a number of ways. The missiles introduced Americans to the nuclear space age and also required unprecedented levels of civilian engagement. For the first time, Americans would be asked to live next door to weapons of war. In promoting its latest missile system, then, the Air Force had many concerns with which to contend: Could the Air Force convince the Pentagon and Congress of the importance of nuclear missiles without eliciting larger public fears? Would Americans accept weapons of mass destruction in the heartland? Was it possible to promote a missile system that, in the end, was to be hidden away? How could you sell the population on a strategy that they were meant to forget?

While the outline of the Minuteman program has been described in numerous Air Force publications, the public presentation of the missile itself has been overlooked by scholars. But the publicity was critical, not only in getting the system built, but also in bringing Americans on board with the idea of nuclear deterrence and the Cold War. The missiles were presented to the American public as a panacea to Cold War security needs. A mere pencil-and-paper sketch in the fall of 1957, the Minutemen were rushed through development precisely as the nation was undergoing a massive reconsideration of weapons and war. In October 1957, the Soviets launched Sputnik into orbit. The era of push-button war was at hand, but it was not the Americans who controlled the lead. "Missile gap" hysteria was not far behind. Over the next few years Americans were repeatedly, though erroneously, warned that the Soviets would soon wield missile superiority, an advantage that purportedly would lead them to launch a preemptive nuclear strike against the United States. Many members of the Air Force Association and the U.S. Air Force encouraged these fears.[9]

Just as Sputnik was more than a beeping ball in orbit, the Minutemen were much more than strategic weapons. The Minutemen and the ways they were sold to the public helped inure the country to an extraordinary military landscape. The missiles were not built in a vacuum, but took careful account of public concerns as well as economic and political pressures. Only in understanding these relationships does the Minuteman program, and the nuclear arms race it was so integral to, make sense. Nothing in September 1957 pointed to the installation of 1,000 thermonuclear warheads across the United States. But just three years later, during the Air Force Association Convention, Minuteman planners were hoping for a force as much as ten times that amount. No one seemed to blink.

Part of the reason the Minutemen were pushed forward so quickly was that in the late 1950s they seemed to provide answers for yawning strategic and political questions. In fact just about everyone with an interest in missiles had some claim to the newest system. Congress needed it to fill the missile gap; the American public needed it to assuage their fears of Soviet military superiority; Eisenhower needed it to quiet those unfounded national concerns about strategic inferiority; in 1961 the new Kennedy administration needed it so as not to look feckless and weak; and all the while the Air Force needed it to keep its status as primary deterrent force. For a time the Minutemen were allowed to fill all of these needs; there were few real limitations on the imagining of the system and therefore few restraints on its development. Well into the early 1960s, the Minuteman program had no specific deployment numbers. Tellingly, from development in 1958 through the start of deployment in 1962, no one was certain how many missiles would be built—600? 1,000? 10,000? When the Joint Chiefs of Staff finally tried to reconcile Minuteman force levels in the fall of 1959, they noted warily the absence of basic statistics that would make their job possible. Not until 1964 did Secretary of Defense Robert McNamara sit down and set the outer limit: 1,000, a number arrived at not through careful consideration but through compromise and because it was a nice round figure. In the Minuteman program this ambiguity is precisely what allowed the perception of the missile's inexpensiveness to prevail for so long. No firm numbers, no clear performance data, and no real cost estimates were available. It was because of this general failure to articulate clear and consistent strategic and operational needs that the Minuteman's inexpensiveness would be seriously and irrevocably compromised. The ambiguity also allowed the missiles to fulfill, however erroneously, the desires of nearly everyone. It was the "ultimate weapon," Reader's Digest's "missile that closed the gap," and President Kennedy's "ace in the hole."[10]

To understand how and why this happened with little opposition, we first have to go back to the days when the Minutemen were on the drawing board. When the Air Force Ballistic Missile Division (BMD) began work on the Minuteman, no one yet realized that the missiles would have to fulfill surprising cultural functions.

In September 1957, the organization charged with building ICBMs, the Air Force BMD, opened a small, one-man office in the back of its Inglewood, California, headquarters. It was there that Colonel Edward N. Hall was put in charge of designing the nation's first instantaneous missile. Hall, by all accounts a rather irreverent but brilliant engineer, worked alone, without a secretary or assistant. Rumor had it he once tried to quit, but his resignation was not accepted. Hall named his project Weapon System Q, not for something, but simply because Q was a letter that had not been taken by another project and also had a nice "air of mystery about it."[11]

The solitary work of an Air Force engineer hardly seemed the propitious beginnings of what, in 1960, Roy Neal would describe as the nation's salvation. And it was not. In fact the difference between the humble origins of the Minuteman program and its unveiling just three years later demonstrates just how much politics, paranoia, and groupthink could influence strategic decisions.

As Hall began work on Q, there was no certainty that such a new missile would be built. Throughout 1957, the pace and size of the nation's strategic missile programs remained a matter of debate. Most strategic planners accepted the necessity of building missiles but disagreed about the resources that should be expended on them. The president was a case in point. Dwight D. Eisenhower tended to take a long view of the nation's defense, preferring measured programs with clear results. He was certain of the importance of missiles but also understood that technology would take time and that there was no point in rushing headlong into something simply because of psychological ramifications. Eisenhower was more perturbed with the "competitive publicity" of the armed services. Well before warning the nation of the military-industrial complex, Eisenhower excoriated the Pentagon for turning weapons spending into a public pissing match. Such public rhetoric would inflame passions without fact; it would escalate the arms race without regard to means, needs, or repercussions. Even if the Soviets developed the first missiles, Eisenhower reasoned, they would be so crude as to be ineffective. The strategic balance would hold.[12]

In the fall of 1957 Eisenhower was quite confident in the nation's missile programs. The Pentagon had more than thirty different missile systems under development, including two ICBMs, Atlas and Titan, both of which were to be deployed by the end of the decade.

So certain was Eisenhower, in fact, that the Department of Defense enacted budgetary restrictions that summer, including caps on overtime spending, slowing the deployment schedule for existing missiles like Titan and Atlas, and ordering the review—and probable cancellation—of redundant missiles. The intent was to avoid knee-jerk developments. Eisenhower hoped that the country would need at most 150 "well-targeted" ICBMs to deter a Soviet first strike.[13]

The men of the Air Force BMD were less sanguine, which is precisely why Hall was put to work on Q. They believed that strategic superiority required nuance; it was no longer about how much mega-tonnage you could hurl at the other side. Rather it was about how well disguised and protected that megatonnage was; how instantaneous you could make your weapons; how well you could *fool* the other side. In this context the ICBMs already being readied, the Titan and Atlas, were obsolete. Both were huge and lumbering and relied on liquid propellants that had to be manually loaded before launch, a process that could take hours and leave a significant window of vulnerability for preemptive attack. For the men of the BMD, national security depended on developing a next-generation rocket, regardless of the resources required.

In creating ever-more sophisticated weapons, the BMD had important allies. As Hall tinkered away in Inglewood, more prominent missile advocates—a group *Time* magazine called the "missilemen"—turned rocketry into a public spectacle. "With every tick of the clock," missile advocate Trevor Gardner warned in 1956, "the Soviet Union is moving closer . . . to knocking this country out. Intercontinental air power and missiles are the new double-edged sword of destruction, hanging by a hair over us all." Gardner assured the public that the Soviets were ahead of the United States in ICBM development. Here were the makings of the missile gap. Weapon System Q would be ideally positioned to plug the perceived hole.[14]

But there was another side to Weapon System Q, one that belied the appearance of prudence. As Eisenhower warned, the armed services were in constant competition for resources and prestige. Q was a pawn in this game. The Air Force was preoccupied with maintaining its position as the nation's premier nuclear deterrent force, but challenges seemed to come from everywhere. The biggest threat was the Navy's Polaris program, a small, solid-fuel rocket to be deployed on submarines. Polaris was actually ahead of Q in development, and Pentagon officials suggested, on numerous occasions, that the Navy's technology be employed for the land-based missile. There were few things that could have displeased the Air Force more. For the BMD, Q was thus a means not only of plugging a strategic hole, but also of solidifying the Air Force as the nation's preeminent power.[15]

In the fall of 1957, Edward Hall was not unaware of these issues, but he approached the problem of a new missile as he did most problems, as an engineer. Like most of the early missilemen, Hall came into rocketry by happenstance. Born Edward Nathaniel Holtzberg in New York in 1914, he received his bachelor's and graduate degrees in engineering from the City College of New York—degrees that *Time* magazine would later term the "essential emblem of the missileman." During the Great Depression Hall had trouble finding work, partly, he suspected, because of anti-Semitism. He changed his name to Hall, without measurable impact on his career prospects. To make a living he worked a variety of odd jobs as an electrician, mechanic, and steam fitter. By the late 1930s he was looking for new opportunities and found the U.S. military. In 1939 he enlisted in the Army Air Corps and in 1941 was shipped to England as an officer. There he applied his varied experiences and capabilities and was both praised as a problem solver and castigated for cocky impudence.[16]

It was at the end of the war that Hall's career intersected with missiles. In the spring of 1945 the young officer was sent to Germany to investigate and gather materials from the Nazi rocket program. During the last year of the war the V-2s had rained terror on

London. From that program everyone realized that truly long-distance rockets—those of intercontinental capability—were possible, and it would simply be a race to see who could come up with them. The Americans desperately wanted to know how the German V-2 was built and to acquire as much of the research, equipment, and personnel as possible. Under Project Paperclip, hundreds of Nazi scientists, such as Wernher von Braun and Arthur Rudolph, were brought to the United States, where they played leading roles in the American space program. Hall did not chase scientists but instead was charged with going to Germany to examine the Nazis' rocket assembly line. Hall himself later insisted that he brought what he had found back to Wright-Patterson Air Force Base in Ohio and got to work figuring out what it all meant.[17]

From there Hall became part of a small cadre of men devoted to bringing American weaponry into the space age. He worked on the Air Force's Navaho and Atlas programs before moving to Los Angeles and the BMD. Hall knew rockets, he knew chemicals, and he was brazen. "I am not going to study [the new missile]," he informed one of his superiors. "You can sit down and study until hell freezes over." Instead, he argued, "we can design a weapon system," which is precisely what he went on to do. Moreover Hall was adept at managing the bureaucracy of the Air Force and the Pentagon. He himself reported that in the early 1950s he faked an intelligence report on Soviet rocket engines so that the Air Force would continue to fund his own similar project. Neil Sheehan has written of Hall: "when his goals were endangered, scruples that might have deterred others aroused no hesitation in Hall."[18]

In September 1957, Hall's instructions were simple: draft a development plan for a "solid-propellant inter-continental missile" available sometime in the "foreseeable future." He took to his new task with messianic fervor. He often worked all night, talking to himself and furiously scratching formulas away on the chalkboard. Nodding to Eisenhower's fiscal restraint, Hall envisioned an inexpensive underground missile deployed in the thousands—as many as 10,000. Producing this new missile in great amounts would make it cheaper—per unit—and less vulnerable to Soviet attack than the Titan and Atlas. "*All* elements of the missile," Hall repeatedly insisted, must be "simple, reliable, highly producible so that they lend themselves to mass production, and be low in cost." Fielding thousands of simple rockets would compensate for their reduced accuracy. According to 1958 BMD planning documents, the first 100 Minuteman missiles would cost $1.1 million each, but the thousandth would be nearly half that, the five thousandth less still. By way of comparison, each Titan cost more than $20 million.[19]

This notion of economic efficiency would be one of the chief justifications for the Minuteman system, no matter how compromised that rationale would soon be. From 1957 through the early 1960s a near constant preoccupation with cost runs through Minuteman planning documents—from Air Staff deliberations down to BMD memos. Similarly, inexpensiveness was promoted to the public. At the Air Force Association Convention in 1960, when introducing the Minutemen, Roy Neal insisted that these missiles had essentially reversed trends in weapons development. While this was true in a relative sense, the Minutemen were proving anything but inexpensive. By the time the first missiles were deployed, each weapon cost nearly $35 million, excluding facilities and maintenance. Every dollar spent tied more and more people and companies into the burgeoning national security state. Their development solidified the military-industrial complex, creating a long-term web of dependencies that connected the Air Force, dozens of contractors spread across the nation, and the politicians who sought to protect them.[20]

Still, in the fall of 1957, Q was a mere outline. The new missile was the project of a single engineer. There was no guarantee that the country would either need or choose to build a new missile system. If Eisenhower was to have his way, the footprint and magnitude of the missile fields, of nuclear deterrence itself, would be contained.

But his nightmare about public hysteria—stoked by interservice rivalries and inflated estimates of Soviet capabilities—was about to come true. Sputnik would change everything.[21]

We may credit Edward Hall with designing the Minuteman, but the Soviet satellite made the missiles a reality.

On the night of October 5, 1957, there may have been no better place to be than the plains of western South Dakota. The inky blackness of the autumn night sky, the wide-open expanse of prairie, and the near absence of lights would have been the perfect platform for viewing history. Don Paulsen, a twenty-seven-year-old Korean War veteran and lifelong South Dakotan, stepped out of his house in rural Wall (population 629), lay down on the cold ground, and waited. While most Americans were told that they could see the tiny object moving overhead, like an orbiting star, if they knew where and when to look, on the eastern seaboard urban lights could bleach out the sky. Their best hope, authorities said, would be to try to pick out the pin-sized speck of light with binoculars. But in Wall, South Dakota, Paulsen did not need binoculars: he could see Sputnik with the naked eye.[22]

With history in the making, the entire world turned its eyes skyward that week. Sputnik was the first man-made object to orbit earth. The satellite was essentially empty: there were no cameras, no devices, no research tools of any kind on board, yet the space age, long the stuff of fantasy and fiction, was here. Unlike long-range bombers, which could be detected with radar on their flight across the seas, satellites and missiles, both shot from rockets, were *in*vulnerable to countermeasures. Missiles, Americans learned, would someday be accurate to a matter of miles, then a half mile, then—sometime down the road—a few feet. Even the most out-of-the-way place imaginable, like Don Paulsen's yard in Wall, South Dakota, suddenly seemed as exposed as a military base along the Iron Curtain.

Sputnik was a watershed moment in the psychological Cold War. It left Americans feeling vulnerable, behind, and scandalized. Senate majority leader Lyndon B. Johnson led the convulsions of national anger and fear. He predicted the day when the Soviets "will be dropping bombs on us from space like kids dropping rocks onto cars from freeway overpasses." The editors of *Newsweek,* mincing few words, declared that a dozen or more Sputniks "equipped with H-bombs" would "spew their lethal fallout over the U.S. and Europe." Sputnik also provided the missilemen with a powerful tool for bashing the president and his Grand Old Party. Senator Henry Jackson, a Democrat from Washington and a fierce cold warrior, argued that Americans under Republican leadership were losing the war for space. He declared that first part of October "a week of shame and danger." With shrill alarms in the nation's dailies and the patterns of election-year politics raising the rhetoric, Americans were soon preoccupied with missiles. The missile gap and the answers of the missilemen were not far behind. It was not that the missilemen were correct, but rather that they seemed to have ready-made solutions to the crisis of national confidence.[23]

Public concern and Sputnik also pried open Eisenhower's legendarily tight fists (though they do not appear to have altered his own assessment of the nation's strategic position). Within months the president was forced to reconsider his defense ceilings, loosening the constraints he had imposed on military spending. The nation's missile programs—Weapon System Q in particular—were the direct beneficiaries. By February 1958, Q was a weapon under development. Funding and support were forthcoming. The name "Minuteman" had begun to adhere. The Pentagon approved Minutemen for research and development by March. In just five months Q had gone from idea to weapon, an extraordinary feat in a time of peace. The Air Force projected that an operational Minuteman ICBM could be available by 1963, but quickly—and seemingly unrealistically to many—that date would be revised to 1962.[24]

Sputnik also revealed the elite world of strategic thinking and planning to unprecedented levels of public attention. Most defense planning remained highly secretive, cloistered in the halls of the Pentagon, the White House, and the armed services. But post-Sputnik fears of a missile gap led to widespread public participation in conversations about Cold War defenses. Suddenly Americans were interested in the types of weapons that were supposed to protect them from nuclear annihilation. Almost overnight newspaper readers learned a new vocabulary; headlines tracked decisions about missile systems, numbers, and war-fighting capabilities. Terms such as "ICBM," "IRBM," and "SLBM" became recognizable acronyms denoting the missiles soon to be in the nation's arsenal: intercontinental, intermediate-range, and submarine-launched ballistic missiles. The language of nuclear warfare, "counterforce," "first strike," "no-cities," "window of vulnerability," and "mutually assured destruction," was cycled into popular discourse. So absurd but ubiquitous was this language that it was quickly satirized in Stanley Kubrick's film *Dr. Strangelove* (1964).[25]

More seriously, the Minutemen were quickly caught up in these public arguments about the size and nature of the nation's deterrent force. Almost certainly some version of the missiles would have been built, but without Sputnik and the missile gap, the Minuteman would have been a different program. Developed in step with the dawn of the nuclear space age, the Minutemen were inextricably tied to larger popular and political concerns about the Cold War. Right away the men of the BMD had to sell their idea to the Pentagon, but soon they would also have to turn their attention to a broader audience. And in the late 1950s the public was listening.

The need for salesmanship was in part why Ed Hall lost his job. In the fall of 1958 he was shipped off to France to work on a NATO program. Given his abrasive character, Hall was not the man anyone wanted trying to sell the new missile to the Pentagon, the president, or the American people. The Minuteman program instead would be left to Air Force officers Lieutenant General Otto Glasser and General Samuel Phillips, both of whom were better suited to the politics and diplomacy of weapons procurement.[26]

It would be up to these men to translate Hall's weapon into a working and sellable rocket. Hall's design was an abstraction—an engineer's match for the questions at hand. Hall had never identified precisely where in the country his missiles would be deployed. Nor did anyone yet know how many Minutemen would be approved— estimates ranged from 47 (thanks to budgetary limitations) to 10,000 (Air Force dreaming).[27] Until 1960 no real estate had been appraised. Like plastic overlays, new ideas about space and war would be placed above and below Hall's own plans, eventually creating the missiles' own peculiar nuclear geography. The map would be messy and transient, shifting with the strategic winds, but Hall provided the first hazy outlines of how, if not where, the Air Force could deploy the Minutemen.

2

Selling Deterrence

An early indication that Weapon System Q would be something quite different was its eventual name: Minuteman. Most missile systems had climbed into the pantheon of mythology—Thor, Jupiter, Titan, Atlas, Nike, and Zeus. Weapon System Q, apparently, was to have more earthly aspirations. Though Ed Hall had initially called the missile "Sentinel," a morning commute changed that. On the way to work in early 1958, before Hall lost his job, Generals Bernard Schriever and Charles Terhune got to talking about the name. Schriever, head of the Ballistic Missile Division (BMD), admitted that he did not like Sentinel because it sounded too foreign, too Old World, "too much like a European type of guard to represent a missile that was based in the United States." The alternative name, Minuteman, "would mean something to the people of the United States." It would make the missile uniquely American. By June 1958, "Minuteman" was in wide use.[1]

The Cold War gave new urgency to the need to borrow from the past. Imagining the Minuteman missile as kin to the musket-bearing Revolutionary minutemen could provide much-needed continuity for what was rather quickly becoming an ambiguous and omnipresent conflict. The reality, of course, was that nothing was terribly similar, but the suggested commonality gave Americans yet another means of envisioning their present predicament as nothing out of the ordinary. Both representations of the minuteman reified the ideal of an antimilitaristic, antiaggressive people, responding only when provoked by tyranny. Moreover, the name and its cultural weight provided a means of mitigating any dystopian associations with this new technology. The memory of the Revolutionary minuteman, in a sense, helped domesticate the Cold War Minutemen.

The popular resonance of the nation's Revolutionary past was not lost on the Air Force. Many official publications about the missile system could not avoid referencing the historic namesake, often graphically. The shadowy figure of a minuteman, circa 1774, with tricornered hat and musket, was often superimposed on a missile. The parallels were too obvious for popular magazines and corporations to pass up: *Life* magazine declared that the new missile was the "Minuteman in modern dress." North American Aviation, the primary contractor for the Minuteman's guidance system, didn't even bother showing the missile in one of its advertisements, instead using a familiar Revolutionary minuteman statue with rifle in hand, vigilantly watching the horizon. Americans were to recall the militiamen of Lexington and Concord who had emerged from their communities in 1775 in order to stop the advance of British forces intent on squashing independence. Both would be defensive soldiers, living within their communities and ready to emerge, armed, when called upon.[2]

American high school students would have understood the imagery immediately. By the 1950s, Cold War–inspired patriotism had thoroughly penetrated textbooks, helping the nation's youth conceive of their country as a global, benevolent power. In fact, in popular textbooks such as Henry Bragdon's *History of a Free People*, much of the nation's past became a mere prelude to the Cold War and the international entanglements that would entail. Since the American

Revolution, the texts claimed, the United States had been a continual beacon of democracy, freedom, and technological progress. Patriotic symbols such as the Stars and Stripes and the bald eagle took on special significance. "Today," historian and journalist Roger Butterfield wrote, "the nation's symbols are more meaningful to us and the rest of the world than ever before." It was the "Minute Man of Concord" who through vigilance and preparation had been able to "turn back" the advancing British troops in April 1775. In actuality the story was far more complicated; the militias attacked the British on their way *back* to Boston. But the perception of American citizens rising from their communities to fight, against the odds, for their freedoms had an intoxicating cultural logic.[3]

Yet while the name "Minuteman" signaled the process of normalizing the ICBM, some incredible leaps of faith had to be made to link the minutemen of the late eighteenth century to the rockets of the Cold War. The minutemen really needed 2 minutes to get ready; the missile could be fired in less than 30 seconds. Muskets did not carry the firepower of a 1.2-megaton thermonuclear warhead (despite the fact that at times the Minuteman missile was described as a "rifle"). Moreover, while the militia was to protect a community under siege, the missiles would actually mark rural communities with giant red bull's-eyes as the enemy's prime targets. Accordingly, the task of Minuteman missile publicity was actually to create an updated version of the minutemen: community warriors in "modern dress," as *Life* suggested.[4]

This imagery was hardly accidental; the Air Force, like its close affiliate the Air Force Association, was no fool when it came to public relations. Beginning with the interservice rivalries of the late 1940s, the Air Force had honed its sales pitch to an unwavering hum. What would later be called "junkets"—flying congressmen, community leaders, and others around on Air Force planes to Air Force events—were already well in place in the 1950s. The use of such planes to ferry people to and from the Air Force Association Convention in San Francisco in 1960 prompted congressional inquiry. Many of the congressmen integral to funding the Minuteman program had taken such flights before the decade was out. Moreover, the Air Force had willing private partners: businesses such as Boeing, the main contractor for Minutemen, were more than ready to go along with the publicity onslaught. By the 1960s the art of public relations was so well mastered that Senator J. William Fulbright accused the Pentagon of having Madison Avenue pretensions. It was exactly this sort of public campaigning that led Eisenhower to warn about the military-industrial complex. So many ads picturing missiles were placed in the nation's glossies, in fact, that upon leaving office Eisenhower decried the "insidious penetration of our own minds" with images of weaponry and war.[5]

The annual Air Force Association Convention was the capstone of such efforts. It was at such meetings that missile contractors, subcontractors, Air Force officers, newsmen, and strategists got together to promote the policies and products of air power. The San Francisco convention boasted 4,000 registered participants, including seventy-eight executives from General Electric. General Motors was there, "showing how the Nation's biggest automobile maker is now fully committed to producing parts for missiles." Seventy-four Air Force generals were on hand to answer questions. Weapons contractors spent hundreds of thousands of dollars transporting and erecting dummy weapons across the plaza.[6]

The convention was little more than a publicity event. To be sure, business took place—albeit behind closed doors in some of the city's finest hotel suites—but at heart the convention and the military hardware deposited in the plaza were advertisements for the idea of air power. "For a man with clearance for secret information," an unnamed "industrialist" told the *Chronicle*, "I am not going to learn anything . . . at the Civic Auditorium." But the general public could. "A trip through the Panorama," *Air Force Magazine* boasted, "provided a broad education in defense . . . part of the USAF-industry-AFA programs to inform the public." Conference organizers hoped that tens of thousands of people would flood the auditorium when the panorama opened to the public. People were encouraged to take pictures. Later the Air Force Association reported that 61,000 had indeed come. Each one of them had passed the Minuteman missile on the way in. Here was the weapon that had solved the problem of deterrence.[7]

Those involved with the Minuteman went to great lengths to promote the missile system as the ultimate weapon. Beyond the name, the graphic imagery, the public unveiling, and a barrage of press releases, the Air Force made sure local and national newspapers ran stories trumpeting deployment. A film on the Air Force missile program, narrated by Walter Cronkite, was commissioned. Air Force commanders were encouraged to attend not only the Air Force Association conventions but also Aviation Writers Association conferences and other public events. Significant program events from missile tests to base openings were primed with publicity. Minuteman program director Sam C. Phillips conducted television interviews in areas where the Minutemen were to be deployed. Tellingly, the Air Force sanctioned its own accounts of the program: one top secret and another intended for public review. Both were completed in 1962 before the first wing of Minuteman missiles was operational. The latter, *Ace in the Hole*, was penned by Roy Neal. According to Hall, Schriever actually conceived of the book in order to "carry the message of the Air Force's greatness to the public." The Air Force Information Office assigned a program officer to the project— someone Neal would later refer to as a "collaborator"—and helped Neal get in contact with his eventual publisher, Doubleday Books.[8]

The Air Force probably got the most bang for its buck in well-placed popular magazines such as *Reader's Digest*, *Fortune*, and the *Saturday Evening Post*. "Minuteman is a military miracle," declared *Reader's Digest* in its celebratory 1962 coverage of the first Minuteman missile wing. Minutemen redeemed many of the failures that

Sputnik had laid bare—in just a few short years the country had overcome its technical shortcomings, recouped from national humiliation, and created the "most important U.S. weapon since the atom bomb." Minuteman "is an achievement few believed could be accomplished so quickly," *Reader's Digest* gushed. "That it is already a powerful force-in-being is perhaps the most impressive lesson yet taught to liberty's enemies."[9]

Indeed *how* the Minutemen came into being was nearly as important to the sales pitch as what the Minutemen would mean for national security. Minutemen are "a great credit to our country," Major General O. J. Ritland, commander of the Air Force BMD, raved to the Aviation Writers Association, and not simply because they signified technological achievement, but also because they seemed to prove American economic might despite overwhelming odds. Alluding to the humiliation of Sputnik and early Soviet advances in ICBMs, Ritland argued that the new missiles signified that the United States had "been able to meet the [Soviet] challenge and to surpass—democratically and through the free enterprise system— Soviet advances in the fields of ballistic missiles." It was no small feat, Ritland reminded his audience, since the Soviets had a state-centered and "highly disciplined" system that could force innovation with singleness of purpose and without the constraints of public opinion. And the public celebrated: Minutemen, it seemed, resolved many of the failures that Sputnik had laid bare. "If a missile gap ever really existed, it doesn't now," concluded *Reader's Digest*.[10]

Ritland was hardly the only one to imagine Minutemen as the glorious product of American business practices. The Air Force frequently played up its relationships with U.S. corporations, claiming that its business-minded approach saved time and money. During the official turnover ceremony of the first wing of Minutemen in Montana, the audience was reminded that the system was the "product of a military-science-industry team," which had created a "bold new concept in defense." According to the Minuteman program director, Sam Phillips, this close partnership both helped ensure competence within the military and allowed corporations to use federally funded research and development for innovations they could also use in commercial sectors. Like the RCA televisions and Sears dishwashers proliferating in the new suburban home, Minutemen could be mass produced. Minutemen were everyman's missile, a Chevy instead of a Cadillac: the "poor man's missile," *Time* called it without derision. The underlying message was that American economic efficiency not only bolstered defense but also enhanced consumer choice. Minuteman missiles were not a monster to be feared, but a product to be embraced. The symbiotic relationship was proof of American economic prowess. Minutemen were thus more than missiles. They were also weapons in the economic and ideological Cold War. Minutemen were evidence of capitalism's triumph over communism.[11]

Connecting Minutemen to national touchstones like the Revolutionary minutemen and free-market ideology would hardly get the system built. Nor would such parallels alone erase the true purpose of the nuclear weapon. But in many ways these images worked because they tapped into long-running national ideas about war and society. Through these ideas Minuteman missiles—like the airplane and naval power before them—were cycled into a cultural narrative about how the United States behaved during conflict. That story looked something like this: American weapons were never offensive or aggressive; instead they were defensive and nonthreatening. The United States was not particularly aggressive or militaristic, but rather a righteous and wary defender, coming to the aid of the world in only the most urgent of times.

From the earliest days of the republic, the nation preferred to present itself in opposition to Old World militarism. No matter how fanciful the notion (pacifist A. J. Muste would declare that the country was "trading in one form of militarism for another"), it was one the nation clung to even in the midst of war. It was for these reasons that historically a large standing army had never been permitted; that the militia of Concord was praised as the ultimate in community defense; that until the Cold War the War Department existed only in wartime; that universal military training had been rejected following World War II. The Cold War, of course, changed much of this—the temporary War Department became the Department of Defense, replete with one of the largest office buildings in the world; for the first time peacetime defense budgets became a topic of national discussion; and civilians were asked to participate in civil defense drills though war had not been declared. But despite this disjuncture, many Americans clung to traditional attitudes about war—searching for ways to avoid reckoning with the nation's new status as a military colossus.[12]

The commander in chief was terrified of the implications of creeping militarism. Eisenhower's "New Look" hoped to stymie military excess by channeling money into powerful weapons rather than armies, into avoidance rather than war-fighting capacity. Deterrence and the New Look fit well into a broad national narrative about war. Americans believed that their country would never strike the first blow and that the goal of the ever-expanding military was to *deter* war, not to fight one. The concept of nonaggressive strategic offensive capability—a deterrent force—provided a powerful rationale for the hundreds of millions of dollars that were soon being poured into nuclear delivery vehicles, namely, missiles.[13]

Eisenhower's firm rejection of ever-escalating military budgets accentuated another long-running trend in American views on war: the idea that technology could solve all problems. Americans had long used the promise of technology to resolve tensions between their fear of a garrison state and the need for national defense. The atomic bomb was the ultimate, though hardly the only, representation of this tendency. Atomic weapons and long-range bombers allowed war to be fought at a distance without ground troops. In the most extreme assessment, technology would make war obsolete.

According to journalist Walter Lippmann, the atomic bomb fulfilled a deep but totally unrealistic American desire to avoid war. The consequence was an inaccurate assessment of what it took to actually fight a war. The bomb, Lippmann wrote, was the "perfect fulfillment of all wishful thinking on military matters: here is war that requires no national effort, no draft, no training, no discipline, but only money and engineering know-how of which we have plenty. Here is the panacea which enables us to be the greatest military power on earth without investing time, energy, sweat, blood and tears, and—as compared with the cost of a great Army, Navy, and Air Force—not even much money." The problem, as Lippmann understood it, was that Americans were removed from the horrendous realities of war, which perhaps were all that could keep them from fighting one. Such weapons allowed Americans to have the ultimate means of fighting without having to sacrifice. As a rancher who had a missile implanted on his land would later admit, he would rather have a missile next door than send his son to battle.[14]

The Minutemen would take faith in technology to the extreme, nearly totally divorcing society from the implements of war. In the space-age Cold War, inanimate objects rather than men would wait in the countryside, constantly vigilant and armed, ready to emerge from the prairie to do battle. The minutemen had been fully displaced by the Minutemen. It was, according to *The Bulletin of the Atomic Scientists*, one of the few critical voices on nuclear strategy in the 1950s, a victory of technocracy over humanity. So complete was this replacement that the men involved in operating and maintaining Minutemen—the missileers—were hardly warriors at all. Certainly, declared the *Bulletin*, they were no relation to the warriors of the past. Instead the missileers were "technicians" who came to work in "white coverall-type uniforms, hard (safety) hats, and bright colored scarves." Much like the white-collar executive of the postwar period, missileers reported to work at missile facilities with "briefcases in hand." Their purpose was to turn some keys, enter a few codes, monitor control panels, and, if it came to it, mete out "biblical justice." For the scientists at the *Bulletin,* Henry Adams suddenly seemed prophetic. In 1862 he had written, "Some day science may have the existence of mankind in its power, and the human race will commit suicide by blowing up the world."[15]

The most important consequence of selling these missiles to the public was not the fact that it helped get the missile built, but that the sales pitch created a justification for the expansion and acceleration of the program even when it was not necessary. In creating the expectation of the "ultimate" weapon, the Pentagon had no choice but to build it, even though by 1961 Secretary of Defense Robert S. McNamara admitted there was no missile gap. Perhaps Eisenhower had been correct and the country would need at most a couple of hundred rockets. The making of the Minutemen demonstrates that when nuclear warheads were divorced from their devastating consequences, there was no psychic limit to their production. The seeds of this ambiguity were established by the missilemen in the mid-1950s and their relentless and somewhat hysterical preoccupation with vulnerability. Vulnerability could mean anything and everything, a haziness the BMD and missile advocates took advantage of perfectly. In the Minuteman missiles, vulnerability was effectively linked to quantity and cost—meaning that one more of them could close any gap in the nation's strategic capabilities. The first Minuteman was just the beginning—the same arguments would be paraded to similar effect during the remainder of the Cold War as Minuteman I turned into Minuteman II and finally into Minuteman III, with *three* warheads and entirely new silo configurations. These were essentially three separate weapon systems using the same name and the same justifications to receive a pass from the public.[16]

While the domestication of Minutemen provided a comforting continuity for Americans confronted with the brave new world of push-button war, the long-term implications of the weapon system were hardly favorable. After the initial burst of publicity, Americans mostly forgot about Minutemen and the policy of nuclear deterrence that the missiles buttressed. For the remainder of the Cold War—and in fact beyond—decisions about the missiles were often made without the knowledge of the people they were meant to protect. Thus, since the dawn of the missile age, Americans have been largely divorced from discussions about nuclear strategy and war, unaware of the principles of massive retaliation, and confused about the meaning of deterrence. Minuteman publicity did not cause this ignorance, but it certainly encouraged complacency.

Since this era, Americans have also remained aloof from critical questions of defense spending. The Minutemen helped enshrine this disconnect, since the program was pressed forward with such urgency, using a language of efficiency as convincing as it was deceptive. The reality was that the Minutemen were never really inexpensive weapons, yet their presentation as such further undermined the country's efforts to restrain defense budgets. Despite rapidly spiraling costs in the late 1950s and early 1960s (when the average cost for each missile grew from estimates of $350,000 to $1.45 million), Minuteman programmers consistently argued that relative and marginal costs would fall—eventually. To be sure, the Minutemen were cheaper than the first-generation Titan and Atlas missiles. But just because something is relatively less expensive, it is not necessarily prudent to buy.[17]

On May 4, 1962, Sam Phillips, who became head of the Minuteman program after Hall's transfer, found himself in a bit of a bind. Working from his office in the California desert, Phillips received a list of proposed questions that Wyoming senator Gale McGee planned to ask him during a television interview. The interview was a public relations coup, part of the sales pitch the Air Force had undertaken prior to deploying a wing of 150 Minuteman missiles around Warren Air Force Base. While most of the questions were innocuous, and the type that the Air Force in fact loved to answer—how does a missile work? what does a launch site look like? how will missile deployment affect the region's economy?—number five raised red flags: does "location of this site at Warren make Cheyenne a prime target?"[18]

Phillips took a stab at answering the awkward query. In his typical upright all caps, he made notes on a yellow legal pad about how to sidestep the question by mentioning the Strategic Air Command's "strength to prevent conflict" and the "defense of freedom and rights." Classification reviewers in the Air Staff, however, wanted no part of it; there was simply no graceful way to answer a question about population targeting. Of the twelve advance questions submitted for review, it was only number five that Phillips was advised not to answer. "This is an extremely 'nervous' subject," the Air Staff review noted. We "feel the Senator would be better advised *not* to introduce the subject of Cheyenne/Warren's target priority." Moreover, the reviewer added, the reality is that Cheyenne was already a prime target, given its Air Force base. Perhaps, he went on, clearly stretching the filaments of truth, "the addition of Minuteman to Warren should make it a *less* likely target in the future than in the past."[19]

As the internal Air Force exchange suggests, the rocket age fostered considerable anxiety. Missiles meant warheads, which led inexorably to the awkward question of nuclear war. Minutemen were nothing really but weapons of mass destruction. And these weapons of mass destruction would be buried in American soil. Minuteman spokesmen had to address both novelties. Here, again, the convention in San Francisco is instructive. Despite all the technical information provided about the Minutemen, of greater note is what was left unsaid. There was no word on how many Minutemen would be needed. Not a hint as to where or how they would be deployed. No indication of how destructive the warheads perched on their tips would be.

Air Force reviewers took a similar sanitizing approach with Roy Neal's *Ace in the Hole*, the story of Minutemen published in 1962.

Neal had worked closely with the Air Force and industry partners in crafting his book as a classic story of American success: brave and innovative mavericks bucking bureaucracy and exceeding expectations to save the world. According to Neal, not only was the successful launch of the first Minuteman a military feat, but it also "created a tidal wave of optimism throughout the free world." Because of the close working relationship Neal had with the Air Force, his hagiography underwent careful review before publication. At least four different people in the BMD, including Sam Phillips, looked at the manuscript, scratching comments in the margins and blackening sections of text. While mostly concerned with issues of accuracy and classification (the range and size of the Minutemen, for example), reviewers also hoped to excise the starkest reminders of the Minutemen's purpose. It was suggested that Neal change "destroy enemies" to "defeat enemies," and instead of "destroy nations" simply say "destroy enemy targets." The "reality of the terrible power of the national defense" was changed to "the reality of the national defense." More than one reviewer balked at the use of "nuclear impasse" to describe deterrence—better to use "credible deterrent." "Egad!" someone wrote in the margins, "impasse implies war-winning capability!" The text was changed accordingly. While not all the requested changes were made, Air Force reviewers clearly hoped to promote a weapon of defense and deterrence, not provide reminders of nuclear war.[20]

With regard to the Minutemen, the Air Force had a few things to hide. The reality, as General Curtis LeMay told the House Committee on Government Operations in 1960, was that the proposed hardened Minuteman sites would help reduce total American casualties in the event of war, but not by sparing residents of the missile fields. ICBMs would, in fact, "draw some of the enemy ICBMs or submarine-launched missiles away from our population centers which would otherwise be their targets." While there was little public discussion of targeting, internal Air Force planning documents made no pretense about the logic of deploying thousands of relatively cheap missiles: it would require the Soviets to build even more missiles if they hoped to disable the missile fields. Ed Hall and the BMD insisted that should the Soviets attempt an attack on the United States they would be *unable* to destroy the Minuteman force—even if they lobbed 900 5-megaton ICBMs at the missile fields. "Even in the face of a most severe attack by Soviet missiles . . . the exchange rate in terms of numbers would be very favorable to the U.S.," a study by the Department of Defense's Weapons System Evaluation Group suggested in deadpan fashion.[21]

The implications of 4,500 megatons raining down on the country amounted to a rather bleak picture. The new bombs were thousands of times bigger than the atomic bomb that destroyed Hiroshima. A small attack would kill 50 million Americans instantly and injure 20 million more. Nuclear fallout and radiation would contaminate the nation's food supply beyond repair. The head of Radiation Effects for the Atomic Energy Commission admitted to Congress: "essentially all milk supplies would be lost."[22]

But what of the Minutemen that survived national annihilation? In keeping with contemporary ideas about retaliatory deterrence, any remaining weapons would be fired en masse at Soviet urban-industrial targets. The goal, according to internal documents, was that enough Minutemen would survive to be able to "destroy 135 enemy cities." For those unclear about the meaning of "destroy," the Air Force provided a precise definition: "destruction of 75% of the floor space." For those who wanted more detail still, a parenthetical aside noted that "this corresponds approximately to 75% population mortalities." That is three-quarters of the population killed, both civilian and military. Clearly these were realities that the Air Force did not want widely circulated. They would make the process of deployment more difficult, but more broadly, dissemination of this information could promote opposition to the actual development and maintenance of the nuclear force.[23]

The Air Force was not alone in trying to massage the implications of thermonuclear war. From the dawn of the atomic age the U.S. government had actively sought to moderate public knowledge and information about nuclear weapons and war. The Manhattan Project—the nation's massive effort to build the first atomic bomb in Los Alamos, New Mexico, hidden even from the vice president— was only the beginning. The nation's entire postwar nuclear complex would be shrouded in layers of secrecy. While often motivated by national security concerns, this secrecy also had a way of taking on its own import, shielding Americans from even the most basic information about nuclear materials. While some protested at the time, it would take decades before a significant number of Americans would realize that the information kept from them in the name of national security—facts about uranium mining, radioactive waste, and testing—had, in some cases, caused them real harm.[24]

Eisenhower did not particularly want the country preoccupied with its own destruction. He believed the public had a right to know about nuclear weapons but that this information should be presented in ways that would not terrify—to "Alert, not alarm." His 1953 "Atoms for Peace" proposal was a case in point: Eisenhower's plan was to put the best minds to work on using the atom for human advancement, not assured destruction. Project Plowshares, the brainchild of nuclear physicist Edward Teller, was aimed at harnessing atomic explosions for civilian needs. One proposal was to use atomic devices to dredge a harbor in Alaska. Another projected that explosions could open gas and oil reserves. Perhaps soil irradiation could help agriculture. Federal Civil Defense materials were also bleached of fearful imagery; the message was defense and survival rather than doom. The *Duck and Cover* cartoon that millions of schoolchildren watched in the early 1950s assured viewers that a nuclear attack was no different from other types of disaster, like an earthquake or car crash; the key was to be prepared. Light clothes would help mitigate burns; wearing a hat and closing your eyes could save your vision.

The intent and effect of this information was to make the bomb seem normal and tamed so that it would not have to be feared. Perhaps more surprising than the innocuous imagery was the fact that it seemed to work: most Americans were content to ignore the bomb. As Congressman Chet Holifield lamented during one of the many congressional hearings he chaired on civil defense, "it is easier, you know, to sweep these things under the bed than it is to discuss them; because when you start discussing them the people have an opportunity then to find out what is in store for them."[25]

Yet efforts at assuaging concerns about nuclear war would become more difficult as the 1950s came to a close. There were worries about Sputnik and the missile gap, and then the peace movement remobilized around the issue of nuclear testing. Organizations such as the National Committee for a Sane Nuclear Policy (SANE) and the Fellowship for Reconciliation published sometimes graphic depictions of radiation and its long-term consequences. In St. Louis, activists initiated the "baby tooth survey," which measured the level of radioactive strontium-90 in small children. The results were grim: radiation from nuclear tests was penetrating kids everywhere in alarming doses. In 1962 the venerable Dr. Benjamin Spock would famously add his face to the cause in a *New York Times* ad telling Americans that "Dr. Spock is worried."[26]

Skepticism about nuclear safety percolated through popular culture. In the burgeoning realm of science fiction, the world of the "quiet fifties" was besieged by a menagerie of mutant creatures roused by testing and transformed by radiation. In 1954's popular film *Them!*, giant mutant ants emerged from the New Mexico testing grounds and found their way to the sewers of Los Angeles. That same year the ultimate Frankenstein for the nuclear age, Godzilla, was awakened from the depths of the South Pacific by American nuclear testing. In 1958 the United States was attacked by the 50-foot woman. By the end of the decade such dystopian visions would permeate the mainstream: 1959's *On the Beach*, about global Armageddon, was a blockbuster.

Set in Australia, the film zeroed in on contemporary fears of radiation. When the movie opens the world has already been destroyed. The only survivors live in Melbourne and are counting the days until a deadly radioactive cloud kills them as well. Their final choice is to either die a slow and painful death of radiation or take the government-issued "sleeping pill" distributed at the town square. It is their lot to ponder how man had come to destroy himself and his world.[27]

While *On the Beach* garnered critical acclaim as well as box office success, government officials took a less sanguine view. The Eisenhower administration worried that it could foment "extreme pacifist and 'Ban the Bomb' propaganda." Utah senator Wallace F. Bennett, a member of the Joint Congressional Atomic Energy Committee, proclaimed the film "distorted" and "unscientific, unrealistic and dangerously misleading." New York's director of civil defense echoed Bennett in arguing that radiation would not kill everyone and that there were adequate and possible defenses against such an outcome.[28]

Official concern about *On the Beach* demonstrates just how sanitized government officials hoped the idea of nuclear war could become. In actuality the movie was decidedly tame, eschewing graphic and gory images. The film lacks both carnage and the grim details of personal suffering. Instead the two American cities shown—San Francisco and San Diego—are structurally intact, just emptied of people. Despite the rather bland images, officials worried that *On the Beach* would make people fatalistic and glum.

The public presentation of weapons systems had to, as much as possible, avoid such pitfalls. It was for this reason that Air Force officers like Sam Phillips moderated their own comments about the Minutemen. To be sure, there was only so much anyone could do to elide the purpose of armaments and avoid the horrible realities of preparations for war. But there were ways to render aggression and destruction palatable. It was an art the Air Force had mastered. For years Air Force publications and popular depictions (including movies like *Strategic Air Command*) had helped Americans get used to the idea of air power. The message was well honed: the vigilance and commitment of the men of the U.S. Air Force could harness modern technological horrors to keep the peace.[29]

Despite the government officials' fears, the Minuteman publicity worked: combined with the nation's new sense of strategic vulnerability, the media blitz helped push the program rapidly forward with little critical thought. Rather than terrify the nation, the technology of missiles provided a safe reprieve for many Americans in the late 1950s and early 1960s. Missiles allowed Americans to ignore their country's burgeoning role as a global military power because they allowed the country, for a time, to fight without having to mobilize, to wage permanent war without feeling militarized. These attitudes would change, of course, though never radically. By the mid-1960s the mechanization of war would lead to dark cultural projections of Armageddon. Movies like *Dr. Strangelove* and *Fail-Safe* would decry the hyper-rationalization and technological takeover of warfare, showing how the missing human link could lead so easily to disaster. But by this point the Minutemen were central not only in the nation's arsenal but also in popular understanding of the Cold War. There would be no turning back.[30]

If Air Force planners, military strategists, and the general public could remain comfortably distant from these fits of absentmindedness, not all Americans were so fortunate. These missiles—whether 150 or 10,000—needed a place to call home. And increasingly it appeared such a place would be over large swaths of land within the continental United States. To make this process as seamless as possible, to "domesticate" this rather extraordinary weapon system, the Minutemen ended up being hidden in plain sight: buried underground in out-of-the-way places, scattered like buckshot in American farm fields. So while much of the country was able to believe that their country was able to avoid militarism during the Cold War, that technology and economic efficiency had secured a uniquely

American way of waging war, the reality was that small parcels of their land were militarized so the rest of the country could avoid the awkward consequences.

Even more startling still, in September 1960, as General Thomas White unveiled the Minuteman in San Francisco, the U.S. Air Force knew precisely where—down to the foot—and how it was going to deploy the first 150 Minuteman missiles. For logistical and psychological reasons, those in charge just didn't want anyone else to know.

3

The Mapmakers

Gene S. Williams grew up next door to a nuclear missile. Born on his parents' ranch in western South Dakota, Williams was a toddler in 1961 when the Air Force demanded a section of his family's land—and not just any plot. What the Air Force wanted—and got—was a nice, flat, 2-acre piece of land in the middle of what the Williamses considered a good wheat field. Not what the family wanted to sell.

Gene's father declared that having a missile on his best field was like having a 2-foot-square hole cut out of the middle of his living room. What had once been a perfectly useful place became a blank spot that could never be used again. Making matters worse, compensation for that hole was prorated based on the amount the property was worth; no consideration was given for long-term damages or general inconveniences, of which, the Williamses could attest, there were many. It was as if a homeowner with a 3,000-square-foot house worth $30,000 was given $20 to compensate him for a hole in his living room. Twenty dollars, Williams would later say, in exchange for a hole that "you're going to have to walk around . . . for the rest of your life." The family never could avoid that hole: Williams and his father always needed extra time to mow the grass around the four extra corners that the missile silo made on their property.[1]

During the Cold War the Williams family was among thousands of landowners who lost a piece of land for deterrence. Throughout the 1960s, just as the American public was introduced to the defensive benefits of the Minutemen, rural landowners learned of the missiles' geographic needs. Beginning in the winter of 1960, Air Force and Army Corps of Engineers personnel fanned out across Montana, the Dakotas, Wyoming, Nebraska, Colorado, and Missouri in order to acquire 2-acre plots of land and hundreds of thousands of square miles of easement rights. By 1967, 1,000 Minuteman missiles were underground in hardened silos, each tipped with a 1.2-megaton warhead, ready to be fired up over the North Pole and intended to land behind the Iron Curtain. The *New York Times* compared the construction of the missile fields to the Manhattan Project. The Air Force estimated that it would take 27 Soviet missiles to eliminate just one Minuteman. Underground hardening and dispersal—scattering missile silos across thousands of square miles—were that good.[2]

While most Americans were granted a reprieve, of sorts, from the immediacy of nuclear weapons and the strategy of deterrence, individuals in the missile fields were not. Each day they opened their kitchen windows and saw strange antennas poking from the ground; they shared their dirt roads—roads upgraded with military money—with armored trucks; they provided water to stranded Air Force maintenance crews; they spent extra time plowing around 2-acre "holes" in the middle of their wheat fields; they drove their children to school past missile silos. Some of them built bomb shelters; most did not.

But for all the changes the arrival of the Minutemen wrought on individuals in the Great Plains, little, if any, thought was given to their plight by distant planners—the "wizards"—who determined where nuclear missiles would go. This was an oversight born of urgency, not malice. The men who designed the weapons of the Cold War were convinced that in their work lay the fate of the nation; they did not think much about the everyday implications of their designs. Colonel Ed Hall, for example, never specified a place for his missiles. He never mentioned South Dakota in all of his work. Yet it was Hall's achievement that would prove Williams's long-term consternation. Many years, dozens of people, and layers of bureaucracy may have separated the two men, but their lives intersected in the deployment of a rocket. Connecting the dots between the two—from Hall's planning to Williams's reality—demonstrates the surprisingly intimate ways strategic policy can affect the everyday, as well as how little strategic thinking actually takes into account the very people it is meant to protect.

Hall's blueprints for the Minuteman were in some ways more staggering than what ended up taking shape. In 1957, from his office in Southern California, he envisioned a vast missile "farm" or "forest"—anywhere from 600 to a few thousand missiles deployed in a single enormous field of underground holes. This technoforest would be a giant no-man's-land, inhabited mostly by subterranean missiles, surveillance equipment, and the occasional Air Force crews that would patrol the area and fix things when they went wrong. The region would be monitored by helicopter and foot patrols. Manpower needs were limited, just five men per missile, compared to the 100 men required for a single Titan.[3]

Hall's initial plan was relentlessly utilitarian, dedicated entirely to the principle of cheap, massive retaliation. It was also potentially huge, turning tens of thousands of acres into a military reservation. Yet if the physical imprint of the Minutemen startled anyone in the Air Force, such concerns were never recorded. At no time did anyone express reservations about appropriating such large swaths of the country in what would ultimately become sacrifice zones. On the

contrary, planning documents studiously avoid nontechnical matters by employing the rationale language of deterrence, calculating
and quantifying probabilities, fatalities, and outcomes with mathematical precision, leaving little room for human implications.

There was ample precedent for such thinking. The Minutemen
were not the first weapons that would rearrange the American landscape. By the late 1950s, the military had already blocked off huge
swaths of land not just for traditional military installations, but also
as broad restricted sites with less obvious purpose. Entire landmasses
in the South Pacific were erased by atomic weapons testing. The
White Sands Missile Range and the Nevada Test Site gobbled tens of
thousands of acres of the American West for secret weapons projects.
Chunks of the map were blacked out, rendered invisible to Americans
without the highest security clearance.[4]

The Cold War took on a more everyday form as well. By 1960 few
Americans avoided some contact with the national security bureaucracy. This was particularly true in the West, where planning for war
and destruction coincided with rising prosperity. Defense installations and dollars proliferated—between 1947 and 1960 the Air Force
increased its active bases from 115 to 162. The Air Force Academy
was constructed in Colorado, and new bases sprang up in Montana,
North Dakota, and Arkansas.[5]

The U.S. government was quite simply used to rearranging space
and appropriating land for national security purposes. When Minuteman planners like Hall thus set out to plan their own nuclear landscape, they did not conceive of their project as anything terribly new.
It was assumed that a map drawn using the correct strategic and fiscal abstractions would be the right one.

Likewise, the problem of where to deploy intercontinental missiles was not a novel one. By 1957 a good deal of thinking had been
done on the subject in anticipation of the Atlas and Titan systems.
The first question was broad—would intercontinental ballistic missiles be deployed overseas or at home? While the choice for their

eventual location is obvious in retrospect, in the mid-1950s the idea
of implanting nuclear weapons in the United States was something
of a departure in strategic thinking. Before then technical limitations meant that the country's offensive weapons were deployed
overseas—either on bombers or short-range missiles—not permanently affixed to the American landscape. The simple fact was that
before the ICBM, no weapon could travel 5,000 miles without stopping. But the advent of *intercontinental* capabilities meant that basing such weapons at home was not only possible, but according to
the Pentagon's own internal think tank, the Weapon Systems Evaluation group (WSEG), increasingly desirable. Such a recommendation was made in the September 23, 1957, report "Geographical Location of Initial ICBM Units."[6]

Not everyone welcomed this change. Former Manhattan Project
physicist Ralph Lapp told Congress that he would prefer that the Air
Force took "the deterrence force out of the US" and put "it at sea."
Lapp's opposition was to making portions of the United States "mile-
wide bull's-eye[s]," which was, of course, precisely the point. According to the WSEG, the greater vulnerability of overseas ICBMs actually "weakens the deterrent effect of the ICBM, and can increase the
total hazard making an attack more likely." Thus, what may have
initially seemed attractive about overseas basing (or the ocean-based
basing favored by Lapp)—keeping Soviet warheads targeted on foreign populations—turned out to also be one of the plan's biggest lia-
bilities. Non-U.S. locations would be more vulnerable to short-range
Soviet weapons, even those of the nonnuclear variety, leaving more
Soviet ICBMs capable of attacking the United States. There was also
the issue of credibility: would the United States really retaliate if the
Soviets bombed Europe or a missile base somewhere in the Pacific?
This was hardly a novel concern, and the WSEG determined that to
maintain a credible deterrence, the United States had to keep its
long-range missiles at home. Credibility would hinge on holding the
population hostage to annihilation.[7]

At the same time, who was to say that a foreign government might not create certain "command-and-control" problems for American weapons? Early on it was thought that ICBMs could be placed in the "Arctic wastes or the Pacific Islands," an idea that would resurface periodically as the Minutemen were deployed.[8] Yet the planned transfer of intermediate-range ballistic missiles (IRBMs) to Europe had provided plenty of reasons for not sharing nuclear weapons. Already that fall the Pentagon had addressed British and Italian concerns over control of strategic weapons (would it be equal?), cost of deployment (who would foot the bill?), and the issue of consultation in the event of aggression (the Europeans wanted it; the U.S. did not). There were not only political and bureaucratic problems, but public relations issues as well. The Italians, for example, wanted all discussion of IRBMs kept top secret because of potential political fallout at home. "We must give no arguments to the [Italian] Communists," the Italian defense minister reminded Secretary of Defense Neil H. McElroy. And while the range of ICBMs made Europe an unnecessary basing location, the lessons learned on the Continent could be relevant in other locations. The primary question, at least for the Air Force, was whether or not the U.S. military would be able to maintain "complete control over the use of . . . nuclear weapons." And so it was decided that ICBMs would be placed at home.[9]

But where? It was to this question that the Air Force turned in 1957 as it made plans for the Atlas and Titan missiles. The experience did not augur well for the Minutemen. The WSEG had made a very specific recommendation in its fall report: "the north-central region, in and around North Dakota, is nearly optimal." But the Air Force would ignore that advice, instead running through its own list of bases.[10]

A primary reason was that territorial disputes within the Air Force and Pentagon stymied the simplest decisions. National security prerogatives did not trump bureaucratic turf wars. Basing plans were made through the rather opaque intersection of the Ballistic Missile Division (BMD) in Southern California, the Strategic Air Command (SAC), based in Omaha, and Air Force Headquarters and its Ballistic Missile Committee, both in Washington, D.C. A great deal more than geography separated the three. The BMD was preoccupied with fielding an operational missile force; SAC remained wedded to air power; and the Air Staff had larger political and bureaucratic concerns with which to contend. Given the personalities and objectives involved, there was bound to be confusion. And there was. While the BMD made operational plans and basing recommendations, it was ultimately up to SAC to deploy weapons based on target coverage. But SAC did not work in a vacuum. SAC's siting recommendations too required approval from the Air Staff and finally the Office of the Secretary of Defense. It was not always a welcome chain of command.[11]

The overlapping and often confusing jurisdiction over ballistic missiles was mirrored in the jumbled criteria used for missile site selection. It seemed that just about everyone involved had a specific idea about where the missiles should go—SAC planners, Pentagon strategists, eager congressmen, and, in some cases, citizens interested in housing missiles of their own. By 1960 the Air Staff listed nineteen different conditions that had to be considered before making basing decisions. Some criteria were more flexible than others. Strategic considerations—such as target coverage and dispersal (criteria 1 and 5), were nonnegotiable. Each launch site was supposed to be 5 to 7 miles from the next. "Geological conditions" were also high on the list (criterion 3), though the exact meaning of those conditions could be up for discussion. "Commuting distances," "other terrain," and "sparse population" were noted, though often ignored (criteria 11, 8, and 6, respectively). In the end it was money that most preoccupied military planners. Siting requirements like "cheap land," "economical logistical support," and "government owned land" were largely efforts to check the tendency for costs to spiral out of control (criteria 7, 10, and 17). SAC, for example, hoped to use "existing military facilities" (suggested criterion 4) as support bases for missile installations and to find regions with ample "community support," good local roads, and a labor force capable of site construction. While the Air Force originally looked to Army and Navy bases as potential ICBM sites, given the interservice rivalries of the era, neither service proved particularly amenable to sharing its property with the Air Force. As a result, by late 1957 SAC-BMD was looking exclusively at Air Force bases for missile deployment. And in case that was not enough to think about, "weather" (criterion 12) was to come into play as well—severe weather, some feared, could limit access to missile sites. Snow and frigid temperatures, for example, could lead to considerable construction delays.[12]

In 1957 the Air Force determined that the first squadron of Atlas missiles would be at Cooke Air Force Base (later renamed Vandenberg) in California, where most missile testing and training was done. In August 1957 Warren Air Force Base in Wyoming was chosen to host the next four Atlas squadrons. These would be "soft" missile bases—the missiles stored in unhardened facilities, dependent on advanced warning, early radar defense, and dispersal for survival. Even with these rudimentary specifications, the first Atlas missiles would not be operational until sometime in late 1959, and then and only then could the United States boast of having an ICBM.[13]

These realities, suitable for most military planners in early 1957, became signs of national *in*security after Sputnik. *Soft* missile bases? *Aboveground* launchers? *One* location for *all* the missiles? *Late 1959?* Hadn't the Air Force been paying attention to anything? To outside observers it appeared that American ICBMs themselves were at risk of being "Pearl Harbored" before they even left the ground.

Here Air Force planning—and frankly Air Force efforts at saving money—ran headlong into a growing hysteria over strategic vulnerability. Defense analysts at places like RAND projected that by 1960 the Soviets would be capable of launching a devastating first strike against the United States, crippling the strategic deterrent force. (Not surprisingly many of the missilemen were involved.) These analysts recommended defensive measures that would cost billions: the Air Force should bury its airplanes in underground shelters, build active defenses around bases, and create an early warning system. Another option was to keep bombers airborne at all times. Others urged a huge national public shelter program. Still more wanted to ramp up military spending—insisting that no money was too much. In late 1957—just after Sputnik—a committee appointed by Eisenhower to examine civil defense presented a report demanding 600 ICBMs.[14]

Clearly, aboveground, lumbering ICBMs like Titan would not solve the problem of vulnerability, particularly not when inflated estimates of Soviet capabilities continued to animate war planning. On the heels of Sputnik, all worst-case *estimates* of Soviet capabilities became instant fact, lending ammunition to the idea of a "missile gap." Throughout 1957 intelligence officials had warned that an "aggressive" Soviet "crash" program in ICBM development was yielding incredible results. The November 1957 National Intelligence Estimates, for example, warned that the Soviets could have a 5,500-mile missile sometime in the early 1960s and perhaps 500 missiles by 1962. That range would allow the Soviets to reach nearly all significant U.S. targets—including all ICBM bases—from relatively secure locations behind the Iron Curtain. Making matters worse, the Soviets seemed to be mastering missile accuracy. By 1960 it was expected they could hit a target within 2 or 3 miles. Add to this smaller and more powerful warheads—say, 10 to 20 megatons—and suddenly significantly fewer missiles were needed to disable the American military machine. Based on these estimates the Soviets would need only one missile to take out an entire Atlas complex; only twenty to eliminate every American ICBM.[15]

These fears were based on particular expectations of Soviet behavior, expectations neither proved nor questioned. American leaders and military planners believed that the Soviet Union was intent on domination, that should it have the capability to use missiles, it would. There seems to have been little critical reflection on how the Soviets themselves viewed the Americans' obsession with missiles, nor on the possibility that the Soviets thought about weapons in much the same way as the Americans—as a deterrent, a means of stymieing an enemy that seemed aggressive. Without this critical thinking, American military planners continued to press for more money, more weapons, and more fantastical war-making scenarios. Indeed, though estimates of Soviet capabilities were soon proved erroneous (they had only thirty-six ICBMs by the end of 1962), the Air Force used these assumptions when making decisions about the Minutemen.[16]

It was directly into this milieu of missile panic, inflated defense budgets, and rapidly expanding concepts of vulnerability that the Minutemen were deployed. And while in theory Minuteman siting teams could have benefited from the experience of basing Atlas and Titan missiles, few lessons seemed to have been learned—other, perhaps, than the perception that everything, even specific geographic boundaries, was negotiable. The WSEG's initial idea that all ICBMs should be in the nation's interior, for example, was pushed and pulled until Air Force missiles virtually blanketed the country, stretching from Washington to New York, from the Southwest to the Canadian border, and into Arkansas. And while Air Force Headquarters still insisted that the interior of the country was ideal for deployment and reserved the right to "consider separately" any location outside of that preferred zone, that zone had become ill defined indeed.[17]

The growing preoccupation with vulnerability also upended the initial operational plans for the Minuteman. Hall had wanted to deploy hundreds of missiles all together in a vast "farm," but such a farm—once thought of as relatively invulnerable—was highly exposed indeed. In step with fears of vulnerability, the idea of the missile farm gave way to a much larger and broader concept of missile "fields," a series of discrete squadrons consisting of fifty missiles and five superhardened launch control centers. Launch orders would be given to each squadron, rather than the entire missile forest, so that fifty missiles (rather than 600) would be launched either simultaneously or in a "ripple." The five launch control centers in a squadron, though technically in charge of just ten missiles each, could, in the event of an attack, fire all fifty missiles in their squadron. This configuration offered two advantages: it required the Soviets to have more targets, and it would provide greater redundancy to the U.S. missile force. But it also required more land, more bases, and, of course, more money.[18]

As these strategic changes were taking place, Minuteman planners discovered an unwelcome technical surprise: the Minutemen could not travel as far as expected. The first derivation fell short by 2,000 miles. For this reason the Air Force decided to deploy the first squadron of missiles to Malmstrom Air Force Base in Montana. Given the base's northern location and high altitude, a missile could easily make it up over the North Pole to targets in the Soviet Union.[19]

That decision was made as early as mid-1959, though the Air Force tried to keep it quiet as long as possible—so quiet, in fact, that in September of that year representatives of the Air Force actually lied to Montana's congressional delegation. They told Senator Mike Mansfield that survey crews were scouting western Montana for "underground defensive installations," which could be related to an antimissile system. The Air Force hoped this information would be passed on to curious residents and help "hide" its true intentions. The Air Force knew its tactics wouldn't work for long; a defensive installation would be limited probably to just one location, whereas engineers were out surveying hundreds of spots in Montana. But it hoped to buy some time.[20]

Nonetheless, inquiries trickled into Senator Mansfield's office, inquiries he passed on to the Air Force. Vernon Taylor, for example,

wanted to know what was happening to his land. Taylor owned the
Peerless Oil and Gas Company, about 25,000 acres in Fergus County,
100 miles southeast of Malmstrom. Taylor's first visit from the Army
Corps of Engineers was in March of 1960. He was told that a few
acres of his land were needed for national security. Other area ranchers received similar visits and were asked to sign right-of-entry permits for survey and exploration. The Corps needed these permits in
order to take detailed core drilling and seismic measures of potential
properties, basically a final check that the terrain was suitable for a
nuclear missile. The Corps would then provide this information
to the Air Force so it could draw up final siting maps—with missile
locations pinpointed to the foot.[21]

Vernon Taylor, for his part, was not particularly concerned with
nuclear Armageddon. Nor was he terribly interested in the economic
impact of missile deployment to the state of Montana. His concern
was for the economic viability of his own ranch lands. The land the
military wanted was 2,500 feet from his front door. Ceding this property would make his ranch and home worthless. While many landowners granted these intrusions, Taylor refused. On April 18 the
Army Corps of Engineers filed a condemnation proceeding against
the plot of land in question in the U.S. District Court, but before the
case was heard, Taylor relented and the appropriate samples were
taken. Taylor's battle, however, did not end there. Rather than take
on the Defense Department alone, Taylor took up the issue with
Mansfield. "I do not wish in any way to interfere with the proper defense of my country," Taylor wrote. "But there are hundreds of thousands of acres in this general area of much less value." Taylor asserted
that the siting of a silo would dramatically decrease the function and
value of his land. He also made a personal plea: the health of his
wife was at stake because she traveled between Texas and Montana
to seek relief from a lifelong illness.[22]

This was not a problem isolated to Vernon Taylor. Landowners
throughout the missile fields were at least partly right to think that

strategic planners in far-off military headquarters were playing God with their pastures. Missile-site selection was based not on local needs, but on the suitability for maximum strategic efficacy. In the rather cryptic words of one newspaper, they were selected for "mathematical and engineering reasons." It was as good an answer as Taylor was likely to get.[23]

While Vernon Taylor in Montana pressed his property-rights case (which he ultimately lost), the Air Force went ahead with its Minuteman plans. In fact, it was at precisely this moment that General Thomas White unveiled the new missile in San Francisco. But while White would laud the missile itself, he remained quiet about where exactly the missiles would go. Not even Montana was mentioned. White understood what kind of news was good publicity and what could elicit unwanted attention. Missile deployment could easily be the latter.

In fact, so reticent was the Air Force about where and how it would deploy its missiles that any premature release of information was cause for alarm. That is precisely what happened on October 23, just one month after the Air Force Association Convention, when the *Los Angeles Times* ran a detailed—and accurate—map of the Montana missile fields. "Vast Complex to Hide Forest of Missiles" announced publicly for the first time the number of Minuteman missiles to be deployed in Montana (150) and precisely how those missiles would be stationed. While correctly showing the missile fields, the article incorrectly assured readers that "the information was cleared for publication." White had never cleared such details for general release. "It is difficult to understand how this could have happened," White blasted the heads of the various Air Force commands in a November memo. He reminded everyone of the "Policy Concerning Release of Information on Minuteman" from April of that year, in which White explicitly spelled out the policy for releasing any information about the Minuteman system: all details had to be cleared at the highest levels. Clearly with the release of the

Montana map, protocol had not been followed. The inspector general would be making a "complete investigation," he warned.[24]

White had no intention of burying the Minuteman story in impenetrable layers of military secrecy. He had, after all, just recently returned from the Air Force Association Convention in San Francisco, where he was named "Aviation's Man of the Year," and shared the spotlight with a Minuteman missile during the weapon's unveiling. But what White likely understood was that Americans might find the map of deterrence startling. It was one thing to learn about the defensive properties of the Minutemen, and quite another to learn how much land they might consume. No one wanted to know that the "ace in the hole" would require thousands of plots spread across tens of thousands of square miles of private property.[25]

Even after the Air Force announced that the first Minuteman missiles would be deployed in June 1960, information remained cloudy. National newspapers reported that fifty-five missiles were slated for deployment in this first "squadron." Even that number—just part of what the Air Force was planning—was "unexpectedly large," according to the *Chicago Tribune*. The *New York Times*, too, declared its surprise at the size. But, as the *Los Angeles Times* story revealed, the originally reported number was actually too small. Instead 150 missiles would be deployed near Malmstrom Air Force Base. This was, in fact, "startling," according to the paper, particularly when "contrasted with present ICBM operational units." Recall that as of 1960 the nation had only 120 ICBMs.[26]

Startling or not, White could not necessarily answer all of the questions that could be raised. The simple matter was that in the fall of 1960 the Air Force still did not know where or how all of the missiles would be deployed. What White did know was that post-Sputnik, the program was on an accelerated schedule and that his ballistic missile team needed to have missiles in place and operational by 1962. He also knew from deploying the Titan and Atlas programs that missile siting could lead to headaches and delay. One possibility was that the map could spark the energy of those Americans interested in protesting nuclear installations. Or, even more likely and potentially time-consuming, the map could encourage politicians hoping to bring military installations to their home districts, turning weapons deployment into the political circus that procurement had become.

Senator Stuart Symington had a lot to think about in the fall of 1959. For one, there was his potential presidential run. According to the *Washington Post*, the Missourian was "the compromise candidate" amidst a field of Democratic hopefuls like John F. Kennedy, Adlai Stevenson, and Lyndon B. Johnson. Symington was in the viable, though not entirely enviable, position of being able to win if everyone else messed up. "Everyone's No. 2" was *Time* magazine's assessment. Hardly the front-runner, the Missouri Democrat had gained some stature since the days of his failed dark-horse candidacy in 1956. Symington's biggest advantage was his appearance: tall and handsome, "dignified" and "statesmanlike." He simply *looked* the most presidential. Though he had failed to make a name for himself on domestic political issues, he was something of "a self-appointed Cassandra" on an issue of increasing importance to the Democrats: defense. In 1954 he set his tone by insisting that "the United States may be more vulnerable than Great Britain was in the late thirties."[27]

The year 1959 was a good one for dark prophecies, if not dark horses. Fears of a missile gap reached new heights, at least partially due to the efforts of Stuart Symington. He was one of the most outspoken and partisan critics of Eisenhower's defense policies and budgets. From his seat on the Senate Armed Services Committee, Symington chaired—and publicized—hearings on preparedness, air power, and the missile gap. "What's the good of being the richest man in a graveyard?," Symington liked to scoff, lambasting Eisenhower's fiscal prudence. He accused Eisenhower of placing "soft living and budgetary considerations ahead of national security." In the spring Symington warned that the Soviets would have four times as many ICBMs as the United States in 1961, a claim echoed in papers nationwide.[28]

Presidential run and missile gaps notwithstanding, Symington also had to think about his constituents. Over the past decade he had proved himself an able advocate for Missouri. In 1959 his interest in defense and his desire to bring federal spending to the "Show Me State" combined in the Minuteman. Symington knew about the missiles, he knew they were going to be deployed somewhere in the continental United States, and he also knew that Whiteman Air Force Base in Missouri was about to lose its main mission, the B-47. Accordingly, earlier in the year Symington wrote to the SAC commander, General Thomas S. Power, about hosting some military hardware. "Dear Tommy," he implored in a February letter, "why can't we have one of the missile bases in Missouri?" Power directed his legislative officer to provide encouragement to Symington. "We have recommended an area which includes the northwestern part of Missouri for the first Minuteman complex," Power noted, but it had yet to be finalized.[29]

Not every senator could get away with greeting the SAC commander as "Tommy" or with hoping a request for nuclear weapons would be rewarded. But Symington was no ordinary senator. From 1947 to 1950 he had served as the first secretary of the Air Force, where his penchant for subtle arm-twisting and charming people in the right places had helped ensure the Air Force's preeminence in the Pentagon. Symington was, quite simply, an airman—he knew the Air Force, he knew its leaders, he knew its mission, and, perhaps most interestingly, he knew its intelligence. In 1956 the *New York Times* noted that "Symington is in a position to receive inside tips from Pentagon sources 'unhappy'" with the president's defense spending. Armed with the same assumptions that animated defense analysts and Air Force planners, Symington took the cause public.[30]

While Symington's connections to the Air Force may have been extraordinary, the relationships he represented between government, the military, and business were not. It was these relationships—both personal and institutional—that would lead Eisenhower to sound the alarm about the military-industrial complex. Symington's own government service had grown out of his business experience. From the presidency of Emerson Electric Manufacturing Company in St. Louis, Symington was tapped by President Truman—a fellow Missourian—to run the Federal Surplus Property Administration in 1945. From there he moved on to posts in the Air Force and then, combining business and military connections, to political office. Symington's was not an uncommon trajectory, and his path to power, the issues that he emphasized, and the connections he utilized reflect the ways that the Cold War had become both larger and smaller than a battle against the Soviets.[31]

As Symington's entreaty for missiles suggests, Cold War defense spending was big business. No respectable congressmen could avoid hungering for the crumbs of military installations, no matter what doomsday scenario they represented. Jostling for Pentagon spending was not, of course, a new political reality. The relationship between military expenditures and economic growth had long been noted, and many politicians were well versed in how to bring defense pork home. World War II, while not the first round of such politicking, sharpened the elbows and pricked the ears of politicians interested in continued federal largesse. No stranger to federal money, the American West logged an impressive $60 billion in wartime spending, dwarfing the hitherto unheard-of amounts doled out during the New Deal. Half of those monies were earmarked specifically for the military. The San Francisco Bay Area boomed thanks to shipbuilding; Hendersonville, Nevada, was born in order to accommodate the government's need for magnesium; the Jet Propulsion Laboratory expanded the holdings of CalTech, and so on. The federal government essentially created the aerospace industry—much of it concentrated on the Pacific Coast, especially in Southern California.[32]

For these reasons, throughout World War II there were more than a few cities fighting to become the "arsenal of democracy." And it was quite clear that it was, at times, a fight. Regions and communities had to make themselves available and attractive for companies, such as Boeing, that had huge government contracts. The Colorado Springs Chamber of Commerce and town boosters lobbied hard for Army and Air Force installations by catering to the military's need for cheap and plentiful land. This relationship continued, to the intended effect, during the Cold War.[33]

In South Dakota, Francis Case, a seven-term congressman elected to the Senate in 1950, fought to bring wartime federal funds home. An agricultural outpost, western South Dakota was hardly ideal for industrial projects and direct war contracts—the sorts of things that would funnel more than $30 billion to California in the early 1940s. Thus, being unattractive for the *business* of war, South Dakota would have to settle for housing war's implements, what historian Gerald Nash has called "the consolation prize." A military installation is really all western South Dakotans could hope for, and they were pleased with what they got. In 1942 the Rapid City Army Air Base opened to train crews of the B-17 Flying Fortress. The base was briefly closed at the end of the war, but then reopened in 1947 as part of the newly formed U.S. Air Force.[34]

The Cold War normalized what was supposed to be the abnormal military geography of the Good War. Few South Dakotans complained. Their experience in war had readied them for the benefits of military alertness. By accepting "permanent" preparations for war as a legitimate form of economic development, they had made a fateful choice about the form and function of federal intervention. Slowly then, South Dakotans—like people around the country—had unwittingly begun to embrace a creeping form of militarism.[35]

Yet it would be erroneous to think this incorporation of cities and regions into the military-industrial complex was somehow accidental. Just as it took work to make the Minutemen missiles palatable to the American public, it took effort to cultivate military-society relationships. It took time and energy to create the sort of attachments that eventually would have towns and regions up in arms about the proposed closing of their particular installations. As missile deployment shows, the Air Force seriously considered community support when making basing decisions. Military officers actively sought the support of locals in regions where they had installations. At the same time, local groups became adept at proving their regions' loyalty.

The middlemen in this military-civilian courtship were politicians like Symington and Case. While Symington's connections were obvious, Case's relationship with the military was more circumspect. By the time of Minuteman deployment, Case, a Republican, was in the twenty-fourth year of a long, though unexceptional career representing South Dakota on the national stage. He was, according to some colleagues, "deadly dull." A more charitable biographer said, "he was happiest in obscurity in the back row on the Republican side." Case, however, knew the benefits of government money, especially money directed at the military. Besides helping get Ellsworth Air Force Base established in 1940, he lobbied hard for an ammunitions depot; pushed for the completion of Mount Rushmore; was instrumental in the Missouri River Basin dams; and—though unsuccessful—wrote to FDR suggesting the Black Hills as a site for the United Nations Headquarters. Since the 1940s the political elite in Rapid City had turned to Case for information about the base. To the Air Force, Case had the dual benefit of being a local politician with a seat on the Senate Armed Services Committee. Good relations with Case were thus important both for smooth operations at Ellsworth and for sympathy during conversations about defense policy and appropriations having nothing at all to do with South Dakota.[36]

Put quite simply, politicians were the linchpin to a smoothly running military-civilian relationship. Major base announcements channeled through their offices so they could issue the press release about the accruing Air Force benefit to the region. "The Pentagon knows

and rewards handsomely its friends," *Washington Post* writer Julius
Duscha noted at the time, "and seldom forgets an enemy." These
were important lessons in the 1950s, when defense spending reached
$42.5 billion annually.[37]

This new Cold War spending, money for the "permanent war
economy," did not flow to all places equally. Already in the early
1950s grumbling about defense inequalities could be heard on Capitol Hill. Representatives from former military-industrial powerhouses
like Detroit and Chicago complained about being given short shrift
in defense appropriations. Money was flowing a bit too steadily to
the West Coast, where the aerospace industry was ensuring California an economic boom. New York, on the other hand, suffered from
rapid demobilization and base closures—a trend that made future
defense dollars even harder to come by. By the time the missiles
rolled around in the late 1950s, it was clear that rising defense budgets did not lift all boats. Rather, national security defense imperatives
were lifting some faster and at the expense of others. This was true
not only for the nation as a whole but within the West as well. While
in general the West benefited disproportionately from Cold War
defense spending, the Great Plains generally lagged behind.[38]

Of course, in the realm of Cold War defense spending, the
Minutemen—and indeed missiles in general—were an unusual case.
Missile installations were not the giant New Deal–style public works
projects that bases, testing grounds, and airstrips could be. Missile
sites did not, for example, conjure up images of long-term housing
booms and civilian support jobs. These were military gumdrops of
a more temporary nature—something perhaps attractive for out-of-
the-way communities with little in the way of organic growth potential. Residents of western South Dakota, for example, already knew
the benefits of Air Force contracts: the just-completed Titan facilities
had reverberated positively throughout the greater Rapid City economy. While not providing exact numbers, a local newspaper noted
hopefully that "deposits have increased substantially" at the First

National and American National Banks and more construction permits had been issued for new buildings.[39]

There is perhaps another reason that missile sites were seen as desirable for some communities. They were an insurance of a sort, a policy taken out on the local Air Force base. This was particularly important for communities whose new Air Force bases had become "significant local adjuncts" to the economy. Committing a missile wing to a particular area would signal SAC's commitment to the long-term maintenance and indeed existence of that base, even in the face of military downsizing. For cities such as Rapid City, South Dakota, and Great Falls, Montana, both increasingly dependent on their Air Force bases, this was an important consideration. It was a reality that the Air Force seemed to understand. One of the siting criteria (criterion 9) was "considering the phase out of the Air Force in the region." While the U.S. military had rapidly downsized immediately after World War II, the Pentagon's real estate holdings had only grown since then. Of course, the missiles would someday be expendable, but not in the immediate future.[40]

Here was why Symington so wanted missiles in Missouri. Whiteman was the state's lone Air Force base, and its primary mission, hosting the B-47 Stratojet, was set to expire in 1960, when the plane was retired. Whiteman was not slated to receive a wing of B-52s as replacement. A suitable mission had to be found or the base could be closed. Symington's letter to Power indicates that he thought he had found one. If missiles were the future of the Air Force, then a base with missiles had a future.[41]

While state and local representatives also lined up for their share of military procurement and deployment, few seemed concerned with the implications of the weapons systems they requested. Lost in all the negotiating, begging, and hand-wringing was the grim reality of what nuclear weapons could mean: in the event of nuclear war, the

missile fields would be ground zero. While no one spelled out specifically what this would mean for the Great Plains, plenty of experts
had projected that nuclear war would devastate the nation's urban
areas. It would not be difficult to draw out those conclusions. For a
10-megaton bomb, ground zero would be reduced to a "crater as
deep as a football field is long" that would radiate a quarter of a mile
in every direction. For another four miles everything in a city would
be flattened and just about everyone would be dead—except for
those who had time to get not to a basement but to a subbasement.
A bank vault would be preferable. At 7 miles out, survival was possible
assuming adequate warning and adequate shelter; 50 percent survival
was expected, though most buildings would be destroyed. The average farmhouse, Ralph Lapp warned, would be destroyed within a
10-mile radius from ground zero. For those who survived the blast,
there was radiation to think about. And this was all for one nuclear
bomb—not the dozens that were expected to hit the missile fields.[42]

Senator Symington did not seem terribly distressed with the possibility. On the contrary, in late 1959 he was upbeat about the prospects of hundreds of warheads replacing the B-47 as Whiteman's
mission. In mid-September the joint SAC-BMD Minuteman Siting
Team had pinpointed 100 Minuteman launch sites and the exact
locations for the first two launch control centers near Kansas City.
On October 2, the same team mapped 197 missile sites in the northern part of the state. On October 15, SAC-BMD gave its official recommendation to the Air Staff: the first 150 Minuteman missiles would
be in Kansas, with the potential for building out to 600. Approval, it
seemed, was a mere technicality.[43]

And yet it was a technicality that did not come. Not only was there
a defect with the first Minuteman missiles (which led to their deployment in Montana), but the Air Staff did not approve Missouri as
a missile base. In trying to keep Whiteman open and appease their
former secretary, SAC-BMD siting teams had defied Air Staff instructions. Missouri simply did not meet all of the requirements for

deployment. White suggested that "more imaginative thought" be given to Minuteman deployment. Secretary of the Air Force James H. Douglas was less charitable: he ordered Minuteman director Sam Phillips "to go back to do more homework." Vulnerability and survivability were, not surprisingly, on the top of that homework list. Air Force Headquarters recommended that missile bases be more widely dispersed and that fallout patterns be considered: missiles could not be sited upwind of large population centers like St. Louis.[44]

These were not arbitrary selection criteria handed down from the Air Staff. Site selection was becoming political in ways larger than Symington's entreaties for a missile base. This had to do with missiles, after all, and this was the era of the missile gap. A handful of congressional inquiries into the missile programs were initiated in 1959, and more would follow in 1960. Politicians were picking up not only on the theme of strategic vulnerability, but also on the implications of nuclear war for the American people. Could Americans survive? Would they even want to? The growing involvement of nonmilitary personnel became evident in March 1960, when the House Military Operations Subcommittee, the Holifield Committee, took up the impact of hardened ICBM sites on the American population. Over the first two days of testimony a gruesome picture of postattack America was drawn. It appeared that surviving a nuclear blast would be the least of one's worries; radiation clouds, ecological disaster, food shortages, and social breakdown would be just a few of the rewards waiting for the survivors. And the picture looked all the more grim if you happened to live downwind of a proposed American ICBM base, presumably ground zero in a Soviet attack.[45]

So when General Curtis LeMay, former SAC commander and current Air Force vice chief of staff, was summoned on the morning of March 30, the committee wanted to know what consideration, if any, the Air Force had given to the American people when siting their new ICBMs. LeMay dutifully told the committee that yes, indeed, the Air Force had given "due regard to the potential danger to the civilian population." However, he added glibly, "when you are upwind, somebody else is downwind." There was simply no way to avoid casualties in thermonuclear war; somebody, somewhere, would bear the brunt of the blast and fallout.[46]

After LeMay's blunt performance before the Holifield Committee, he quickly turned around and informed SAC and BMD that the hearing had serious implications for ICBM siting. Congress had "reemphasized" the importance of thinking of "possible collateral damage to major cities and heavily populated areas" in the event of a Soviet attack. "Future proposed ICBM sites," he thus cautioned, "will be critically reviewed."[47]

LeMay also picked up the Whiteman cause, despite the fact that Missouri quite specifically did not meet all of the parameters. Though the next few Minuteman deployments were slated for Ellsworth (South Dakota) and Grand Forks (North Dakota), LeMay continued to press for Missouri and Pease Air Force Base in New Hampshire. In doing so LeMay argued that while neither place was as remote as the Dakotas, each had the benefit of above-par support facilities and "excellent" community support.[48]

In the case of Pease, LeMay's sentiments were premature. While a whiff of defense dollars could entice the needy, it could also alert the opposition, which is precisely what happened in New England. On January 6, 1961, the *Boston Globe* reported that Pease Air Force Base, just 55 miles north of Boston, had been selected to host a wing of Minuteman missiles. Bostonians could be forgiven for not noticing the news. Filed out of New Hampshire, the story was buried on page 23, after the "women's pages." There were frankly grander things to think about that week: John F. Kennedy—and seemingly the entire state of Massachusetts—was preparing for the inauguration of the thirty-fifth president just two weeks away. What would Jackie wear? But for those who made it into the bowels of the paper, the *Globe* noted that the potential missile sites—150 of them—would be scattered across New Hampshire, Maine, and yes, Massachusetts.[49]

The *Globe*'s announcement was premature. In reality no final decision had been made about hosting the next round of missiles. The secretary of the Air Force had tentatively agreed that Pease could house a wing of missiles, but a verdict awaited more testing and higher Pentagon review. But some Bostonians did make it to page 23, and they did not at all like what they saw. The Greater Boston Committee on Sane Nuclear Policy (SANE) did not think New England needed a new version of the minuteman. The organization was under no illusions about what nuclear deterrence—and actually housing its instruments—would mean: "these are not defensive weapons to protect our cities and towns against attack," SANE declared in a flyer distributed around the region. Instead the Minutemen "are aimed at Russian cities and towns as retaliatory and revenge weapons." This clearly made New England ground zero. Reprinted on the flyer was also a small copy of the *Globe*'s January story. In conjunction with the Boston Committee for Disarmament and Peace and the Massachusetts arm of the Women's International League of Peace and Freedom, SANE asked that area residents write to the president and their congressmen to stop the deployment.[50]

The Boston flyer quickly found its way to Southern California and the desk of Minuteman program director Sam Phillips. At the same time Pease Air Force Base was rather quietly removed from the list of potential Minuteman bases. Though the two events cannot be linked directly, the evidence is certainly suggestive. Perhaps the Air Force realized a little negative publicity was not good for its missiles. While initial community support—including the active lobbying of New Hampshire senator Styles Bridges—seemed positive, the involvement of urban Bostonians demonstrated that, in the nuclear world, "community" was taking on new dimensions. No longer would the Air Force have to consider just the people in the immediate base area. Suddenly residents many miles away, in a potential fallout zone, could also get involved.[51]

In fact, though most Americans were predictably placid in the face of nuclear weapons, the Pentagon had found that the peace lobby was not an inconsiderable foe. What they lacked in numbers they seemed to make up for with energy. For example, in 1960, the Committee for Nonviolent Action began protesting the deployment of Polaris missiles to Groton, Connecticut. "Fish of Death," the fly-ers called the armed submarines. Polaris Action garnered a good deal of media attention. The same group took aim at the possibility of missile bases in New England with its pamphlet *The Strange Case of the Disappearing Woodlands*. In order to publicize Air Force in-tentions, activists canvassed regional newspapers and communities in order to piece together the where, what, and how of potential mis-sile deployment. In all, the group determined that sixteen communi-ties in New Hampshire and Maine had been surveyed for Minute-man sites. Most important, the pamphlet sought to debunk the widespread notion that the sites were for "anti-missile" and "defen-sive" missiles. On the contrary, the Minutemen were "pushbutton" weapons of offensive capabilities that made New England a prime Soviet target.[52]

The peace groups also raised questions most Americans seemed to be avoiding, namely, the long-term efficacy of the military-industrial complex. Literature from SANE and the New England office of the American Friends Service Committee asked trenchant questions about the potential legacies of using defense spending to prod growth, about the use of missile imagery to sell products, and about the proliferation of military gear in children's toys and books. The groups sought to debunk the notion of any economic benefit of the missiles and other military bases. In fact, on the contrary in Maine and New Hampshire, the Committee for Nonviolent Action warned, the presence of nuclear missiles would discourage outside industries from coming to the region.[53]

The Air Force could have forced its missiles onto New England. But why? The very idea of nuclear deterrence depended on its invisibility. The dilemma was emblematic of the larger, long-running problem for national security planners to make deterrence—in push-button form—acceptable, credible, and forgettable. Indeed Minuteman publicity and deployment were aimed as much at obfuscating these grim possibilities as they were at selling a weapon to the American public and fielding a strategic weapon system. In the end, then, the missiles would be deployed to places long considered invisible: Great Falls, Rapid City, Cheyenne, Minot, and Grand Forks. In 1962 Missouri would also get its own missiles. Not only would outsiders not think of these locations, but rural Westerners would be more likely to accept the missiles. As one peace activist begrudgingly admitted in 1959, "the West is something of a stepchild in this country in regard to involvement in world affairs. . . . The missile base is seen as something of an honor that really makes Cheyenne a part of the United States, and a partner in the missile 'prestige.'"[54]

The role of politicians in missile siting is ambiguous. Clearly Symington was crucial to the deployment of missiles in Missouri. In other places the involvement of politicians was clearly beneficial but overall not determinative. In fact, the Air Staff specifically hoped to keep site selection criteria and plans quiet so as not to "trigger" unnecessary attention and put the Air Force in the "untenable position of trying to justify to every source why their locations were not chosen if they can show it meets these criteria."[55]

But given the politics of land and place across the American heartland, the Air Force could not help but "trigger" at least some attention, particularly when time was of the essence and the Minuteman program was slated as a national priority. Perhaps the Air Force could avoid arguments over what states would get missile installations, but it would be unable to avoid some contention about what particular plots of land would be appropriated for missiles. As the case of Vernon Taylor in Montana suggests, rural western landowners were not always willing to silently accede to losing their

property. The same issues would continue to plague missile deployment. And so it was that in January 1960, when the Air Force sped
ahead with the second round of deployments in South Dakota, "representatives from our National Defense" found their way to the
Great Plains and into some trouble.

4

Cold War on the Range

W hy hold a meeting when you have nothing to say? That, at least, was Harold Schuler's assessment of the Army Corps of Engineers' efforts in April 1961. Schuler, secretary to Senator Francis Case, acted as a stand-in when the senator was out of state. On the night of April 6, Schuler traveled down to the American Legion Hall in Wall, South Dakota, where the Corps of Engineers was holding the last of three meetings about Minuteman missile land acquisition. For several months, representatives from the Corps had been traveling through western South Dakota seeking rights of entry for construction. But many landowners were skeptical; thus, the meetings. The first two, neither of which Schuler could attend, had been in Rapid City and Union Center. But on this final night, Schuler showed up with a yellow legal pad, where he scribbled notes to be transcribed for the senator. More than 120 people filled the hall, nearly all ranchers with a few journalists, a member of the local chamber of commerce, and a lawyer thrown in.[1]

The opening moments of the meeting were inauspicious. A technological glitch left the thirteen-minute Air Force film about the Minuteman without sound, though the film was played nonetheless.

Then, Colonel Arthur George, base commander at Ellsworth, mis-identified the real estate agent for the Corps of Engineers, calling him John Kent rather than Dale Kent. Schuler quickly scribbled "Frankly—great confusion" in thick black graphite.[2]

Things did not get much better. Over the course of two hours, Schuler's assessment of the Corps and Air Force officials in charge became increasingly incredulous. "In general," he wrote, there has been a "lack of attempts to acquaint people" with the most basic in-formation. "No one has any authority or knows what he is talking about." "Dale Kent," he jotted, is "massively unable to get ideas across." Toward the end of the meeting Schuler put down his pencil and got up to address the group. "We know that everybody is hurrying this project," he said. "But maybe we ought to take five minutes longer here and there . . . maybe we should have tested this film before it came here. . . . There are a lot of things that aren't explained prop-erly and they haven't been explained tonight."[3]

Schuler's assessment of the ranchers was equally unexpected, though far more generous. "Never heard so many," he declared. "Showing spine in back," he scrawled, and then added "not recalci-trant." Schuler was surprised that the typically reticent ranchers could so well articulate their cause. So impressed was he that he quickly dashed off a memo to his boss in Washington, D.C. "Imme-diately get on the side of the landowners," he advised Senator Case. Why? "It would be good to keep on the better side of some of those strong conservative stockmen." Finally, Schuler recommended, "transfer Dale Kent . . . [who] is very inept in his public relations."[4]

The problem was larger than one of personnel or publicity, how-ever. This had to do with land, property, and national security, a po-tent triad under any circumstances. But the problem was inflamed by the fact that the groups involved understood the stakes in differ-ent ways. As Kadoka-area rancher L. G. Weller fumed, "as represen-tatives of the Government, you got nothing to lose. . . . But us as individuals lose. . . . It makes quite a bit of difference." The Corps could have just as quickly shot back that their jobs were on the line, that national security dictated expediency, and that they didn't make the rules anyway; they just followed "rules of higher authority" that could not be broken.[5]

So concerned were the landowners that they had been meeting since January, when the Air Force publicly announced the deployment of missiles to South Dakota. On February 14 the ranchers created the Missile Area Landowners Association (MALA), with the explicit purpose of using collective power to assert their property rights. The organization's "Articles of Association" declared that the group existed for "the consideration of common problems for the securing of information affecting our property and the value thereof and the use to be made of the same." These ranchers did not oppose the missiles program per se, but had questions about what was going to happen to their land.[6]

Their response was, in fact, quite normal and expected. Rural South Dakotans had long come together to promote local interests in the face of outside intrusion. Different this time were the forces arrayed against them. From the start the landowners were quick to assert their patriotism and basic acceptance of the Minutemen. In no way, admonished rancher Leonel Jensen, did they want to "slow the progress of defense." But what they did want was information and perhaps something to say about what was going to happen to their land. A faceless bureaucracy had arrived on their doorsteps and told them, that piece of land, there, that piece you value most—that is what we want. There were no negotiations, no give and take. It was that, the impersonal, seemingly arbitrary taking from above, that made some western South Dakotans insert themselves into the making of American nuclear policy.[7]

This small group of South Dakota ranchers would not, ultimately, get very far in their battle. But their efforts provide a brief window into the ways that nuclear deterrence directly influenced Americans. Moreover, how this particular story played out over the early 1960s demonstrates the difficulty many Americans would have grappling with the new Cold War bureaucracy. The overwhelming majority of South Dakotans—even those who had to cede land for the project— embraced the missiles and their responsibility. But that broad acceptance should not hide the ways that national security requirements transformed ideas about politics, place, and land. On the western plains national security needs brought into sharp relief traditional western tensions between land and government, individual and state. But the means that South Dakotans had long used to manage the federal presence were largely impotent. As a result western South Dakotans were forced to redefine their own ideas about patriotism and citizenship. The resolution of these tensions, however tenuous, demonstrates how South Dakotans, and indeed all Americans, were persuaded that deterrence—the threat of global thermonuclear war and the militarization of the plains—was an acceptable way to fight the Cold War.

Leonel Jensen was among the first South Dakotans to learn that his state was about to host the Minutemen. He was not a military man so he did not learn of deployment through those traditional channels. Rather, Jensen was a rancher with some land. And, like Vernon Taylor up in Montana, Jensen owned some land that the Air Force had taken a keen interest in—not for its proximity to the Jensen front yard or its worth as a good winter wheat field, the reasons that Leonel Jensen liked that particular field, but rather because it was relatively flat, within a specified distance from other predetermined missile locations, and near enough to a road that the Air Force would not have to create an entirely new one to gain access. It was for those reasons that in early November 1960, Jensen received a rather odd visitor in search of soil samples for "a possible missile base." Like Taylor in Montana, Jensen was asked to sign a right of entry for survey and exploration (which he did) and was told not to share information about the Air Force program with anyone; the Minuteman was an issue of great national importance and the authorities would provide information on a need-to-know basis only. For the time being, Jensen was to sit tight and stay quiet.[8]

Jensen could stay quiet for only so long. The next week a larger, better-equipped survey team returned to his ranch and began taking soil samples. Jensen did not know it, but these were Army Corps of Engineers personnel making final soil borings. This time they answered his queries with "courteous" though "abrupt" responses and told him that almost definitely the missile would be sited where they were boring, on a spot, according to Jensen, not amenable to his ranching operations. At this point Jensen decided to make some noise. In a November 16 letter, Jensen presented his quandary to Senator Francis Case—not that the missile should be sited on someone else's land, but that it should be sited somewhere else on his land. "We have five thousand acres in the ranch and we have plenty of places where a defense installation would not be objectionable . . . we can not quite see the practicallity [sic] or the fairness of the Defense Command just plotting on a map where the base should be and then putting it there." Case's response was prompt, if not totally satisfactory. In it he explained that through a conversation with the Air Force he had learned that no money was yet allocated to missile construction, so there might still be time to get the site moved.[9]

For the rest of 1960, Jensen battled alone. He did not yet know that Gene Williams, just 30 miles to the east, and Cecil Hayes up north in Elm Springs, were also questioning government right-of-entry forms, worrying about land values, and seeking answers to what seemed a tangled web of bureaucracies, rationales, and expectations. In all, 198 landowners spread over 13,000 square miles of western South Dakota were approached by Army Corps of Engineers real estate agents that November. And all received the same information—some part of their land was needed for national security, and it was a secret program that should not be discussed. Publicity should be left to the experts.[10]

For a while the landowners complied. But by late January the absence of clear information about the ranchers' property proved bothersome. Williams had heard nothing since he had been contacted in November. Perhaps, he hoped, they had decided to move the missile away from his best wheat field. Any additional information Williams had gleaned from newspaper stories or word of mouth. Rumors spread quickly: "A young guy up near Enning and his family are being asked to move—they want to put a missile next to his house"; "Did you hear that it is harder to put a missile on federal grasslands than on private property?"; "I heard that we won't be able to use the land ever again." For Williams the most intriguing rumor of all may have been the most implausible: Leonel Jensen, just up the road, was able to get a missile site moved.[11]

In search of answers, information, and perhaps a little confirmation, area ranchers did what they had long done: they got together and talked. Following the Air Force's official announcement of deployment in January, the landowners organized. Throughout February and March they gathered information, conducted polls of area residents, sent newsletters, and lobbied politicians, community leaders, and agricultural groups for information. There was no master list of how many or which people were affected by the Minuteman program, so the newly formed landowners association compensated by holding frequent meetings in towns scattered throughout the region. Gatherings were announced in local papers, and whoever showed up and paid $1 was in. By mid-March the group had its own letterhead. By April, President Eugene Pellegrin reported at least 100 dues-paying members; many more came to meetings. Eventually regular meetings were called for the group's directors, twenty-seven ranchers from all corners of the deployment area, who served as liaisons with their neighbors. The membership fee—increased to $10 that spring—was used to help defray the cost of disseminating information, largely by the organization president and vice president, Pellegrin and Cecil Hayes, respectively. Following a series of well-attended meetings and the formation of subcommittees, at the end of March, Pellegrin could confidently write, "we are already beginning to realize the benefits of being organized and acting together."[12]

No one should have been surprised. No one should have underestimated the degree to which western South Dakotans held sacred their right to property. By the 1960s there were few fools left among South Dakota's farmers and ranchers. This stretch of the western plains had proved itself one of the most intractable agricultural regions in the country. Most of the original homesteaders had long since moved on, selling or in some cases simply abandoning their claims. The people who remained, those whom author Wallace Stegner labeled the "stickers," had a well-earned attachment to the land. In this part of the country land was money, land was livelihood, and, in many cases, land was family and history.[13]

Western South Dakota's first land boom occurred relatively late in the country's homesteading history: the first land bonanza was not until the early 1900s. There were reasons for this late start: early travelers labeled the Great Plains "barren," a "wasteland," "useless for civilization," and perhaps most sweeping of all, the "Great American Desert." Teddy Roosevelt, who found his manhood on the Dakota plains, noted its tremendous "sameness." Average annual precipitation is just 17 inches—some of which comes in the winter, when, for seven months of the year, a blizzard can whitewash the state for days on end. In 1936, a strange year by every measure, the state's low was −57 degrees Fahrenheit and its high was 120 degrees Fahrenheit. There are few trees and fewer people. The sky and the land open up for hundreds of miles in every direction—"the biggest sky anywhere," wrote Stegner. The wind, which can blow hot or cold, can take a grown man's breath away. A tornado, of course, could take his life.[14]

The extremes of South Dakota are almost a cliché, written into state mottos and slogans. For a while it was "the Blizzard State," and then "the Sunshine State." Now it is sometimes referred to as "the Land of Infinite Variety." It was against these extremes that homesteaders had to contend—to figure out how to build houses without trees (soddies were the answer); what to use for fuel (twisted ropes of hay for cooking; buffalo "chips" for warmth); and how to get water (haul it for miles or dig a well). The government also required that homesteaders break a few acres of the native sod in an effort to have something grow—a proposition that turned out to be far more difficult than some may have expected. Area farmers labeled western South Dakota's soil "gumbo" soil. It was silty and claylike, with poor drainage, basically suitable for semiarid short grasses, but not much else.[15]

Early homesteaders like the Williamses and Fauskes learned quickly just how unforgiving the region could be. A major drought in 1910 and 1911 led to a mass exodus—some counties lost as much as half their population. The grasshoppers came in 1930, swarms of them that moved across the state somewhat haphazardly, destroying a thousand acres while leaving one in the middle untouched. Those spared from the locusts were left to the mercy of the drought and the dust. John Steinbeck's Joads were not from western South Dakota, but they could have been. In the 1930s western South Dakota lost 14 percent of its population—most of them moving west, drawn to the possibilities of labor and wages.[16]

Inglebert Fauske and his bride were part of this exodus. They fled the dust, the bugs, and the short grasses and went south to New Mexico in search of federal employment. The New Deal was kind to them, and both found jobs with the Soil Conservation Corps on an Indian reservation. They managed to eke out a living but missed home enough that they returned to South Dakota and, with the help of the Farmers Home Administration, bought back their family's land seventeen and a half miles south of Wall. There they took part in what was to emerge as a specific type of agricultural production and ownership in South Dakota: somewhat large, family-owned and -operated farms dependent on livestock for the primary source of income. Indeed, for the families that stayed on during the Depression, the era was an opportunity to buy adjacent lands and increase the average size of ranches. The Jensens purchased lands from neighbors who could no longer pay their taxes.[17]

Cattle were, of course, not new to western South Dakota. But the general dependence of small farmers on them was. During the range-cattle bonanza of the nineteenth century, the Great Plains was found to be ideal "grazing domain." While the industry and its giants were decimated in the 1880s, stock production remained a regional mainstay, often supplemented with the cultivation of forage crops and hay. Gradually, as homesteaders moved in and tried to become farmers, the acreage devoted to crops—wheat, corn, and alfalfa—grew, while the number of cattle dropped. What the Great Depression did was provide a stark reminder that the "Great American Desert," regardless of Herculean agricultural efforts, could not be tamed. No degree of crop rotation or diversification could disguise the region's inherent inhospitality to intensive farming. In a sense the native short grasses—which appeared magically drought resistant—called for grazing. In the 1930s and 1940s government policies and environmental realities made this increasingly apparent to the region's holdouts and returnees. New Deal programs such as the Soil Conservation Act encouraged the shift from soil-depleting to soil-conserving crops and a return to grasslands—and thus range-lands—in the west. The native short grasses had defenses against drought that wheat, corn, and alfalfa simply did not.[18]

Throughout the 1940s and 1950s, livestock production grew in importance to South Dakota's economy and cattle ranches were doing well. William Bielmaier was able to buy up neighboring farms to add to the original 3,100 acres he purchased from his parents when he returned from the Korean War. Indeed the acreage of South Dakota farms grew as their numbers shrank. The end result was large ranches owned and operated, in many cases, by the children or grandchildren of homesteaders. Leonel Jensen raised his family in the farmhouse his parents built. Lyndy Ireland still lives in the home her grandmother purchased in installments for $1,969 from the Sears, Roebuck and Company "Modern Homes" mail-order catalog in 1920. The Alhambra-style home is just a stone's throw from the log cabin her grandparents originally built.[19]

Western South Dakota may have seemed remarkably distant from the centers of power, but its residents had learned how to manage the levers of democracy, should it come to that. There was ample precedent for the landowners association, and these South Dakotans understood their efforts as part of a continuum of direct agrarian democracy. South Dakotans had been active in the Populist Party of the 1890s, casting their votes for William Jennings Bryan. Dakotans also pioneered the ballot initiative and were not shy about using it. In 1960 these landowners still believed, as Thomas Jefferson had articulated more than 150 years before, that agrarian producers—family farmers and ranchers—were integral to the success of the nation. They were the most "virtuous" and "independent" citizens with the "most lasting bonds" to the country. As historian Catherine McNicol Stock has demonstrated, rural people have often used arguments about their productive importance to promote political causes, sometimes radical ones. Many missile-area landowners continued to understand their place in these terms. Put simply, it was their duty to protect their hard-earned property rights and ranching interests against unknowing outsiders.[20]

By 1960 this was also a group long accustomed to—and wary of—the federal presence in their midst. A complex matrix of government regulations and bureaucracies, mostly remnants from the Great Depression, already determined much of their lives. Soil-conservation protocols, land-use regulations, and grazing allotments were administered by a blend of local, state, and federal agencies. For those ranchers who leased grazing allotments in the public domain—about 620,000 acres in western South Dakota alone—leases were arranged with either the Forest Service or the Bureau of Land Management (BLM), and sometimes both. To reconcile the often contradictory needs of federal largesse with a heritage of fierce autonomy, South Dakotans had worked out strategies for managing the federal government. The key was local control. State government was kept small and federal monies were channeled appropriately to local needs with a minimum of oversight. Local administration of federal programs, such as soil conservation, ensured more personal and less intrusive regulation. In many cases it was your neighbor who met with you about ranch management and land needs. Stock growers' advisory boards, generally made up of area ranchers, ran BLM and Forest Service grazing-allotment programs. From the Depression, South Dakotans had learned to use federalism to their own, independent advantage. And so when ranchers met throughout that unseasonably warm February of 1961, they were merely trying to figure out the best ways to "manage" this latest government intrusion. This latest government intrusion, however, could not easily be managed.[21]

There are many ways to see the same place. In western South Dakota, where ranchers saw a sense of place and history, military planners saw vast open spaces, "ideal" terrain for a missile system. Colonel Sidney T. Martin had a different view still. When the young engineer arrived in South Dakota in the summer of 1961, he saw a problem—a vast logistical problem. As lead engineer for the U.S. Army Corps of Engineers, it was Martin's job to oversee the construction of 150 Minuteman missile sites on the western plains. His blueprints came from faraway places: construction specifications from the Los Angeles–based architectural engineering firm Parsons-Saven, and maps that Air Force planners in Southern California drew up based on abstract principles of deterrence, vulnerability, and dispersal. Few of those planners had actually been to South Dakota, where Martin had to make it all work. Martin had to turn the tiny black dots and lines of contour maps into high-tech missile silos, to set into motion one of the largest construction projects of all time:

moving 20 million cubic yards of dirt. And he had to do it all as quickly as humanly possible.[22]

The actual construction work did not trouble Martin. He had previously worked on the Atlas system in Wyoming, and these new missiles were far less complex. The Minuteman facilities were designed to be highly replicable—"a simple, low-cost repetitious task," according to the *Military Engineer*. Construction crews were sent out in teams to perform repetitive tasks at different sites: one crew excavated, another poured concrete, another lowered the prefabricated silo into the hole, more came to backfill the hole with leftover dirt. These engineering concerns Martin had a handle on. What caused Martin real angst was the geographic reach of the project, the vast distances that made up the missile fields. His crews would have to get materials and men across 11,000 square miles on a 3,000-mile "road net" of dubious quality, often during extreme weather conditions. This was going to take some clever management and would ultimately prove the source of greatest tension once the construction program began. Making matters more difficult, Martin took command precisely as the country was in the midst of a new bout of missile-gap hysteria. Whether he recognized it or not, Martin's work would be scrutinized by not just his superiors in the Corps of Engineers, or the Air Force brass that oversaw the missile programs, but the nation as a whole. The combination of difficulties and scrutiny, as well as the grumbling coming from the ranchers in the missile fields, was going to make Martin's task far more contentious than anyone had imagined.[23]

In 1961 the Cold War was coming closer and closer to home. The Soviets seemed to be everywhere, particularly above and right next door. On April 12 Yuri Gagarin began his two-day stint orbiting the earth. Like Sputnik three and a half years before, the event reminded Americans that if the Soviets could launch a man into space, they could certainly launch much more. Perhaps more ominously the Soviets seemed to be making friends just 90 miles off the American mainland in Cuba. The miserable failure of the Bay of Pigs invasion, launched on April 17, seemed to demonstrate just how far Americans were falling not just in the space race, but also in the overall Cold War.

The Soviets were quick to combine the April events. After the Bay of Pigs, the Soviets warned the Kennedy administration against further actions in Cuba by suggesting that the same rockets that vaulted Gagarin to space had clear military applications. Most worrisome, the Soviets insisted that Gagarin's safe launch and return proved their mastery over accuracy, a key component of ICBM technology. So while technically the missile gap had been laid to rest, Americans were once again whipped into a frenzy over control of the heavens and all that was beneath.[24]

All the while the newly elected Kennedy administration was studying the nation's defensive posture and reviewing military needs, including the strategic missile program. It was a program that had already had its fair share of scrutiny. For years the ICBM force was a cause célèbre of lawmakers concerned with both guns and butter. In the era of "missile gaps," the nation's ICBM program became everyone's business. People wanted to know why it was taking so long, why nothing seemed to work, and why, given these dismal results, it cost so much. The Air Force and the U.S. military had to do better with the Minutemen.

But a strategic review by the new secretary of defense, Robert S. McNamara, showed that the Air Force was not actually doing any better at all. McNamara realized that the Minuteman program was over budget and increasingly behind schedule. In January 1961 Secretary of the Air Force Eugene Zuckert warned the new secretary of defense that the missile program was probably behind by sixty days. By February, Bernard Schriever, head of the Air Force Ballistic Missile Office, was concerned. Operational schedules at all ICBM bases were slipping. Schriever acknowledged that concurrency, shortened operational schedules, and a lack of resources were all seriously hindering the Minuteman program. But he would cede no ground. Borrowing from Kennedy's public remarks a week earlier, Schriever reminded his own staff in the Ballistic Missile Division that "the next four years [will be] the years of greatest peril to this country." For Schriever the Minutemen would play a central role in "reducing this peril." But in order "to maintain the seemingly impossible operational schedules" laid out for the Minutemen, "super human efforts" would be required. "I have worked with each of you for years," Schriever wrote, "and know that you can make the impossible possible." If his personal plea was not enough, Schriever reminded his colleagues that "the national security" as well as "the prestige of the USAF and the [Ballistic Missile Division] demands no less."[25]

This pressure, in turn, came crashing down on the Army Corps of Engineers. Construction delays—whether foreseeable or not—reflected poorly on the Corps. And there had been plenty of delays—so many, in fact, that the continued employment of the Corps as principal player in missile site construction was in doubt; perhaps another organization would do better. The Corps of Engineers thought not, and to prove it the Corps conducted extensive internal studies of ICBM construction. So too did the Air Force, the Defense Department, and ultimately Congress. The results often pointed not to failures in weapons development, but to problems in construction and site management. While both the Air Force and the Corps of Engineers were held to account for management lapses, much of the onus to improve fell on the Corps.[26]

Back in July 1960, nearly a year before Martin took over South Dakota's program, the construction and site activation program for ICBMs had been completely reorganized. No longer would district offices for the Corps of Engineers oversee deployment. Instead all control was centralized in the Corps of Engineers Ballistic Missile Construction Office (CEBMCO), located in Los Angeles near the Ballistic Missile Division. The aim was to centralize decision making and link more closely together the operational and construction phases of the ICBM program.[27]

That fall CEBMCO began a "deliberately ambitious" publicity effort to demonstrate the complexity and urgency of its work. While the campaign strove for "objectivity," the ultimate goal was to show that "the Corps is doing a good job on ICBM construction." The Corps had experience in this area: good PR regarding the Corps' work on North African bases provided "a testimonial that did much to deter untoward criticism, particularly in the responsible elements of the press willing to recognize the truth."[28]

To highlight missile-site construction, the Corps of Engineers was contemplating a "vigorous motion picture production" program along with strategic reports to be landed in key magazines such as *Fortune, Engineering News Record*, and perhaps *Parade. Business Week* hoped for an interview with CEBMCO head General A. C. Welling. For Welling's benefit an advanced list of possible questions was available, obtained through "close relations with the men controlling the magazine's end of the undertaking." Perhaps even more important, the prospect of a "picture story" in *Life* "appear[ed] favorable."[29]

Despite the management changes and PR push, missile site construction continued to lag. In early 1961, congressional hearings grandstanded the problem. The House Military Construction Subcommittee, chaired by Representative Harry R. Sheppard, Democrat of California, was distressed to discover that Minuteman construction at Malmstrom Air Force Base in Montana was no more efficient and no less prone to delays and expense than construction at the Titan and Atlas sites. In February 1961, Sheppard declared the program a "sloppy job." The Senate, too, found cause for alarm and the Preparedness Subcommittee launched its own investigation. The Minutemen were proving to be anything but the "ultimate" weapon, as they had been heralded.[30]

It was under these conditions that the Corps of Engineers began working in South Dakota in 1961. To be sure, the Army Corps of Engineers had a Herculean task ahead of them. Martin himself would write that it was the "greatest construction effort in history." But even before the excavation could begin, land had to be acquired. And it was here that Martin and the Corps of Engineers had a problem. The Corps of Engineers' Real Estate Acquisition team was having trouble getting all of South Dakota's landowners to sign rights of entry for construction. Real estate officers began seeking signatures in March, hoping to have all the property acquired by summer. Many ranchers refused to sign. It looked like the planned-for August ground breaking would be delayed. Making matters worse, the failure to acquire the missile sites had a cascade effect: without the missile sites purchased, the Corps could not negotiate easement rights for the thousands of miles of underground cables that would connect the missile silos to their launch facilities and to one another. Hundreds, if not thousands, more landowners would be involved in that process. Such desperate times did not provide for flexible measures. Major Edmund R. Preston of the Omaha Corps of Engineers Office told South Dakota landowners that the Corps was "substituting accelerated land acquisition in the interest of speeding up the defense program."[31]

By late March 1961, the Corps of Engineers realized it had a problem on its hands. Corps agents quickly created a pamphlet of "facts" about land acquisition and scheduled the April landowner meetings. South Dakota's landowners were ready. Through meetings and letters they had distilled their message down to three main issues. First, many wanted to know if they could get the proposed missile site moved. They didn't mind a missile on their property, but they wanted to be able to choose which plot of land they would lose. Second, landowners wanted to know how compensation would be determined. Finally, landowners were upset about their relationship, or lack thereof, with the Air Force and Corps of Engineers. These South Dakotans were accustomed to managing or somehow personalizing outside programs. The last point Leonel Jensen stressed. "One thing we have lacked up till now has been authorative [*sic*] sources," Jensen admitted. And "one thing we have learned is that even the Government Agencies that are working on this project are not always in accord on what can or can not be done."[32]

Jensen, in all likelihood, had no idea how accurate his assessment of government discord was. In reality, communication between the Corps of Engineers, the organization charged with building the missile fields, and the Air Force, the group that designed and would ultimately be in charge of the missiles, was poor, and guidelines for missile land acquisition were still being determined. The very same problems that complicated missile site selection from afar thus plagued land acquisition and construction on the ground. This was a totally new program that required new land-acquisition protocols, but none had yet been drawn up. By its own admission the Corps was using the same land-acquisition procedures it would use for civil works projects such as dams or highways. The main difference, as landowners would soon point out, was that dams and highways tended to increase the value of surrounding properties, yet most landowners were pretty certain nuclear missile sites would not be viewed as neighborhood enhancements. In addition, multiple agencies were involved in deployment but no one group seemed capable of making binding decisions. Individuals carried out their jobs on the ground but were often ignorant of changes that had been made at higher levels. And it was all complicated by the demands of national security and extremely short deployment plans for the Minuteman system. Toward the end of the land acquisition process Senator Case noted warily that western South Dakotans had been used as "guinea pigs" in the whole process.[33]

For many of the landowners the injustices began the moment faraway strategists plotted missiles on their property. The ranchers rightly suspected that no thought had been given to their own use of the land in question. "When the first sites were spotted," Jensen demanded during the Wall meeting, "why weren't the rights of the individuals considered to the point where they might change that site a half a mile where it would be out in a pasture instead of right in the middle of an alfalfa field?" The experiences of a dozen or more landowners confirmed Jensen's point. In letters and at meetings they recorded the hardship they would suffer if the Air Force went ahead and buried a missile on the "only spot of decent farm ground" that "I consider quite valuable." Many landowners offered to *donate* their land as long as they had a say in which parcel was taken.[34]

If the landowners were looking for a personal answer to their questions, or at least some acknowledgment that their property rights had been considered, they were disappointed. When asked about missile siting, one of the Air Force officers attending the meeting from Ellsworth told the group in Union Center on April 5 that "they are working on the final computations." (Whom he meant by "they" was left to the imagination.) On the April 6 he was only slightly more illustrative: "Mathematics that are applied to the geography," he began, tapering off. And then: "the man who computes does not know how it is going to actually affect the countryside." "When you enter into the mathematics," the colonel tried to clarify, the ability to "shift [the missiles] one way or another becomes hard." Likely he was not the only one confused.[35]

Jensen stood up and eviscerated the Air Force's theory of mathematics: the proposed missile site on his own property had been moved. Back in November Jensen wrote to Case asking for help. According to Jensen the Corps of Engineers survey crews had tested a plot of land on "some of the best farm land we have." Couldn't it be moved a little? Case, in turn, passed the complaint on to Strategic Air Command (SAC) Commander General Tommy Power. In December Power wrote to Case indicating that a "mutually agreeable" location had been found on the Jensen ranch. That location was about a mile north of the original spot in the middle of relatively useless prairie land. While giving no indication of how the site had been moved or who had approved the relocation, Power thanked Case for "bringing this matter to my attention." Moreover, Power informed Case, and Jensen then informed the landowners and the Corps, "the policy of this command [SAC] is to avoid siting missile facilities on [used and productive] property wherever possible."[36]

Some ranchers wondered, given all the siting specifications, why the Air Force didn't simply put the Minutemen on federal lands. There were certainly enough of them—nearly 20 percent of the state was "public." Since the 1930s the federal government had been buying up delinquent or abandoned rangelands and turning them over to the Forest Service. It was to that department that ranchers turned when they wanted allocations of grassland for their herds of cattle to graze. So why the Air Force couldn't go there too confounded ranchers, particularly Gene Williams. In his estimation a section of the federal land was about 200 yards from the field the Air Force had selected for launch facility Delta-6. The reasons provided, according to Case, were merely meant to "fool" the landowners—suggesting that missiles had to be placed *exactly* where they had been mapped, despite the fact that they had a 6,000-mile range and could clearly be refigured. Case's own entreaties to the Corps of Engineers, the Air Force, Zuckert, and McNamara yielded nothing. "This question was not answered," Case told his colleagues, "in any way, shape or form." Perhaps one of the reasons was purely bureaucratic, as was hinted at in internal Corps of Engineers documents. Apparently acquiring land from other government agencies was often more time-consuming than acquiring it from private individuals.[37]

The seeming preference for private over public lands only helped confirm what many western ranchers long believed: the federal government was grossly inefficient. More than a few ranchers suspected the entire missile program was a waste of taxpayer money. And so despite the fact that this was a military program and South Dakotans

considered themselves immensely patriotic, landowners understood
the missiles in the same terms that they had come to see all federal
programs: sometimes necessary but always to be guarded against. No
government agency was to be fully trusted. That spring Cecil Hayes
warned his fellow ranchers: "There is one thing we deffinitely [sic]
must not lose sight of. . . . If we do not get a good precedent established in this taking now [of land for missiles], we certainly will not
be in any position for further takings by the Government for military
installations." He concluded ominously, "and I am sure there will be
many more."[38]

The same mistrust percolated through conversations about compensation. Landowners were uncertain of how much reimbursement
they could expect for their sacrifice and when they would receive it.
Early reports were not encouraging. Landowners had initially been
told that government takings should proceed under land negotiations like those that would take place "normally" between a "willing
seller and a willing buyer." But a Corps of Engineers representative
disabused them of that notion, declaring that the Corps would find
it "difficult" to negotiate with landowners who refused to sign rights
of entry for construction. To landowners it sounded like they would
have to cede their land *before* the value of that land had been determined. What, then, would be the point of negotiations later on? It
would be hard to get a fair price after you had already signed your
rights away.[39]

Nor did government policies seem to take account of the true
meaning of the land in question. Landowners did not want direct
payment simply for silo lands—what would amount to about 2
acres—but also for the depreciation of lands adjacent to silos, for
damages incurred, and for lost productivity. "No one seems to like
the thoughts of a missile on their back steps," Gene Pellegrin wrote
to Senator Case. "When an area is chosen for a missile installation,
land values go down." The landowners association came up with
their own valuations and depreciation schedule for lands: $10 per

acre for lands extending out one-quarter of a mile from the site down to $2.50 per acre for lands one mile out. The group also decided that each landowner should be compensated no less than $2,500 for land, damages, and depreciation. They hired their own appraiser to provide a nongovernment value for lands (a development welcomed by the Corps of Engineers).[40]

Senator Case took up the landowners' cause. The usually quiet senator spent a good part of the spring meeting with military representatives; he wrote letters; he talked to Corps of Engineers personnel; he even asked the secretary of defense and chief of the Air Force for assistance in speeding up decisions and changing acquisition procedures. Where he could, Case inserted his concerns into the federal record. A favorite tactic was to ask officials to put themselves in the boots of a rancher. "Mr. Secretary," he implored McNamara during hearings on defense appropriations in 1961, "do you own a farm?" When McNamara demurred, Case switched tack and told him to feel like a farmer nonetheless. "If the farmer," Case demanded, "were reluctant to sign on the dotted line" because he feared that "his gates would be left down, that trucks would be running across his fields," and that there would be "interruption of his operations for the next year or two," Case asked, "could you understand his reluctance?" McNamara admitted that he would. Later Case asked the acting head of the Corps of Engineers if he would, himself, live on land with a missile site. The colonel said he would need some time to think about it.[41]

"I find it impossible to believe," Case declared to Pellegrin and later to his colleagues on Capitol Hill, "that a program which will cost billions should find it necessary to chisel farmers and ranchers out of just and fair compensation for land taken and damaged." And "chisel" it certainly seemed to be doing. Reports from the field indicated that men were making $30 per day working on survey crews. That was about how much ranchers were offered for each acre of land. Case went further and insinuated that cheapness was perhaps

getting in the way of site relocations: reportedly each soil boring cost
$3,000. Was it the case that the Corps did not want to have to redrill
soil samples for new sites and spend the extra money? While Case
did not explicitly charge the Corps of Engineers with stinginess, he
certainly seemed to imply it was their shortcoming. After all, why
not pay each landowner their minimum asking price of $2,500?
Given that the missile construction program in South Dakota
would ultimately cost $75,719,004, wasn't $2,500 per site—for a total
of $412,500—a small price to pay for landowner cooperation?[42]

If the Corps refused that option, ranchers also knew that condemnation could work in their favor. When landowners refused to sell
their land voluntarily, the government would sue for procession, a
process known as eminent domain. While the landowners would
still lose their land, the value would be determined in court, not by
Corps representatives. That seemed only fair; in fact it was their
constitutional right, as the landowners liked to point out. And it
was hardly unusual. In 1962 the Justice Department reported that
120,000 eminent domain cases were working their way through
the courts. To be sure, not all of them were for missile installations.
Land was also needed for flood-control projects, water conservation,
and other civilian needs, most notably the interstate highway system.
But more than three-quarters of government land requirements were
for national defense, and the majority of condemnation cases involved missile sites.[43]

Summing up sentiment in the missile fields, Case told the Senate Defense Appropriations Subcommittee that landowners were
"baffled" by the approach. Assuming the Minutemen are of the
highest national priority, Case argued, then this problem "deserves
consideration at the highest level, the cutting of some red tape, and
the establishing of new regulations as a basis of compensation."
Case tried, unsuccessfully, to have some new regulations written
into the appropriations bill. These landowners required more cre-
ative and thoughtful approaches. While his colleagues on the

Armed Services Committee were sympathetic, no one wanted to mess with federal purchasing requirements through binding legislation. Better to have these things taken care of on a more local level.[44]

The problem, of course, was that the Corps and Air Force agents involved in land acquisition argued that without appropriate legislation there was nothing they could do. While they wanted to smooth over the rough edges, they simply could not make cash payments or individual contracts with landowners that were not already government approved. Land values would be determined based on fair market value in the area—which was $15 to $40 per acre. While damages would also be compensated, there would certainly be no land depreciation taken into account. Landowners were clearly unhappy with the amounts being discussed. Corps of Engineers offers ranged from $100 to $650. As Case reminded his colleagues, "men who have had sales pending for their ranch, about to retire, find that nobody wants to come in" and buy their land.[45]

What Case and his constituents didn't quite seem to grasp was something that the Corps of Engineers and Air Force understood all too well: this was national security and there really was no room for negotiation. All the years South Dakotans had spent managing government agricultural programs could not, it appears, have prepared them for this. While President Eisenhower, on his departure from office, had spent much time railing against the perils of a garrison state (with South Dakotans nodding along eagerly with him), it looked like a little corner of South Dakota was about to become just that.

While ranchers spent much of 1961 griping about their predicament, there were some who had it worse than others. In fact nearly everyone could agree they didn't have it as bad as Ernest and Nona Niederwerder. While most people wondered how they would move cattle around missile sites or deal with Air Force patrols, Niederwerder had to figure out where he would put his family. The Air Force had not simply plotted a missile site on the Niederwerders' land; they had put it in spitting distance of their home. But instead of moving the missile site, the Air Force decided to move the Niederwerders.[46]

Adding another layer of strangeness to the entire project, the Air Force had taken the time to determine how close an "inhabited dwelling"—or home—could be to a missile silo. In 1961 it was 800 feet; that number would rise to 1,200 feet the following year. The reason: blast effects from either a missile launch or an accident within the silo. If a missile was launched, the heat and fire from the boosters would burn and destroy all buildings and occupants within a certain radius. Presumably, if deterrence had any meaning, in the event of a missile launch—thus nuclear war—the missile's neighbors would be vaporized even at a distance of 1,200 feet, but that did not stop the Air Force from mandating where Ernest and Nona Nieder-werder could raise their growing family. Their home was some 400 feet into the blast circle of a missile site that had been mapped despite the fact that there was a home right there. Rather than tweak a missile's location, the Air Force preferred to relocate a family.[47]

The Niederwerders' predicament pointed to one of the many absurdities in the Minuteman program: a nuclear missile was being implanted in someone's backyard; in fact, hundreds of missiles were being implanted in hundreds of backyards. This was no Department of Forestry reclamation or agricultural subsidy program. This was the federal government quartering weapons—its cold warriors—on a citizen's property. And while the Corps of Engineers promised that the Minuteman "would create no hazards for its neighbors," from where the Niederwerders stood, things looked a bit less serene.[48]

Of course the logic of deterrence, the very abstraction that had created this very real problem for South Dakotans, was meant to be ignored. As nuclear strategist Herman Kahn intoned with typical circularity: "when one has to depend on something working, one cannot afford to question the underlying assumptions; it would be too disturbing, if one did, too disturbing . . . if we raised questions that shook our faith in the notions." To accept the missiles in the ground, then, meant one had to believe that they would never come out. And here is where Ernest Niederwerder's communication with the government seemed so disquieting. In mandating an uninhabitable radius around each missile site, the Air Force had signified that—contrary to all expectations—one of those missiles could, in fact, be launched someday.[49]

There were those who would not have found this terribly surprising. The launch of a Minuteman—particularly the accidental launch of a Minuteman—had troubled military planners from the first. For this reason the Ballistic Missile Panel recommended that extra fail-safes be included in these new "push-button" missiles. Perhaps the Minutemen should be outfitted with automatic "destruct mechanisms." Or, more fantastically, at some future, undetermined date, "strategically positioned satellites" could be used to shoot down accidentally fired missiles. At no point were the American people apprised of these possibilities.[50]

By April 1961, around the time Niederwerder got his resettlement letter, none of these troubling issues had been resolved, at least not suitably for the Lauritsen Committee. The panel, chaired by the eminent physicist Charles C. Lauritsen, was established in 1960 by the Ballistic Missile Division to conduct an outside review of the Minuteman program. And in 1961, though not tasked with considering the possibility of accidental launch, the committee highlighted the issue in its final June report. First, the committee noted, "accidental firings" had indeed occurred "in many of the systems currently in operation." As a result, it was possible that accidents would occur in this new system. Second, the complexity of the Minuteman, particularly its electrical wiring, would only increase the probability—no matter how small—of such an accident. Moreover, though the committee did not want to point any fingers, it appeared that no agency really had the expertise to properly assess safety systems for missiles.[51]

The real problem, however, was in the operational plans for the Minutemen. Ed Hall had designed the system back in 1957 for salvo or ripple firing: a launch order would trigger no less than fifty missiles all at once. This was not only cheaper, but also well suited to Eisenhower's strategy of mutually assured destruction. The Minutemen would be used only in total war. There was no need for individual Minuteman launches or retargeting capabilities. The primary target of this devastation would be urban-industrial centers: large, immovable targets. A salvo or ripple firing of 800 missiles would signal global doom.

But by 1961, when the Minuteman missile was quickly moving from a design to an operational weapon system, the Lauritsen Committee and the new Kennedy administration were prepared to consider other outcomes; whereas salvo firing was initially accepted for its simplicity and totality, those characteristics suddenly seemed rather harrowing indeed. While the accidental launch of a 2-megaton Atlas missile was horrifying enough to contemplate, it would be a mere pinch when compared to the launch of a Minuteman squadron— some 50 megatons of nuclear force. Such an "unintended obliteration of cities outside of the U.S. through improper launch," the Air Force noted dryly, should be avoided. The Lauritsen Committee took a dimmer view of the possibility. "The committee feels most strongly," they warned, "that regardless of the precautions taken against inadvertent launch, the threat to world security implicit in such a system required application of the highest level of approval and control." In other words, more study was necessary.[52]

The Office of the Secretary of Defense concurred. It recommended that the Air Force add selective launch capabilities, so that one missile could be fired at a time. It was also hoped that stop-launch and retargeting capabilities could be added. These changes, of course, could only add cost to the program, which is exactly why they were not originally planned. Insisting that existing "fail-safe" measures were adequate, the Air Force estimated that these extras would cost tens of millions of dollars for each wing of missiles. These changes would also add extensive delays. To retrofit the missiles at Malmstrom Air Force Base in Montana, for example, would set the program back no less than three months.[53]

But there was another, more sweeping logic behind the Pentagon's interest in new Minuteman capabilities, and it had less to do with safety and more to do with how to win a nuclear war. Faith in Eisenhower's all-or-nothing nuclear strategy—mutually assured destruction—was far from unanimous. Throughout his administration strategists at organizations such as RAND had devised plans for fighting limited nuclear wars, for responding to Soviet aggression with discrete and pointed retaliation. In his top-selling 651-page tome, *On Thermonuclear War*, strategist Herman Kahn took these ideas public. "A thermonuclear war is quite likely to be an *unprecedented catastrophe*," Kahn admitted. "But an 'unprecedented' catastrophe can be a far cry from an 'unlimited' one." The question for Kahn was how to prepare the nation to fight and survive the "limited" variety of war. Henry Kissinger was just one of the many policy wonks who had already thought up an answer to Kahn's question: what the country needed was a strategy that provided for the selective use of nuclear weapons. While the capability of a massive retaliatory blow remained essential to deterring all-out war, more limited uses of nuclear weapons would prevent the Soviets from challenging the United States in smaller conflicts around the world—for example, another Korean conflict.[54]

"Flexible response" was the call sign for this type of deterrence, and McNamara was an early convert. In the spring of 1961, as the Kennedy administration consolidated its control over the nation's bureaucracy, McNamara shifted the focus of American nuclear strategy from total war to a more limited, winnable variety. He wanted, as Kahn implored, to keep all "options" on the table. This included counterforce targeting, which meant that missiles would be aimed at military rather than urban-industrial targets. By March 1961—just as South Dakotans were beginning to learn of their role in nuclear deterrence—Kennedy was making public statements about "controlled response" and the capability to use nuclear weapons in a limited war. If each side could limit its nuclear strikes to nonurban areas, it was hoped, then population centers could be spared and perhaps outlast hostilities. While many people doubted whether anyone would want to survive in a postnuclear world, Kahn and his cohort were quick to assert that we would, indeed, be able to.[55]

This shift in strategic policy had immediate implications for the Minutemen. Salvo firing clearly did not allow for the nuance of controlled response; how could one hope to negotiate after simultaneously launching fifty warheads at the Soviet Union? What was needed instead was individual launch capability—the firing of discrete missiles aimed at specific Soviet military targets—and the concurrent ability to withhold a large force for follow-on retaliation. By containing damage to nonurban centers, the logic went, a nuclear exchange could take place without global devastation. And so while concerns about Minuteman safety and capabilities reached back into the previous year, the new administration's ideas of controlled response provided the final impetus for missile revisions. In late 1961 it was determined that the Minuteman missile system should be revamped. All wings would be retrofitted with retargeting and individual launch capabilities. Why not throw in new safety features to boot?[56]

Though the specifics of these deliberations were far removed from Ernest Niederwerder and other South Dakotans, the implications for their own lives were important. The good news was that the threat of accidental launch and its accompanying horrors—however remote to begin with—were further diminished. The bad news was that this new strategic posture—the idea of counterforce and targeting military installations—relied on the (unsubstantiated) premise that the

Soviets could be doing exactly the same thing. In other words, western South Dakota—and the Niederwerder home—had just become a potential ground zero.

These considerations were hardly on the minds of ranchers in 1961 as they continued to debate the merits of signing away their property rights. Despite much discontent, by June, Jensen suspected that nearly 75 percent had signed rights of entry for construction. Jensen himself was getting tired of the fight, particularly since most of the rest of the state seemed more than happy with the Minutemen. The local papers, Jensen reminded Pellegrin, were promising $650,000 in road improvements. Moreover, the Wall Chamber of Commerce was getting antsy, concerned that perhaps the Air Force would decide to relocate the project to another township. While Pellegrin and Hayes both reminded Jensen that their refusal to sign rights of entry was actually not going to hold up deployment or road improvements, Jensen was concerned. While such attacks were limited, many ranchers continued to report that they were being branded unpatriotic and subversive by Corps of Engineer agents. Jensen signed in late May, on the condition that the Corps codify his right to negotiate for property damages in the future. In a final parting shot Jensen channeled the nation's Revolutionary past in a letter to the Corps: "I am sure that our founding fathers who gave us the basic principles on which to build a true Democracy would blush with shame if they knew how present administrators of our Bill of Rights and Constitution were choking legitimate land owners."[57]

A few of the state's powerful agricultural groups were coming to a similar conclusion. The plight of the missile landowners was of great interest to them, not only because many of the missile landowners were dues-paying members, but also because the Air Force was going to need a lot more land. Each of the missile sites had to be connected to the launch centers and to Ellsworth Air Force Base so that launch orders and signals could be sent back and forth. This "spiderweb" communication system would consist of tens of thousands of miles of underground cables. Laying those cables required aboveground access and the involvement of hundreds more landowners. In anticipation of conflict both the western South Dakota Stockgrowers Association and the Farm Bureau passed resolutions condemning the current approach to land acquisition. They wanted money put into accounts for the landowners immediately and demanded appropriate compensation for damages. The latter became particularly relevant as the first reports from the missile fields trickled in: careless construction crews had left trenches open and cut irrigation lines. In the worst cases cattle were maimed and killed falling into open pits.[58]

The missile sites also remained contentious. Even after Jensen and others signed, many landowners continued to press their cases. During a June 8 meeting in Rapid City, the directors of the landowners association decided to persevere. In their assessment, Corps of Engineers representatives were still making "false and misleading statements." For those left, the battle lines had calcified into ugly scars and the conflict was becoming deeply personal. Gene S. Williams recalls that what made his parents refuse to sign a right of entry had less to do with the site of the silo (which was a problem) and more to do with the way his family was treated by the military. The Williamses were angered by Corps of Engineers personnel who would drive across their winter wheat field instead of parking and walking. At one point his mother was called unpatriotic. "That kind of rubbed her the wrong way," Williams noted. "Considering that she lost a brother in World War II . . . that probably was the straw that broke the camel's back about, you know, we're fed up with this."[59]

In late June, Senator Case had in hand a list of the seventeen individuals (out of fifty in Squadron 1) who had still refused to sign. The federal government took them to court. By early fall another sixteen landowners in Squadron 2 were served papers. None of them could win, of course. Even Cecil Hayes knew that. But in his estimation they could wait for the best possible government offer, which would certainly be above the $100 to $650 talked about. In the end the Williamses received $1,500 for their land and damages—much more than the $100 offer originally made, but hardly compensation for the time and fees that federal court proceedings demanded. Fortunately, too, for the Niederwerders the work of the landowner's association and Senator Case paid off. After some investigation it was determined that the resettlement letter was sent in error. The Air Force issued waivers for houses already built too close to a proposed silo.[60]

That fall while construction began on most of the missile sites, landowners continued to simmer. Harvey Haidle could not help but compare the worth of his farmland to the multimillion-dollar construction contract that had been awarded to a Nebraska company to build the missile sites. Calculating the cost of each missile site, Haidle wrote, "A little sum of $3,748,000 will be sunk in this hold of mine plus the minute man itself." All the while, he continued, "we have to sit here and take a little $950 for our land and continued nuisance to our farming operations. I'm not so sure we hadn't better give her to Russia." Hayes was coming to the same conclusion. The chaos of construction was beginning to drive people away. "Joe Topinka moved this week," he reported to Senator Case. "He did not like the idea of his front yard being a garbage dump" during construction. "He has been a good neighbor," Hayes lamented. "We all will miss him and his family. It doesn't seem to me necessary to force someone to move in an area of this kind where places are few and far between. Too many farm families are finding it necessary to move, without being forced to do it. . . . I don't know how long I can take it." In fact Hayes wondered if the recent rumor that the Air Force was going to turn the entire area into a giant "permanent Military

Reservation" was true. Senator Case, after asking the Air Force, assured Hayes that no such reservation was in the works.[61]

The South Dakota MALA did little, in the end, to hold up national defense or to stymie the militarization of their land. The Minuteman missiles were built with little or no discernable delay, at least none that could be attributed to landowners. In fact on September 11, 1961, ground was broken for the first missile site, L-6, during a ceremony called "partners for peace." Hundreds of Air Force and Corps of Engineers representatives, reporters, and locals came to inaugurate the Minuteman construction program. Underscoring the importance of the event, Governor Archie Gubbard drove down from Pierre for the occasion.[62]

Of course halting national defense was never the landowners' intentions. South Dakotans did not fight against becoming ground zero or the potential environmental implications of military installations, but rather against the threat to their seeming sacrosanct rights as property owners. They were willing to fight for what they thought most important, though in the end they would be forced to give in.

The true importance of this story resides in that failure. Despite the fact that the landowners lobbied the necessary people, garnered the support of powerful local agricultural lobbies, and had strong conservative credentials on their side—indeed did the very things that had long proved successful for them—there was simply nothing they could do to effectively challenge the national security state. In many ways Cold War necessity presented rural Americans with precisely the uncompromising, highly centralized authority that had long made them shudder. But rather than simply glom old notions of the faraway "Government" onto the defense establishment, which would have meant treating the military like a distant authority that had to be managed and somehow contained (something like the

BLM), rural Westerners began crafting a twofold understanding of the state. There was that old Washington that continued to meddle where it should not. And then there was the military. By splitting the state into two entities it would be possible for rural Westerners to continue their general skepticism about the federal government while simultaneously revering the U.S. military.

This bifurcation was made possible by two related factors. First, good old-fashioned patriotism made criticism of the defense establishment difficult. It is hardly an exaggeration to say that in the rural West opposing the national security state was to flirt with subversion. As a statewide editorial declared in May 1961, landowners ought to stop complaining and accept that the real inconvenience would be "a Russian missile dropping on South Dakota." At the same time the economics of defense spending were becoming increasingly clear. While residents of the missile fields were not as intimately connected to these realities or dollar signs, South Dakotans living near Ellsworth were. As we shall see, those Westerners had already accepted national security doubling as economic stimulus. A federal bureaucracy created out of necessity—out of crisis—was a necessary evil. Just think of World War II's "arsenal of democracy." Patriotic fervor thus legitimized the creation of the Cold War state while also providing the fuel for its expansion.[63]

This line of thinking had important long-term political implications and helps explain the seeming disconnect between voters rejecting social welfare while favoring a massive defense. Western South Dakotans accepted the need for federal assistance in developing their economy, but by channeling it through Pentagon funds they could shun the more redistributive programs of the liberal state. In other words, their politicians, such as Francis Case, could accept militarized welfare while deploring the welfare state. Bruce Schulman has shown a similar calculus in the South, where politicians used federal defense expenditures not tied to "support for welfare, labor, blacks." Indeed, for many rural Westerners, the goals of many federal programs—tackling racial inequality and urban poverty, for example—seemed far removed from their own problems.[64]

For the next few decades landowners in the missile fields would periodically scrape up against these new realities. But always they carried with them the thought that this would be temporary, that someday the Cold War would end and those missiles would come out. What they did not count on was the permanence of this project. As the Minutemen were nestled into the ground, the defense bureaucracy was insinuating itself into every congressional district, countless industries, and thousands of local economies. When the Cold War came to an end, none of these things—not the hardware, not the political institutions or defense dependencies—could be fully pulled from the ground.

The location of Minuteman II missiles in the United States. Beginning in the early 1960s, the U.S. Air Force deployed 1,000 Minuteman missiles across the heartland. (Library of Congress)

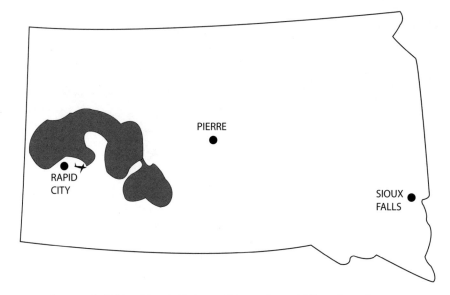

The missile fields of South Dakota: 150 missiles and fifteen launch control centers were spread out over 12,000 square miles. (Map by Heather Dart)

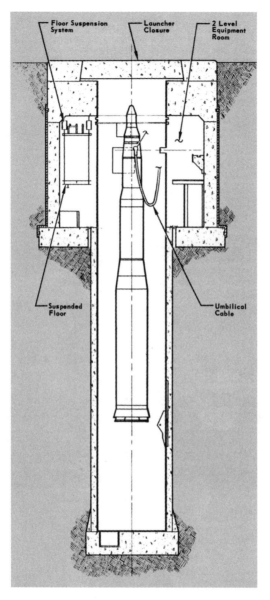

A drawing of a Minuteman I missile silo. The Minuteman was the first missile that could be stored in and fired from a concrete silo sunk 80 feet underground. (Courtesy of the National Museum of the United States Air Force, Wright-Patterson Air Force Base, Ohio)

A view of the Rockies, looking west from missile silo F-8, near Clemons Coulee, Montana. The first Minuteman missiles were deployed to Malmstrom Air Force Base in the early 1960s. Today, 150 Minuteman III missiles remain on alert there. The missile sites were meant to be invisible, so they were designed to blend into their surroundings. (Courtesy of John Hooton)

Fashion and military hardware meet as models pose before a Minuteman missile erected at the Air Force Association's annual convention in San Francisco, 1960. Images such as these led President Eisenhower to warn of the "insidious penetration of our own minds" with images of weaponry and war. (Courtesy of *Air Force Magazine*)

A model poses in front of a corporate display during the Air Force Association Convention in 1960. The association reported 60,000 visitors. (Courtesy of *Air Force Magazine*)

A child poses inside a rocket booster on display in the Aerospace Panorama at the annual convention in San Francisco. The antinuclear organization SANE demanded of such images in 1961: "Is this a healthy way to bring up children?" The companies involved clearly thought it was good for business. (Courtesy of *Air Force Magazine*)

Missileman General Bernard A. Schriever (1911–2005) stands amid
models of Air Force missiles, including some of the systems created under
his leadership. Schriever is considered the "Father of Air Force Space and
Missiles." (Courtesy of the National Museum of the United States Air
Force, Wright-Patterson Air Force Base, Ohio)

A Minuteman missile rises in front of City Hall in San Francisco. The Minuteman was officially "unveiled" on September 22, 1960, during the Air Force Association's annual convention. While many other missiles and airplanes were on display, the Minuteman was the main event. (Courtesy of *Air Force Magazine*)

A launch control facility under construction near Malmstrom Air Force Base in Montana. An Army Corps of Engineers representative described the task of building out the missile fields as the "greatest construction effort in history." Once complete, this capsule is where missileers sat, ready to launch the missiles. The Army Corps of Engineers Ballistic Missile Construction Office and its contractors built 1,000 silos between 1961 and 1966. (Courtesy of the National Museum of the United States Air Force, Wright-Patterson Air Force Base, Ohio)

"A Minuteman in Modern Dress": A transporter-erector truck, which was used to carry the missiles; notice the artwork on its door. The Air Force and its corporate partners often used the image of the Revolutionary minuteman in depictions of its missiles. In many cases, the missile itself is not even pictured. (Library of Congress)

Missile silo K-8, near Spearfish, South Dakota. Beginning in 1961 the Air Force deployed 150 missiles to Ellsworth Air Force Base in western South Dakota. South Dakota's missiles were on alert until 1991. (Courtesy of John Hooton)

A promotional image welcomes the arrival of the Minuteman missile in South Dakota. The deployment of 150 Minuteman missiles was generally met with enthusiasm. Local politicians and the chamber of commerce were particularly avid boosters and worked with the Air Force to cultivate Ellsworth Air Force Base. (Courtesy of National Park Service, Minuteman Missile National Historic Site)

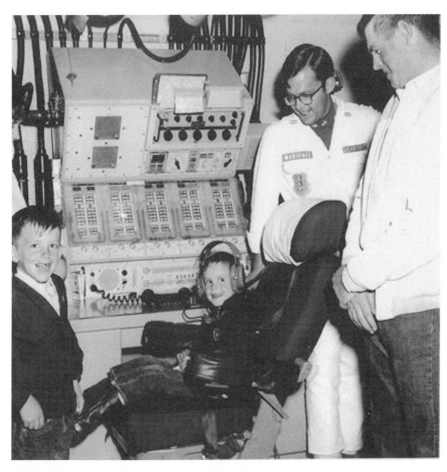

Two boys at the controls of a Minuteman launch control center during a "community day" at a facility in South Dakota in the 1960s. The Air Force cultivated local support through efforts such as annual open houses, adopt-a-missile programs, and other outreach activities. (Courtesy of the National Park Service, Minuteman Missile National Historic Site)

Missile silo O-3, near Knob Noster, Missouri. The "Show Me" state
housed 150 Minuteman missiles until they were dismantled in the 1990s.
(Courtesy of John Hooton)

NO-LONE ZONE
TWO-MAN
CONCEPT
MANDATORY

A mural from the blast doors at Minuteman site D-1 in South Dakota. Murals were painted on many of the blast doors in the Minuteman launch control centers. (Courtesy of the National Park Service, Minuteman Missile National Historic Site)

South Dakotan Marvin Kammerer. Kammerer ranches the land his grandfather homesteaded in the 1880s. In the 1940s, Ellsworth Air Force Base was built on the edge of the Kammerer land. He is a vocal opponent of the military as well as a social justice activist in his state, fighting for preservation of the Black Hills and Lakota rights. (Courtesy of Marvin J. Kammerer)

A bomber roars over the Kammerer ranch, Elk Vale, South Dakota. In July 1980, Kammerer and participants of the International Black Hills Survival Gathering crafted huge rock peace symbols on his property so that airmen could see them when taking off from Ellsworth Air Force Base. (Courtesy of Marvin J. Kammerer)

Minuteman Missile National Historic Site. Only one of South Dakota's 150 Minuteman missile silos remains, not as an active missile site, but as part of a historic site operated by the National Park Service. A glass dome covers the old silo. Inside, an inert replica of a Minuteman missile waits. (Photo by author)

5

Nuclear Heartland

At any given moment during the Cold War, no fewer than 200 Air Force officers lived underneath the Great Plains. Their job was to sit, and wait, and hope that the job they had been trained to do would never have to be done. The officers rotated through four-day shifts of 12 hours underground, 12 hours above. They ate belowground. They slept there. A toilet was furnished for their comfort. The necessities were provided. It was something like a submarine under the soil, only one that would never surface. In the event of thermonuclear war it was expected that these underground airmen—the "missileers"—would survive (and much went into ensuring their survival), at least long enough to launch their nuclear missiles.

Should the missileers complete this task, what would become of them was left to the imagination. There were a few things of which they could have been certain. If they were asked to launch their missiles, then almost certainly it would have been as part of global thermonuclear war. Nuclear deterrence would have failed. In such an event the missileers would probably have felt a jolt as a Soviet warhead hit close to their launch center—harness seat belts, to be worn at the consoles, were provided for just this possibility. The power would have gone out until the backup generators kicked in. Perhaps the air would start to go stale, and then the men would have used the hand-pump oxygen regenerators provided. The aboveground support facilities and their access elevator would have been vaporized. The Great Plains above them—and indeed the entire country—would surely lie in ruins. No one would be left to help them get out. There were a few days' worth of food and water, a shovel, and an escape hatch. Each missileer carried a sidearm. But no one had ever actually tried to dig his way out from 31 feet belowground—where would you put all the sand? What would you find when you reached the top? Like any apocalyptic scenario, this one ended badly. The message was clear: in the event of nuclear war, there were no winners.[1]

Yet by 1968, Air Force officers stood on guard for this doomsday in Montana, North and South Dakota, Wyoming, Missouri, Nebraska, and Colorado. While ranchers and farmers carried on aboveground, trying to ride out cycles of drought and deluge, missiles in silos and missileers in white coveralls were ferreted away underneath, ensconced in concrete bunkers, fed with artificial air and fluorescent lights. When the missileers left their posts, it was in official Air Force vehicles, traveling the back roads of the plains and coming into contact, periodically, with the ranchers and farmers who worked above them.

This peculiar landscape was incorporated into plains life remarkably well, precisely as the Air Force had hoped. Yet the general quiet masked an intriguing problem: Why did Americans accept this condition so easily and for so long? To be sure, shared fears about the Soviet threat and the need for Cold War defenses played important roles in normalizing the ICBM; so too did Minuteman imagery and publicity—so much so that in the late 1950s and early 1960s, many Americans believed that extraordinary measures were necessary to check global Communism. But there is a difference between extraordinary and bizarre, a line the Minuteman system in many ways breached.[2]

In western South Dakota, a far more elemental motivation helped people accept the missiles: money. As many Americans were coming to understand, national security dollars could make the difference between the haves and the have-nots; between those regions that advanced and those that remained mired in the agrarian past. Rapid City, South Dakota, was not a modern, industrial hub, but that did not stop its residents from dreaming of bigger and better things— visions that, in 1961, were hitched to the prospects of neighboring Ellsworth Air Force Base. Rapid City was a good candidate for becoming what Roger Lotchin called the "martial metropolis," a city developed through and "molded by its alliance with the U.S. fighting services." Read in this light, the deployment of Minuteman missiles was one step on a longer path that linked western South Dakota to Pentagon largesse. And so it was that as landowners organized into the Missile Area Landowners Association, other Dakotans moved to signal their unwavering support for the Air Force. An editorial in the *Sioux Falls Argus Leader* chided the ranchers for "trying to get every nickel out of Uncle Sam that the traffic will bear." It would be good "for the ranchers who want that last dollar to think about the last thing that anybody—including the Russian people—wants: a rain of missiles over the North Pole." Patriotism, it turned out, was going to be a respectable cover for self-interest.[3]

If the benefits of defense dollars were increasingly clear in the early 1960s, less understood or anticipated were how addictive and transformative those funds would become. Defense dependency was not intentional, but over time it became nearly proverbial. In 1966, for example, Rapid City resident Almon "Hoadley" Dean wrote to his senator suggesting that Ellsworth Air Force Base look into getting "50 more missiles," this time "possibly aimed at Peking." His rationale was not that the nation needed additional security, but that "our Rapid City community needs this shot in the arm." No wonder landowners like Cecil Hayes fretted about the Air Force turning their lands into a giant "military reservation."[4]

Through the end of the Cold War, residents of the missile fields lived not merely under constant threat of Soviet attack, but also with the nagging apprehension that something more could be done to their land. Shifting views of deterrence and a constant preoccupation with vulnerability would lead to new derivations of the Minuteman. In the late 1960s South Dakotans watched as Minuteman II missiles replaced Minuteman I. During the next decade the Air Force periodically contemplated new ways of deploying their rockets. And in the 1980s a new missile system altogether was proposed. South Dakotans eyed each step along the way with nervous—or in some cases, rapt—attention. Exploring how this relationship unfolded over the course of the Cold War, including moments when it began to fray, reveals the subtle process and consequences of Cold War militarism.

During the winter of 1961, as South Dakota landowners chafed against the capricious requirements of the national security state, nothing about the Minutemen seemed particularly arbitrary to Dean. On the contrary, where ranchers sensed trouble Dean saw opportunity. The Minuteman program would expand Ellsworth Air Force Base; Ellsworth Air Force Base would help grow the community. A self-described "business consultant," Dean wore horn-rimmed glasses and the obligatory western cowboy hat. He was not a rancher, but he was born and raised on the plains of western South Dakota and by the early 1960s he had made a name for himself promoting the region. His goal was to help Rapid City turn from cow town to destination, to help modernize the agricultural outback. In the early 1950s Dean led a tourism promotion group. Over the next decade he founded the Western South Dakota Development Company, an organization he would run for fourteen years. He also served as vice president of the Air Force Association. Dean's boosterism eventually won him a spot in South Dakota's Hall of Fame.[5]

Already in the early 1960s the survival and overall health of Ellsworth Air Force Base was central to any modernization plans. The reasons were obvious: by 1950, just ten years after the base's founding, Rapid City's population had doubled to 27,000. Outsiders moved in; construction jobs proliferated; new money was infused into the area. By the 1960s Ellsworth contributed nearly $55 million annually to the region's economy. Where once Rapid City had looked to the agricultural hinterland for economic sustenance, it would now turn to Ellsworth. In the early Cold War, cows were not nearly as lucrative as bombs.[6]

Dean was not alone in his embrace of the Air Force base and its missiles. After the official announcement of Minuteman deployment in January 1961, the state's congressional delegation was appropriately pleased. Neither GOP senators Karl Mundt and Francis Case, nor the state's western representative, Ellis Berry, also a Republican, could claim much credit for bringing the Minutemen in, but they would certainly not shun additions to the state's only remaining Air Force base. Senator Case wrote to his constituents suggesting the potential hidden benefits of missile deployment: more people meant increased demand for locally produced milk and meats. Nuclear missiles could thus sprinkle military crumbs on even the least suspecting South Dakotans: far-flung farmers and ranchers.[7]

The powers in Rapid City, too, welcomed the news of Minuteman deployment with hopeful expectations. Rapid City Chamber of Commerce president Tom Walsh predicted more than a boon for just meat and milk interests. He saw bigger and better things. The economic benefit, he wrote, would be "a continuing thing," not just a quick, one-shot boost. While the Dakota Steel and Supply Company had yet to hear from any military personnel, the company was confident that "the Minuteman [would] be of benefit" to its bottom line. In keeping with its role as regional booster and educator, the *Rapid City Daily Journal* ran a three-part series on the impact of Minuteman deployment. A January 17 story proclaimed, "Minuteman

Promises Economic Lift." Based on interviews with expectant real estate agents, labor groups, and construction firms, the paper asserted that "there is little doubt" the missile program "will herald vast economic benefits for the entire West River region, as well as Rapid City." Picking up on the enthusiasm, a Belle Fourche biweekly suggested that the Minuteman project would be a "$60 million undertaking." Subsequent articles in Rapid City examined the suspected effect on the region's power, transportation, and schools. While no firm data could be ascertained and very few companies had actually been contacted by the government, everyone interviewed agreed that good things were to come.[8]

The citizens of Rapid City generally provided their support. "We are certainly watching the development of the 'Minute Man' Missile program with great interest," chamber of commerce manager Larry Owen admitted. Owen informed Case that the announcement of the missiles had "stabilized" business sentiment in the region. The chamber not only paid close attention to what was happening on the base, but also became increasingly adept at anticipating and ferreting out information before it was made public.[9]

In 1961, response to these new national security programs thus reflected a barely disguised sense of entitlement. These rural residents *expected* the U.S. government—in whatever guise—to work for them. Nowhere was this more apparent than in letters to congressional representatives begging for missile installations. B. B. Hodson, a cashier for the BlackPipe Bank, wrote to Case that Martin, South Dakota (population 1,184), was ideally suited—and due—for a defense construction project. We have "never had any government construction," Hodson wrote. "We even built our Auditorium without federal assistance, even when we were quite sure that it would be used later for an Armory." Should anyone come to scout the area, Hodson continued, "Mayor Thompson, or the Martin Commercial Club will be most happy to drop everything to assist." Even less demure was Donald L. Cammack of Buffalo, who insisted that his township receive a Minuteman missile because it would "furnish a much needed economic boost to our community." Doyle Grossman, of the Lemmon Chamber of Commerce, pleaded, "we have an unemployment problem in this area. . . . Building a Missile Base would help this community a lot."[10]

Many rural residents greeted the Minuteman in much the same way they greeted other federal programs: with palms up and expectation of moderate economic gain. If nothing else, construction of the missile fields suggested that new federal money would be poured into the region. During the Great Depression, $55 million had been disbursed in South Dakota for soil conservation and range building. For many in western South Dakota, the memories of how important those programs had been to their survival, and the exodus of so many others, were still fresh. New Deal programs remained mainstays of the agricultural economy. In the first three months of 1961, farmers and ranchers in Butte County received $270,780 in direct loans through the Farmers Home Administration. Soil Conservation district offices bought cooperative equipment, provided access to information, and helped organize community projects and outreach. More recently, too, federal largesse had found its way into the state through construction of the interstate highway system and Missouri River Dam project. For ranchers the extra money they made working on the flag crew could make the difference between a winter of want and one of comfort. The missiles would serve the same purpose. In all this prodding and planning, the unique nature of this particular government project was rarely mentioned. Federal money, it seemed, was federal money, whether for conservation programs, bomb shelters, or nuclear missiles. In any case, South Dakotans could find a good use for it.[11]

Local politics also helped inure rural residents to nuclear missiles and the strategy of deterrence. Far inland and far removed from the centers of power, western South Dakotans tended to stick to themselves and distrust outsiders. They generally believed in a small but strong defense and limited international obligations. A strand of isolationism percolated. One of the state's longest-running politicians, Republican senator Mundt, started out in the 1930s as a card-carrying member of Charles Lindbergh's America First Party, and in 1940 he hopped across the country warning his compatriots of the dangers of intervention. While Mundt, like the rest of his state, would eventually embrace the cause of World War II in Europe, he remained wedded to what he called "insulationism," a term that allowed him to support the war while remaining, with caveats, an isolationist.[12]

Such sentiment remained strong even as the nation embarked on a more active Cold War foreign policy. In 1952 South Dakota Republican Party delegates went to Chicago to cast their convention ballots for Ohio senator Robert A. Taft. While half of South Dakota's delegates ultimately sided with the odds-on favorite, General Eisenhower, half remained committed to the losing side, not only of the ballot but of the party. It was the year that the Grand Old Party turned its back on nationalist isolationism (signified by "Mr. Republican," Taft himself) and began its headlong plunge into internationalism, headed by, appropriately enough, a war hero. And while South Dakotans came to accept Cold War internationalism—the necessity of fighting Communism worldwide with American economic, military, and cultural power—it was in muted form. In 1960 the majority of South Dakotans, of all political persuasions, wanted foreign aid programs reduced or abolished.[13]

In general, western South Dakotans, true to their geographic isolation, remained far removed from Cold War decisions, both military and other. They had their Air Force base; young South Dakotans fought in relatively large numbers in the Korean War; many area ranchers were decorated—and proud—veterans. But this was a local patriotism, rooted in a sense of place and time, a sense of community and belonging, more than a national impulse. South Dakota exhibited a "moderate conservatism" that emphasized moral leadership, limited government, and local control, a political culture closely linked to South Dakotans' past as agrarian populists. The electorate mistrusted bigness on all fronts; large federal budgets and standing armies would not be tolerated. Most South Dakotans would have thus appreciated President Eisenhower's exhortations about the capacity for runaway spending to bring ruin to the nation. So, too, they ultimately appreciated Eisenhower's defense goals: the Air Force and nuclear deterrence seemed to provide the most cost-effective and least intrusive means of preserving the nation's security in the face of the Communist menace. Like most Americans, South Dakotans did not like to think of their country as particularly aggressive or militaristic; deterrence helped them think it wasn't so.[14]

In the early 1960s, engineers were not the only people digging up western South Dakota. So too was Leonel Jensen. If an underground shelter was going to protect the instruments of war, Jensen reasoned, then perhaps one could save his own family. And so while Leonel's eleven-year-old son, Paul, played in the construction site that would soon become Minuteman missile silo site B-9, his parents began searching for the most appropriate bomb shelter to add to their home.[15]

The Wonder Building Corporation of America, headquartered in Chicago, had a few suggestions. In full-color brochures, the company proudly featured three unique shelters: the Farm Living Shelter, the Group Living Shelter, and the more diminutive Family Shelter kit. While the farm shelter allowed you to save "your prized breeding stock," the Jensens ultimately opted for something more manageable—a family shelter attached to their basement with an escape hatch.[16]

Jensen was not alone that fall in his quest for nuclear security. In 1961 the Wonder Building Corporation of America sold 5,000 shelters, including one to the Jensens, 15 percent more than the previous year. A new industry was, albeit temporarily, born. In Dallas, the

Acme Bomb and Fallout Shelter Company opened; Sacramento welcomed Atlas Bomb Shelters; and in Southern California the Fox Hole Shelter Company commenced operations. Swimming pool manufacturers discovered they could turn their product upside down and sell pools as fallout protection, not a bad option for the winter months. This was a movement driven not by ICBM deployment, but by international events. It just so happened that precisely as the Minutemen were heading to South Dakota, the nation was on the verge of a full-fledged civil defense boom prompted by renewed tensions in Berlin and President John F. Kennedy's exhortation for Americans to think about their own survival.[17]

According to the president, 1961 was the time to consider the unthinkable: to "recognize the possibilities of nuclear war in the missile age." In his July 25 national radio address, Kennedy reminded Americans of their responsibility to West Berlin, an island in the middle of Communist East Germany. Since the end of World War II, Berlin had been the Cold War's primary flashpoint. Tensions flared again in the spring of 1961 as the East German Communist government sought to stymie the mass exodus of its citizens to the West. In August those efforts culminated in the construction of the Berlin Wall, a literal concrete and barbed-wire barrier between East and West. Kennedy responded by requesting supplementary defense appropriations and expansion of the U.S. Armed Services. If West Berlin should fall, Kennedy warned, if the Soviets could destroy freedom there—which they seemed intent on doing—then the fate of the free world was in question. But he also asked Americans to begin preparing for this new space-age war. An attack was possible and it was the responsibility of the government and citizens to take measures to protect themselves. Nuclear war could be survived: "In the event of an attack, the lives of those families which are not hit in a nuclear blast and fire can still be saved—if they can be warned to take shelter and if that shelter is available." The task at hand was to identify and develop those shelter spaces.[18]

Accordingly Kennedy implemented the national shelter survey, which would, unintentionally, demonstrate the total inadequacy of South Dakota's own preparations. The program would also litter the country with black and yellow fallout-shelter signs. While $3.8 million was being poured down the 80 feet of each future Minuteman missile silo, the state of South Dakota spent much less than that on civil defense. The National Fallout Shelter Survey, released in 1963, estimated that for a population of 680,514, South Dakota had some 143,769 available shelter spaces, none of which, it should be noted, were provided for the express purpose of civil defense. In Jackson County, home of fifteen Minutemen, there were approximately ten approved shelter spaces for a population 200 times that. Perhaps the survey had not counted Leonel Jensen's addition to the family ranch. In any case, the population of South Dakota was certainly not as protected as their warheads.[19]

Residents of the missile fields could be forgiven for not immediately understanding that counterforce, the policy of the Kennedy administration, had made their homes potentially ground zero. Public information about deterrence was vague and confusing. Few missile-area residents grasped that the "no cities" doctrine of targeting weapons at military installations was intended to work both ways. The same ignorance surrounded the missiles themselves. As we have seen, the Minutemen were presented as "defensive" weapons only, the ultimate stopgap protection for the United States, "the most effective deterrent force" and "the greatest retaliatory force" the country has ever seen, according to a Boeing pamphlet sent to South Dakota residents. Missile-field residents thus expected, as they were constantly told to expect, that the missiles would never be used *except* in the event of total nuclear war. No one would want to survive.[20]

This reality troubled Herman Kahn. The high priest of the defense intellectuals, Kahn had, as of late, devoted his considerable brainpower to thinking about surviving nuclear war. In his estimation it was foolish to prepare only for a single, apocalyptic postnuclear scenario in which no one lived. On the contrary, there could be many degrees of survivability, many of them quite livable, what Kahn called "Tragic but Distinguishable Postwar States." The key was to be prepared, something Kahn found the American people astonishingly ill equipped to consider. Kahn bemoaned the very attitude of fatalism that pervaded the missile fields—a sense of "'If we're all going to be dead anyway, there's no use thinking about it.'" On the contrary, Kahn exhorted readers of the *Saturday Evening Post*, "To know what I have come to know about thermonuclear war is to be worried. Yet I am even more troubled that so many Americans today seem so unconcerned." Kahn blamed public apathy on the so-called experts who "contradict one another and confuse the public." But also there was a failure of leadership from the highest levels. As a result "the average American senses a futility." Kahn hoped that a vigorous civil defense program would both overcome apathy and also bolster the nation's credibility, suggesting to the Soviets that the country was ready—if it came to it—to fight, rather than surrender. Kahn, however, was an unlikely—and unsuccessful—popular agitator.[21]

For many Americans, particularly those in the missile fields, more was at stake than merely not understanding nuclear deterrence. As Kahn argued, the American public lacked the information needed to make good choices. But perhaps even more critically, in the missile fields there was quite simply too much to do; the abstraction of nuclear war—the perception that such things would be left to the experts—was an idea solidified through the daily grind of surviving life on the plains. Getting cattle to market, wintering calves, and finding good water were far more immediate concerns than the variegations of strategic theory and the rhetoric of rational analysis favored by the secretary of defense. William Bielmaier recalled that landowners were "much concerned about money and too far into debt" to consider building fallout shelters. "Times weren't good, and there was no extra money." This is not to suggest that rural South

Dakotans were willfully ignorant of the world or the meaning of the weapons in their soil—quite the contrary. Lyndy Ireland recalls nights in front of the television and conversations with her parents about nuclear warfare and deterrence. In a way, she suggests, the missiles signified a "loss of innocence." But, at the same time, like people around the country, these landowners believed in the principles of deterrence and were confident that the experts were making the right decisions.[22]

This line of thinking was corroborated by the events of October 1962. At the height of the Cuban Missile Crisis, the first squadron of Minuteman missiles, up in Montana, were rushed to operational readiness. Kennedy declared the Minutemen his "ace in the hole." For the American public the importance of this new weapon system, still really in its infancy, was sealed. There was no need to question its efficacy, its ambiguous deployment numbers, or its impact on communities in the missile fields. No, all that most Americans needed to believe was that the Minutemen would stand and guard the country from Soviet aggression, protecting its people through the threat of total annihilation.[23]

Still, the Air Force did not leave everything to chance, or to the promise of financial reward. Nationally the Air Force could never shake public concerns about accidental war. As weapons got more technologically sophisticated, the problem only grew. In July 1960, a study from Ohio State University predicted that a "major accidental war" could happen within the decade, with a 1-in-100 chance that it would involve a nuclear weapon. The general disquiet was reflected in popular culture, where accidents became a prominent plotline for exploring the nuclear world. The novels *Red Alert* (1958) and *Fail-Safe* (1962), both made into major motion pictures in 1964 (the former as *Dr. Strangelove*), ridiculed the idea that rational analysis—and men such as Herman Kahn—could somehow predict and control every contingency. Somewhere, someone, somehow, something could go wrong. As *Fortune* magazine noted in 1963, "in fictional portrayals [of missile sites] there must be at least one big scene in which a claustrophobic officer runs amok."[24]

Mishaps did happen. On October 5, 1960, the U.S. early warning station in Thule, Greenland, picked up radar signals that led to fears of a missile attack. Strategic Air Command (SAC) declined to take action, realizing that the message must have been a fluke. Crisis averted. It would take the Air Force two months to report the incident, begrudgingly admitting that the high-tech radar equipment had been duped by its own radar signals, bounced off the moon. Most news outlets ignored the episode, but *The Progressive* magazine had some unsettling questions: How many other such instances had there been? Given the number of different "official" versions being offered, did the Pentagon even know what had happened? What good was a radar system that didn't work? And finally, what if the general at SAC had thought the warning was the real thing?[25]

In 1963, equipment malfunction sent SAC commander general Tommy Power into four minutes of overdrive. While no date was given, the *Los Angeles Times* reported that Power had scrambled his bombers and put all missile crews on alert after communication with the Thule radar base and North American Air Defense Command went dead. Not knowing the cause of the silence—could they have been taken out by Soviet bombs?—Power did what he thought most prudent and prepared for total war. Within minutes it was determined that "a serious electronic failure" was to blame, and the alert was canceled. "So quickly was the truth determined," the article claimed, there was "not the slightest chance of accidental war." But the fact that a warning had occurred at all suggested a less hopeful alternative.[26]

South Dakota had its own incident, though the details would not be made public until the 1990s. In December 1964, just as the missile fields were activated, the top section of a Minuteman missile—

the reentry vehicle containing the warhead—blew off the missile during maintenance work. The silo door at site L-2 did not open, but the warhead fell off the missile and bounced down some 75 feet. A 1-megaton surface burst from this nuclear bomb would have destroyed everything for 70 square miles. That did not happen. Instead the two maintenance workers were checked for radiation—and their cigarettes confiscated—but they eventually were cleared and released. Five days later the warhead was lifted from the silo with a crane. Residents were not informed. A monthlong investigation concluded that during repairs Glenn Dodson's screwdriver had "crossed the wrong wires." Dodson was thereafter confined to base duty.[27]

While the Pentagon compensated quietly and quickly for such problems, it also understood the wide extent of its public-relations challenge. It could not allow Americans to be whipped into hysterics over the unintended consequences of technological failure or the random chance of a high-placed mental breakdown. Accordingly, the Air Force widely publicized fail-safes. In part this was done to combat the novels and movies that promoted images of accidental war, but it also attempted to preempt new concerns. Any contingency had been planned for, the Air Force assured the public, and every system had multiple redundancies in the event of unexpected failure. Even if a crazy missileer existed, it would be impossible for him to launch a nuclear war alone.[28]

As with Minuteman publicity, the Air Force response to accidental-war hysteria took the form of well-placed newspaper and magazine stories. Journalists were given high-level access to commanders and command centers, in order to see and learn about Air Force and other Pentagon fail-safes. In June 1961, Peter Wyden investigated the issue for the *Saturday Evening Post,* and two years later the *Los Angeles Times'* Donald Robinson received an exclusive look at the intricacies of missile launches. In both cases the verdict was the same: "The world," according to Robinson, "need not fear that the United States will ever start an accidental war." Each article went into painstaking detail about the number of people, red buttons, codes, safe combinations, and gold phones required to initiate war. The process was seemingly so full of checks and double checks that William F. Buckley complained it made the nation's deterrent seem *less* credible. Buckley worried that all of this preoccupation over preventing accidental war had led the Pentagon to err "too far in the direction completely opposite." Given all the fail-safes, would the United States be able to launch a retaliatory blow at all when it was needed?[29]

Buckley offered a solution, admittedly out of science fiction: he recommended an automated deterrent force. His inspiration had been a fictional account of a floating space platform filled with hydrogen bombs that would detonate if it sensed a nuclear explosion below. He just as well could have used the Doomsday Machine of *Dr. Strangelove*. During the Cold War, the line between fantasy and reality was never terribly clear when it came to the nuclear landscape. The more absurd a possibility, the more it seemed to catch on.[30]

In the absence of automation, the crucial fail-safe variable was the missileer. A bomber once aloft can be recalled, but a missile cannot. Moreover, missiles were deployed in far-flung locations, connected through wires and underground cables to launch crews who the public thought were solely responsible for activating the rockets. By 1964 there would have been little time to sit around in a "war room" discussing human extinction; global devastation could have happened in 30 minutes. What *Reader's Digest* praised as "instant deterrence" could also be called "instant destruction."[31]

Faith in the Minuteman system hinged on the question of human reliability. Accordingly, the American public was introduced to the warrior of the modern age. From publications such as *Time, Fortune, Reader's Digest,* and major newspapers Americans were informed that the men in control of the missiles were educated, trained, and highly competent officers, known more for their equanimity than their daring bravery. Missileers were chosen for their "stability of character" and "maturity of judgment." The men were screened using the most up-to-date psychological testing and were given unprecedented "checkups by [an] Air Force mental-hygiene clinic." It was not a job for just anyone. Missileers were all college graduates, and most studied for their master's in aerospace engineering, taking advantage of a unique program of study at "Minuteman U."[32]

If that were not enough, the Air Force wanted everyone to know that extra fail-safes were built into the Minuteman system. No single individual could launch any missiles—the reason that there were two missileers in any launch center at any given time. In addition, launch orders had to come from the control center nearby, which, in turn, had to receive the appropriate code from SAC. Finally, if someone did go nuts, well then, that was what each missileer's handgun was for.[33]

What if someone tried to break into the missile silo? This is one instance in which the remote, far-flung deployment of the missiles seemed troublesome. If the base and its security teams were hundreds of miles away, couldn't someone get into the site and tamper with the equipment? Again the Air Force had an answer ready—it had practiced just such a problem. In 1962 the Air Force had hired a "tunneling contractor with the most modern" equipment to break into a site. It took an hour and a half to get through the reinforced concrete lid, which was more than 3 feet thick. But it had taken just minutes for the security detail to arrive. "This is one sort of illegal entry we don't have to worry about," SAC declared.[34]

In the missile fields the Air Force had more intimate ways of getting residents involved. In 1964 South Dakota landowners were asked to become "Vehicle Spotters" and report military traffic problems to the base as soon as possible. "Please call us *collect* to prevent any personal financial obligation to yourself," the letter suggested. In 1966 the base started an adopt-a-missile program to link area towns to nearby launch centers. Townspeople would become "honorary members of the squadron" and the launch centers would bear the name of the community. Launch Center L-1, for example, would take the name "Sturgis Launch Control Facility."[35]

Activities like these were meant to "improve and extend the excellent military-civilian relationships" in rural South Dakota. As Ellsworth base commander Brigadier General Richard C. Neeley realized, "mutual cooperation" was good for his mission. To that end, at least through 1966, landowners were invited to a yearly dinner with airmen. Individuals seen as particularly important were taken on junkets to other Air Force bases, for example, to California, where they were treated to watching missile launches at Vandenberg. Annual "community days" were held at Air Force bases and missile launch centers, during which time members of the community could tour the facilities and ask questions. Most intriguing was that missile-area landowners and residents were able to tour the top secret missile launch control sites—even taking the elevator down to the launch capsule, where they could sit at the controls and simulate nuclear Armageddon.[36]

Even more than the outreach efforts, nothing normalized the Minutemen and the Air Force like the gradual infrastructure upgrades that took place across the missile fields. The needs of the missile facilities were years—if not decades—ahead of local capabilities. Rural dirt roads and makeshift bridges would not carry the heft of missiles and trucks as they made their way hundreds of miles from the base. As a result they were improved—some paved, others graveled over, most frequently maintained, largely on Uncle Sam's dime. Across the missile fields, road maintenance became part of a cost-sharing program between the Defense Department and local governments. "Basically, the counties were subsidized," reported Tim Pavek, a missile-site engineer in the 1980s. They "enjoyed this windfall profit of [a] million and a quarter dollars a year, roughly, shared in the missile fields." Few locals would have complained. As Norman Fauske recalled, his own county, Jackson, could never have afforded such upgrades. "Our roads were so poor that most of them had to be rebuilt," acknowledged Wyoming rancher Kenneth Kirkbride. "The government spent fifty thousand dollars on a new bridge!"[37]

The missile sites also required extra power, something that many rural South Dakotans had only recently acquired for themselves. In 1939 residents of Pennington County had gotten together to create the West River Electric Association, which took advantage of federal Rural Electrification Act (REA) funds to construct and maintain electrical service in the region. The war slowed things down, but by the mid-1950s much of the region had been wired, thanks to continual REA grants. The missiles ratcheted things up a notch. The Air Force needed upgraded three-phase power lines and services as well as a substantial power allocation. As a result the rural electric cooperatives were able to purchase power at lower rates, passing the savings on to local customers. Telephone services, too, were upgraded. As a resident who worked for Golden West Telephone, Don Paulsen knew that ranchers were not likely to spend extra money upgrading telephone lines, but the Air Force would.[38]

Missile-field construction projects were also a boon. And in this area, for a while at least, local optimism was rewarded. Though the main contractor for Minuteman construction, Peter Kiewet and Sons, was headquartered in Nebraska, the project manager promised that local hires would be used whenever possible. Between 800 and 2,400 workers would be needed at any given time. The Army Corps of Engineers advised interested skilled workers to contact Rapid City unions regarding employment. "Non-skilled local residents," meanwhile, were told to approach Local 205, International HOD Carriers' Building and Common Laborers' Union of America. The policy of Local 205 was to accept applications every morning and sort them based on skills and residency. Ranchers and farmers living in the far-flung missile fields were particularly welcome to apply since it would be hard to move laborers across such vast distances. For those who did have the time and inclination, surveyors were making about $30 per day. For William Cissell and his father, such wages could not be ignored. According to Cissell, his father made about $75 per week as a parts man for the John Deere dealership.

When he began working construction in the missile fields, Cissell recalled, "it allowed us to have a bit better life style." William himself would later work in the missile fields when crews were needed to upgrade facilities. He brought home about $130 a week, more than enough to cover his rent of $40 and $20 transportation costs.[39]

While the people of the western plains were doing their patriotic duty in getting used to the nation's "ultimate" weapon, there were plenty within the strategic community who had doubts about the Minuteman's longevity. As physicist Ralph Lapp had warned Congress in 1960, "all modern weapons systems are essentially obsolescent before they are produced." Lapp did not mean that the weapon itself was unusable, but that technology and evolving ideas about strategy made even the newest weapons seem out-of-date. Precisely as the Minuteman I missiles were buried in western South Dakota, the Air Force began testing the Minuteman II system. This new missile had eight times the "kill" capacity of its progenitor—meaning it had a larger warhead, was more accurate, and could travel farther. The cost for procuring each new Minuteman II missile was nearly $40 million.[40]

Hoadley Dean of Rapid City understood the idea of military obsolescence. In 1966 he had written to Senator Mundt not only about acquiring more missiles, but also about getting Minuteman II upgrades started at Ellsworth. Dean knew that the latest equipment signaled a base's importance, and thus its chances of sticking around. Also, changes brought jobs and money—another "shot in the arm" for the local community. Conversion to the Minuteman II required minor construction, installation of new systems, and upgrades to communications networks, all of which happened in 1971, when South Dakota's Minuteman I missiles were replaced with Minuteman II missiles. While missile-area landowners may have been irritated about renewed activity on and near their fields, more than 300 locals found jobs.[41]

Work began on the third derivation of the Minuteman as early as 1964, though it would be another seven years before any were deployed. With the Minuteman III, the nation could essentially triple the number of deployed warheads by simply swapping out the old Minuteman Is and IIs. This was because the Minuteman III had a multiple independent reentry vehicle (MIRV) that carried three separately targeted warheads, all accurate to within 800 feet. It was the Air Force's "big stick." It was also, essentially, a new missile: the Minuteman III missiles were longer than their predecessors, so major work had to be done on the silos, as well as on the communication infrastructure. In many cases, this again meant jobs for missile-field residents, though not in South Dakota, which never received the Minuteman III upgrade.[42]

Few Dakotans seemed to be bothered by what these changes signaled about their country's nuclear strategy or global politics. For most Americans the idea of nuclear deterrence remained fixed: nuclear weapons existed to deter total war. But transformation in the Minuteman program suggested the bizarre twists and turns that strategic thinking continued to take. Fears of vulnerability, that great aid to defense budgets and interservice rivalries, played a starring role. Not only were new missiles developed, but changes were made to existing systems. Soon after deployment of the Minuteman I, it became "obvious" to defense intellectuals that merely burying missiles underground would not protect them from ever-more accurate Soviet bombs. So more and more extreme safety measures were developed and added to the missile fields—from super-hardening missile sites with extra reinforced concrete, to creating shields against electromagnetic pulses. The deployment of both the Minuteman IIs and IIIs included "penetration aids" and decoy warheads to help stymie Soviet air defenses. The height of absurdity came in 1969, when President Richard Nixon funded "Safeguard," a scheme to protect the Minutemen from attack. Dozens of small nuclear missiles would be deployed at a few strategic locations, initially North Dakota and

Alaska. These missiles would be used to shoot down any incoming Soviet ICBMs. By 1975 the program was abandoned as impractical, but only after it had cost the taxpayers $5 billion.[43]

By the mid-1970s, Cecil Hayes's earlier warning about losing more land to a "military reservation" was beginning to sound prescient. Throughout the decade strategists dreamed of yet more ways to make the Minuteman less vulnerable. The "wagon wheel," "garage mobile Minuteman," and "shell game" were various names for a plan to dramatically expand the size of the missile fields, taking land from many more missile-area landowners. A single missile would be driven around among five different shelters, any of which could serve as a launchpad. The idea of mobility had been around a long time. In fact nuclear weapons were deployed on submarines for this very reason, and the first Minuteman planning documents argued for a rail-based system of missiles. Moving a missile about would mean that the Soviets could never be certain where any given weapon was, thus making it relatively *in*vulnerable. In the missile fields this would presumably mean that current missile-area landowners would lose more land—could you farm around the roads and garage shelters, or would the entire region be off limits?[44]

Yet none of these plans—no matter how extraordinary—could save the Minuteman's place as the ultimate deterrent. Just as early frenetic missile efforts in the United States were motivated by over-blown assessments of Soviet capabilities, so, too, often exaggerated claims of Soviet military intentions continued to shape weapons procurement. By the mid-1970s a new "missile gap" was in the making, led by defense intellectual Albert Wohlstetter, formerly of RAND. The feared missile gap of the 1950s and 1960s had failed to materialize, but by the 1970s the Soviets had caught up with the United States in quantity, if not quality, of missiles. This led to shrill cries about a rapidly approaching "window of vulnerability" (again an eerie echo of the 1960s), which, in turn, encouraged the massive arms buildup of the Carter and Reagan administrations. Each advance on one side was met by a countereffort on the other. The arms race had created its own internal logic, from which defense companies, the armed services, and interested politicians could profit. "One of the ironies of recent history," the *New York Times* editorialized in July 1978, "is that the United States invented most of the weapons that, in Soviet hands, now frighten them the most." Anticipating the Pentagon's moves, the *Times* predicted that "to meet that menace, we are drifting toward a new invention that could have the same boomerang effect."[45]

Indeed, precisely at that moment the Air Force was promoting a new missile—the MX, later christened "Peacemaker" by President Reagan. Echoing the sales pitch of the Minuteman decades before, the Air Force insisted that the MX would provide an invulnerable deterrent force for the coming decades, one that would require the Soviets to expend 5,000 missiles to be certain of destroying the entire missile force. This was important because based on assessments of Soviet capabilities, strategists estimated that by the mid-1980s the Soviets could destroy all of the Minutemen with just a third of their missiles, a line of thinking particularly terrifying when wed to strategists' other primary assumption: the Soviets wanted to launch a nuclear attack on the United States if they were confident it would be successful. Under these expectations, largely unquestioned, the Minuteman of the 1970s practically invited a Soviet attack. It was for these reasons that, in 1979, President Jimmy Carter approved the mobile MX, a decision that publicly broadcast the absurdities of the nuclear landscape.[46]

Ray Bradbury could not have scripted a more fantastic apocalyptic landscape than that concocted by the U.S. Air Force. Forty-five thousand acres of barren, scorched desert would be crisscrossed with single-lane asphalt; 4,600 concrete bunkers would loom, like mirages, at the end of barren cul-de-sacs. From the air it would look like a giant suburban construction site—roads preceding subdivisions; scrappy sand to be turned green with shrubbery; perhaps a school and football field at the end of the lane. But the houses, greenery, and people would never come. Instead this was a world devoted to Armageddon: the roads would be used not by moving vans and family sedans, but by huge tractor-trailers hauling missiles. The entire complex would be built so that 200 ICBMs could be shuttled among 3,000 silos, creating an elaborate shell game, all aimed at fooling the electronic eye of the Soviet Empire. The Soviets would have to guess where the real missiles were deployed. Making the entire scheme more absurd was the fact that the MX had to be developed under SALT II guidelines and verification procedures: though not implemented as planned, the weapon system and ground configuration actually had to be calibrated so that clusters of missiles could be verified by Soviet reconnaissance. Apparently the only people to be fooled by the MX were the people willing to house it.[47]

Given past precedent, the Air Force expected little trouble when deploying the MX. But this time rural Americans were less obliging. In 1980, when the Great Basin of Utah and Nevada was identified as the best site for the missiles, local reception was at first encouraging. Jobs and money were hinted at on more than one occasion. The Air Force predicted that the vast construction project, influx of outside workers and airmen, and new skills brought to the area would usher in an "era of general prosperity." Mirroring the response of rural areas to the Minuteman decades before, many Great Basin businessmen and community leaders applauded.[48]

But opposition mounted, driven ironically by new federal legislation. The Environmental Policy Act of 1969 unintentionally became a useful tool in confronting the national security bureaucracy. That act required all federal agencies to conduct studies and solicit public comment before beginning major projects. In general, rural Westerners were wary of the sort of legislation that lodged more power in the federal government, particularly when it meant reviewing public lands. But in the case of the MX, it proved useful. Unlike in the 1960s, when the Air Force could keep quiet about its plans for missile deployments, in the 1970s and 1980s the Air Force had to hold public meetings. When residents of the Great Basin learned about the racetrack basing model, they were alarmed. Unlike opposition to the Minuteman in the 1960s, opposition to the MX was not a protest of area landowners concerned about property values. Rather it was a broad-based coalition of ranchers, American Indians, Mormon leaders, and environmentalists, who put aside considerable differences to oppose the new missiles. Even "sagebrush rebels"—landowners who wanted federal lands turned over to the states—were involved. The coalition had surprising political power, turning Cold War hawks and Reagan allies like Nevada senator Paul Laxalt into anti-MX advocates.[49]

The No-MX coalition in the Great Basin was not a critique of nuclear deterrence or a questioning of the need for weapons of mass destruction. There were antinuclear activists involved, but broad political support for the No-MX movement came from arguments about preserving a "chosen way of life," rejecting federal intervention in local affairs, and the right of individual landowners to make the best use of their lands. For some Westerners this was a classic states' rights argument about the overreach of federal power. For many others it looked a lot like a "not in my back yard" argument, grounded in the fragile realities of life in the high desert. The latter view was supported by the fact that many No-MX activists—including Senator Laxalt—supported the deployment of MX missiles into the Minuteman missile fields. Let the people who had already accepted nuclear missiles continue to live at ground zero, they reasoned.[50]

Though the general consensus about nuclear weapons held, the public rejection of the MX was recognition that the benefits of military-driven development could be unpredictable. MX deployment would have brought jobs and money—a near certain "boom." But as rural Westerners knew, busts always followed, and no one was confident that the region could survive both. The MX would be a temporary phenomenon, with a life span of twenty years or so. What would happen to the area when the federal dollars, people, and services left? The Great Basin did not boast existing military installations that could help redirect what remained after the MX. As a result it was easier for people—even those who favored a strong national defense—to resist the deployment of missiles.[51]

The story of the No-MX campaign in the Great Basin has two important implications for the story of the Minuteman. First, since the MX was not going to be deployed on a racetrack system in the Great Basin, Reagan decided that the new missiles would be deployed in existing Minuteman missile silos. That meant that residents of the Minuteman missile fields were going to have to get used to another new weapon with a potentially devastating new deployment pattern. Second and related, the apparent success of the No-MX coalitions in the Great Basin encouraged other rural Westerners to organize against the MX in their own communities. In the Dakotas, Wyoming, Colorado, Montana, and Nebraska vibrant local organizations emerged that not only targeted a new weapon system, but also questioned the missiles that had already been buried for so long in their midst. Rural Westerners no longer wanted to live next door to nuclear missiles.

6

The Radical Plains

The clown was fiddling with his bolt cutter. He soon realized that it was not easy to maneuver the blades around a lock when wearing a prosthetic nose and oversize shoes—particularly not when it was hot and humid and his face paint was beginning to run, smudging his thick glasses. But once the clown had the cutters in position, the steel padlock "gave way like butter [and] the gate swung open easily." It was then that the clown and his companion entered Missouri's Minuteman missile silo K-8 carrying balloons and a small flute. The two tied balloons to the antennas that sprouted from the ground; they threw seeds on the barren soil and lay photos of children on the missile lid. They hung banners and ribbons. When they were done, they stood on the concrete missile silo, faced the open gate, and waited for the Air Force to arrive. The companion played the flute. It was just after 7:00 AM, Monday, August 15, 1988.[1]

Meanwhile, nearly 30 miles away and 32 feet belowground, lights began to blink at Launch Control Center K-1, one of fifteen launch centers surrounding Whiteman Air Force Base. Each control center was responsible for watching the computer consoles that monitored ten Minuteman missiles. According to the alarm, something was inside the security fence at missile site K-8. For the two missileers sitting in the launch center, it would have been an unusual and perhaps not totally unwelcome break in the routine: most 12-hour shifts they merely had to sit and wait, perform maintenance checks and conduct occasional drills. The job, according to one missileer, was "sheer boredom punctuated by seconds of panic." They were trained, in fact, to perform a task no one ever wanted them to do: turn the keys and enter the codes that would launch the Minuteman.[2]

A security breach at a missile site could mean many things. In the early years of Minuteman deployment, back in the 1960s when the missiles went in, the sensors were so sensitive that "high-jumping grasshoppers" seemed to set the darn things off. More often than not it was just the wind. While the sensors had been updated since then, alarms still sounded on occasion; sometimes large animals were found roaming the 2-acre plot, unable to get out. (How they got in was another matter entirely.) In South Dakota it was rumored that two camels had escaped an area Nativity play and were found rubbing up against a silo fence. On a few very rare occasions people had been found on the sites. Regardless of the type of alarm, the protocol was clear: when a breach occurred, a security team was dispatched to the silo in question. Only then could the Air Force be certain of what was going on. The Minuteman missile sites themselves were unmanned. Isolation was the best security around.[3]

This same protocol was followed on August 15, 1988. But this was not a drill or a computer glitch; there were no grasshoppers or strong winds that day. As the security detail headed out on the drive to K-8, the missileers would have noted that it was not the only silo sounding an alarm: lights went off on K-6, then L-9 and G-11. Perhaps this would be one of those moments of "panic." The tension level in the launch capsules and at Whiteman would have begun to rise: what was happening in the missile fields?

The answer began to take shape shortly after 10:00 AM at the county courthouse in Butler, Missouri. The clown, activist and journalist Samuel H. Day Jr., and his companion were brought in hand-cuffed. They were soon joined by other "Missouri Peace Planters"—as the protestors called themselves. By the end of the day it was clear that fourteen individuals had entered ten different Minuteman sites in Missouri. Countless others had aided the protestors that day, including witnesses and "transporters," those who drove the protestors to the sites and then left before the security teams arrived. Their goal, according to a written statement, was to "reclaim this land for ourselves." Nodding to the no-end-in-sight farm crisis, they wrote, "we are particularly mindful of the interdependence and fragile nature of all creation . . . into this delicate environment come weapons of indiscriminate mass destruction, placed here by a small cadre of white North Americans purportedly to secure our well being."[4]

The Missouri Peace Planters were interrogated by "courteous" Air Force investigators and then were released with "ban and bar" letters warning of the consequences should they ever trespass on Air Force land again. The Peace Planters were prepared for such a fate, so much so that some headed out again over the next week—climbing fences, setting off alarms, burning their "ban and bar" letters in the process. They were determined to "call attention to the danger posed by the missile underneath, and to register personal opposition to the governmental policy which goes by the name of nuclear deterrence but is in truth a policy of global intimidation." They would not be deterred.[5]

What the Missouri police and Air Force security teams did not realize was that the Peace Planters' action of August 1988 was not an isolated event. This was the culmination of years, if not decades, of less visible protest in the missile fields. Since the moment the Minutemen were deployed in the 1960s, people had found ways to register their displeasure. Some posted signs at missile sites, others held prayer vigils at bases, still more sent letters of complaint about Air Force crews and tried in small ways to insert themselves in the unanimous and omnipotent operation of the U.S. Air Force. The individuals involved were as varied as their actions: the fiercely independent rural Westerner angered by the defilement of his land; the Christian pacifist moved to action through religious conviction; the mother of three concerned about the future of her family. By the late 1970s and early 1980s local protest became more provocative. Prayer vigils turned to nonviolent civil acts of resistance. From 1980 to 1988 more than thirty acts of protest took place in the Minuteman missile fields; dozens of people were arrested and hundreds more stood in support. In Montana, Silence One Silo tried to rid the state of a single missile. The Easter Lily Peace Project in South Dakota hoped to raise awareness of the state's militarism through annual vigils and protest in the missile fields. Wyoming Against the MX sought to stymie the deployment of a new weapon.

None of these groups were successful in getting rid of the Minutemen. That would happen only later, when the Soviet Union crumbled. For this reason, and because the efforts of rural peace groups seemed so quixotic at the time, their story has gone largely unreported. But the story is important for three reasons: it complicates the narrative of the antinuclear movement, it undermines the standard story of conservative ascendancy in the rural West, and it suggests new ways of thinking about modern agrarian politics. Protestors in the rural West were certainly inspired and in some cases assisted by the peace movement. But usually their protests were small and took shape with very little outside involvement. They were the product of grassroots organizing centered on highly local concerns, namely, the plight of small-scale agriculture. Where the global antinuclear movement of the 1980s highlighted the emotional and psychic toll of the nuclear arms race, antimissile activism could demonstrate its daily costs—in dollars, land, crops, and community.

Antimilitary protest also reveals a vibrant agrarian politics that remains outside of what scholars have described as the "conservative capture" of the populist heritage in the 1980s, leading to the contemporary idea of "red state America." To be sure, for years—even during the 1960s Vietnam War protests—missile-field residents had been largely complacent, if not outright willing partners in the Cold War. They housed the missiles without complaining and supported a strong defense. But by the late 1970s and early 1980s, here, too, in the rural heartland, consensus fragmented. Some rural Americans became disillusioned with promises that seemed to favor missile silos over grain silos, that privileged weapons over rangeland. While most missile-field residents remained quiet, a few did not. And it was their protest that exacted a reckoning not just with the abstract notion of nuclear Armageddon but also with its physical legacy. As one South Dakota activist declared, "there is more to our rural conservative state than meets the eye." Alienated by Cold War policies that seemed to treat rural areas as military reservations at best, or totally expendable at worst, individuals in the missile fields began to demand a return to a more traditional agrarian-community-centered form of governance.[6]

Sam Day began to discover these activists in the early 1980s as he traveled around the country writing about nuclear facilities and industries. "Restless ranchers" is what he called them. It was their example that led Day to cross the line in 1988 and protest the missiles in Missouri. In fact, without these broader efforts Day's own protest would have been impossible: they laid the groundwork for the Missouri Peace Planters. And it just so happened that one of those "restless ranchers" lived on the edge of Ellsworth Air Force Base in western South Dakota.[7]

Marvin Kammerer remembers the worst day of his life. As these things happen, it started out normal enough. A crisp spring morning in 1979, the sun was rising a little earlier, staying a little later in the western sky. As he did on most mornings, Kammerer climbed to the top of the southernmost ridge of his ranch to survey the scene, scout his cattle. This was the land his grandfather had homesteaded nearly a century before. He could see his two youngest daughters on horseback heading to the one-room schoolhouse three generations of Kammerers had attended.[8]

Behind him Kammerer heard the roar of engines, the thin whistle as wings took flight. He barely turned because it was a sound he was well accustomed to: B-52 bombers taking off from Ellsworth Air Force Base. The Kammerer ranch edged the runway. But something made Marvin turn that morning—it was not the sound of a B-52's engines, but the sound of hundreds of engines. "This was bang, bang, bang," Kammerer later recalled. "These suckers were pouring on as hard as they could go. I mean, there is a lot of difference between a normal flight, a touch down and wrap around and fly around and touch down again." To Kammerer it looked like every single bomber had taken off and was soaring up and out toward the North Pole, presumably the shortest distance to their Soviet targets. It would take about 30 minutes for the Soviet ICBMs to arrive, Kammerer knew; he did not have enough to time to find his family. All he could think of was that on that morning he had not hugged anyone good-bye.

It was not nuclear war, of course, but what Kammerer identified as a "broken arrow," the term used for military accidents involving nuclear weapons. But that did not matter to Kammerer. The moment changed his life. A few weeks later he heard that it had all been due to "a bad chip" or some sort of electronics malfunction. Marvin Kammerer was not entirely comfortable relying on "a piece of machinery" for global survival.[9]

Kammerer also knew that few of his neighbors shared his ire. That the missile fields had never been a hotbed of antimilitarism was something the Air Force well knew. In fact the first attempt to protest an ICBM base—back in 1958—had been a complete failure. That year members of the newly formed Committee for Nonviolent Action (CNVA) had traveled from Philadelphia to Cheyenne, Wyoming, to see if they could get some locals incensed over the construction of the Atlas site. For six months activists spoke with locals, conducted surveys, organized, and tried to get petitions filled. They got nowhere. While a handful of Easterners and a few radicals from Chicago showed up to stop trucks and hang signs, the residents of Wyoming remained uninterested—or worse, annoyed. The CNVA concluded that the "Cheyenne Appeal" was not to be emulated. In fact it seems it was not to be mentioned. The Cheyenne Appeal does not appear in histories or stories about the CNVA.[10]

Not a lot had changed in the intervening decades. Rural South Dakotans in 1979 exhibited the same wariness of outsiders, the same disapproval for anything that smacked of radicalism. To be sure, by the late 1970s ranchers who lived near missiles were often fed up with the Air Force and its strategic weapons, but they were more apt to complain and grumble about the problems with fellow Legionnaires or at meetings of the Stockgrowers Association.

Kammerer understood these realities. In fact his activism in the 1980s was not a total conversion. For most of his life he had been a Democrat in a Republican stronghold. Rather than join the popular local Stockgrowers Association, Kammerer threw his lot in with the National Farmers Organization, a group convinced that the nation's success depended on individual producers without the help of big government. When his brother was drafted in 1967, Kammerer began protesting the Vietnam War, hanging signs on his gate or over the ridge facing the Air Force base: "Keep the bombers on the ground." As such, Kammerer's increasing activism in the 1980s only seemed to affirm what his largely conservative neighbors long suspected: he was a "pinko," or at least a fellow traveler.[11]

But Kammerer had more in common with his neighbors than even he may have cared to admit. He was not an outsider, and for this reason he would be a particularly visible and important activist in western South Dakota. Kammerer's politics were enmeshed with the land, a sense of place and duty, a deep commitment to a particular vision of American republicanism that seemed increasingly under assault from outside forces. For Kammerer the ultimate goal was to be left alone to ranch, raise his family, attend church, and take care of his community. "Bigness is not everything," he would lament, echoing a standard western refrain. In fact it was bigness in government—particularly one in collusion with "fly-by-night" corporations—that received the brunt of his ire. "We have to get back to the rural concept of what land is," Kammerer proclaimed. Land was not a commodity but a precious resource to be cultivated and respected. Agribusiness, invasive mining, and massive developments were out; so too should be government policies that supported such practices. It was the only way that the founding principles of the country—something Kammerer took very seriously—could be upheld. "The farmer and rancher are becoming the next Indians," he moaned, and with them would go the strength of the nation.[12]

Kammerer's antimilitarism grew from the same soil. "We are a great nation with great strengths," he boasted, but "our Founding Fathers feared a military government and Eisenhower warned of the dangers." Kammerer worried that the country relied on defense spending rather than on the hard work of individual men and women. He knew the country needed a military; "I am not a pacifist," he proclaimed. Nor was he an isolationist. But he questioned the size of the Cold War defense establishment, particularly as he watched it take hold in western South Dakota. Kammerer's gradual move toward activism rested on more than principle. It was also deeply pragmatic: whenever Ellsworth Air Force Base needed to grow, it did so at the expense of his land.[13]

So in 1979 Kammerer started making new friends. But this was not going to be politics as usual. Rather, Kammerer melded new concerns and constituents with traditional ideas about the land and its stewardship. That year he helped form the Black Hills Alliance, a group of ranchers, Lakota Indians, and environmentalists devoted to fighting uranium mining and protecting the area's water. "We started putting the two and two together," Kammerer later explained about the highly unusual alliance. They realized that the uranium used for nuclear power could also build nuclear weapons, which, in turn, were deployed to Ellsworth. Kammerer thought often of the broken-arrow incident he had witnessed. He was not certain that the next time it would be an accident; worse, he feared it would be an accident gone too far.[14]

While Marvin Kammerer contemplated nuclear Armageddon in his own small corner of the world, Sam Day, the clown of the Missouri missile fields, embarked on a crusade of his own: a solo tour of nuclear America. Since the early 1970s Day had been at the forefront of journalists trying to highlight the dangers of the nuclear complex. From 1974 to 1977 Day was editor of the *Bulletin of the Atomic Scientists* and then, from 1977 to 1979, managing editor of *The Progressive* magazine. In 1979 he left the "official" world of journalism for the world of direct action. One of Day's goals was to travel around the country (and sometimes the world) exposing the invisible nuclear complex—both military and civilian (a distinction Day himself would have insisted did not exist). Day was not alone in his efforts to publicize the extent of the nuclear landscape; rather, he was part of a long, if generally overlooked, continuum of activists who had railed against the national security state. Since the dawn of the atomic age a vocal minority had agitated for greater transparency. Day's own former publications, *Bulletin of the Atomic Scientists* and *The Progressive*, were both early critics of nuclear secrecy. In the 1950s the *Bulletin* lamented that the government seemed reluctant to face the "unpleasant facts" of the atomic era. More aggressively *The Progressive* charged the American government with "willful secrecy" and "planned ignorance" that undermined the tenets of democracy. But like so much dissent in the early Cold War, such charges were largely buried in the staccato drumbeat of defense and preparedness and often painted with the broad brush of subversion. Few Americans, least of all those living in the missile fields, paused to ask if nuclear deterrence was the right or best policy; whether the creation of such bombs and weapons was moral and safe; what the long-term implications for humanity would be in creating materials that could not be destroyed. No, through most of the Cold War these were the concerns of experts. The issues, many Americans believed, were too complex for the average citizen.[15]

But in the 1970s a broader antinuclear sensibility was stirring and Day was at the leading, radical edge. In 1981 Day joined Nukewatch, the nonprofit arm of the *The Progressive*, created to educate the public and combat government propaganda relating to nuclear secrecy. It was at Nukewatch that Day helped spearhead "direct action" campaigns aimed at "[raising] public consciousness about the Government's continued preparations for nuclear war." In a clear escalation of the type of advocacy work with which he wanted to engage, Day hoped that Nukewatch could act as a clearinghouse of information and activism that could bring people out to protest. Those campaigns included the "H-bomb truck watch," which enlisted volunteers to stake out truck routes and follow Department of Energy convoys that carried nuclear bombs, taking pictures and notes when appropriate. Prospective spotters were given checklists of things to bring (a map, field glasses, and reading material), what to do (sing songs, hold hands, take pictures but not right in the windshield—no use in causing an accident), and what not to do (jump into the street, interfere with the vehicle). Another early campaign exhorted individuals to divest from the military-industrial complex by refusing to purchase goods and services from companies with defense contracts. Indeed the vestiges of the Pentagon were everywhere—from the salt on your table (Morton's was a branch of Thiokol, the maker of solid fuels for the Minutemen) to the thermostat on your wall (Honeywell, maker of missile guidance systems).[16]

By this time the antinuclear movement was on its way to being a national phenomenon. Though small clusters of peace activists had continued to plod along through the 1970s, particularly in Europe, in the United States their numbers remained small, their impact negligible. Things changed in the early 1980s when church rectories and suburban living rooms became the nerve centers of the "Nuclear Freeze," a proposal for a bilateral halt to nuclear weapons production, testing, and deployment. The brainchild of Randall Forsberg in Brookline, Massachusetts, the Freeze had the benefit of being optimistic yet ambiguous; it served as a large umbrella under which a variety of antinuclear groups could stand. It was wildly popular. Forsberg did not articulate the Freeze idea until early 1980, yet by the spring of 1982, 320 city councils had passed their own Nuclear Freeze proposals; that fall nine states followed suit. Major religious bodies, such as the National Council of Churches, endorsed the Freeze, adding legitimacy and manpower. Much of this energy culminated in the summer of 1982, when one of the largest political demonstrations in U.S. history littered the Great Lawn of Central Park with "No More Nukes" leaflets and "Ban the Bomb" buttons. In South Dakota, Kammerer helped lead the region's Nuclear Freeze—declaring his own ranchland, on the edge of multiple megatons of nuclear weapons, "nuclear free."[17]

The very success of the Nuclear Freeze was based on this limited vision and broad appeal. It was a somewhat ingenious tightrope walk between the extremes of abolition and escalation; nothing could have been more politically neutral and thus widely acceptable. You could be both an advocate of a freeze and strong on defense; you could be part hawk, part dove. Senator Henry Jackson of Washington liked the idea of a weapons buildup followed by a freeze (ensuring nuclear "parity" with the Russians). Senator Edward Kennedy of Massachusetts favored a mutually verifiable freeze.[18]

For many Americans, the Freeze was an answer to the cowboy militarism of the new president. Ronald Reagan charged into office a fierce cold warrior intent on bolstering the military budget, using a firm hand with the Soviets, and proclaiming his willingness, according to the administration, to engage in limited nuclear war. In the

fall of 1981, both Reagan and Secretary of Defense Caspar Weinberger suggested it would be possible to contain nuclear war to Europe (the administration would quickly distance itself from these remarks, though never repudiate them). Reagan pushed forward new
weapons such as the MX missiles and the Strategic Defense Initiative, otherwise known as Star Wars, while also resurrecting programs
that had already been deemed of dubious merit, such as the neutron
bomb and B-1 bomber. Strategically Reagan held to the idea of "peace
through strength": the United States had to establish preponderant
power before negotiating with the Russians. The problem, as Reagan
saw it, was that during the 1970s the United States had squandered its
military superiority, allowing the Soviets to take the lead. To compensate Reagan oversaw the largest peacetime military buildup in
U.S. history. The defense budget ballooned from $325.1 billion in
1980 to $456.5 billion in 1987. It was a buildup actually initiated by
Carter, but Reagan's bellicose rhetoric, dating back to his days as
spokesman for General Electric, seemed to raise the stakes. His 1983
declaration that the USSR was the "evil empire" was the capstone of
such thinking.[19]

Only later, once strength seemed to have been achieved, would
Reagan turn to strategic arms negotiations. In fact, during the 1986
Reykjavik Summit with Soviet premier Mikhail Gorbachev, the two
leaders nearly came to an agreement on eliminating all nuclear weapons within ten years. Reagan, it turns out, was something of a nuclear
abolitionist. He abhorred nuclear weapons, despite the fact that his
defense policies actively escalated the threat of nuclear conflict. His
own dreams of a nuclear-free world were partly dashed on his equal
insistence on the Strategic Defense Initiative—a program that, despite billions of dollars, today still remains more fantasy than reality.
Despite the moniker "the Great Communicator," Reagan was either
unwilling or unable to communicate these sentiments—and "dreams,"
as he put them—to the American people. As a result, he left office
having increased the number of strategic nuclear warheads deployed (START limited the number of launchers deployed for those

warheads). Moreover, Reagan explicitly criticized the popular anti-nuclear sentiment percolating throughout the country, suggesting that the Freeze was part of a vast Kremlin design.[20]

Whether or not Reagan's defense actions and rhetoric scared the Soviets, it certainly terrorized the American public. Not even one full year into Reagan's first term, 76 percent of Americans—nearly 20 percentage points more than just six months earlier—believed a nuclear war was "likely." The first lady worried that her husband was being seen as a "warmonger."[21]

The antinuclear movement fed this fear, perhaps hoping that graphic depictions of nuclear war would generate greater antinuclear sentiment. Between 1979 and 1982, *Publishers Weekly* noted, 130 "nuclear fear" books and essays had been published. An instant classic was Jonathan Schell's *The Fate of the Earth*, originally published in *The New Yorker* but quickly turned into a best seller. Through these books, Americans were inundated with information about how effective fallout shelters would be (not very, was the general consensus); how much fallout there would be (so much that you would not see your own hand in front of your face, perhaps for weeks); how long it would take to die from radiation sickness (sometimes hours; sometimes weeks of agony). In the end the world would resemble, as Schell wrote, "a republic of cockroaches," the only creatures sturdy enough to survive.[22]

Many of these gruesome possibilities were made abundantly and graphically clear to 100 million Americans on November 22, 1983. That night the largest TV audience ever assembled watched the slow and painful demise of the Dahlberg family—and much of the Kansas City area—during ABC's *The Day After*. The made-for-TV movie was the first network depiction of nuclear war; many more would follow. The Dahlbergs' farm was perched on the edge of a Minuteman missile field, not close enough to house a missile but certainly near enough for a firsthand look if there was ever a missile launch, which is exactly what the Dahlbergs—and 100 million Americans—saw when two Minutemen roared from their silos and rose into the blue sky. Minutes later the Dahlbergs' youngest, Danny, was blinded by an atomic flash from an incoming Soviet warhead. The second half of the movie followed the Dahlbergs through postapocalypse Missouri. When the family emerged from their fallout shelter two weeks later, all lines of communication were broken; all electric circuits had been destroyed. The Dahlbergs' oldest daughter began bleeding and losing her hair. She died of radiation sickness; the father was shot by roving bandits in search of food. The fate of the rest of the family was left unknown. The case of the Dahlbergs seemed to reconfirm many American suspicions that in a nuclear war, it would be best to live at ground zero and die instantly.[23]

It was precisely the grim possibilities of *The Day After* that made some antinuclear activists, including Day, more radical in their prescriptions for the arms race. Day advocated nothing short of total nuclear disarmament. The Freeze was only a small step—a tactic, not the goal. Most peace groups urged their members "to save the world—but not at the risk of sounding unpatriotic, of being controversial, of offending the neighbors, of upsetting the status quo." Day was tired of receiving hundreds of leaflets imploring him to study conflict resolution, to use moderate language so as not to alienate anyone, to send a cash donation to a peace organization in lieu of action. But these "served as substitutes—as the thermonuclear equivalent of the mouthwashes, pills, and deodorants used to lull the innumerable lesser anxieties of everyday life." These groups and their flyers were wrong, Day argued, because to effect change the political status quo had to be subverted. Perhaps the Freeze was an important vehicle for dialogue, but far more radical ideas were required to rid to the world of the nuclear menace. It was just such a conclusion that some rural Westerners had come to about the nuclear peril in their own backyards.[24]

On July 18, 1980, Marvin Kammerer threw a party. It was the biggest political gathering in South Dakota's history. Over ten days an estimated 10,000 people came and went from the Kammerer ranch for the International Black Hills Survival Gathering. Organized by South Dakota's social justice networks, including the Black Hills Alliance, the event drew people from around the world to protest uranium mining. College students and environmentalists arrived with tents; a few cowboys slept in campers; American Indians rolled out teepees. They listened to lectures, held rallies, and attended concerts by Jackson Browne and Bonnie Raitt. The event was considered a boon to the local economy. Rapid City pizza places were especially pleased, though perhaps not as much as the Black Hills Catering Company, which provided much of the food for the event. Employees were amused to discover that the gathering's participants preferred salads and buckwheat pancakes to the "meat, potatoes and gravy" usually served to local folk.[25]

No one at the Survival Gathering actually hopped a Minuteman fence (at least not that week), and no acts of civil disobedience were performed, yet the people and issues that would make antimissile activism possible were present. The gathering was the first evidence that a meaningful network of social justice activists had formed in South Dakota. It was a fundamental reordering of South Dakota's political culture, without which protest in the missile fields would be impossible. As local activist Jay Davis realized, in "a small state with only a small group of left wing and progressive organizers," it was critical to mobilize a community of support—people who could raise money, hire or serve as lawyers, and provide support, food, and logistics. Not everyone would participate in active protest, but the support community could sustain those few who did. Like the No-MX alliances forming in the Great Basin, South Dakota's peace and justice community drew from disparate sources: Lakota Indians, white ranchers, environmentalists, and religious groups. In the past these groups had organized independently, but never before had they come together. What initially united them was the fear of uranium mining, but rapidly their attentions turned to the MX, the arms race, and the loss of the family farm.[26]

Disenchanted Westerners had other political options, some far
more obvious. In fact, the very same day that the Survival Gathering
opened, Ronald Reagan, the GOP nominee for president, faced a
rousing crowd in Salt Lake City. There, on the steps of the state capitol, Reagan proclaimed his allegiance to the Sagebrush Rebellion.
Over the past few years that rebellion had argued for local, rather
than federal, control of public lands. The self-declared rebels were
tired of huge swaths of land being made off-limits to agriculture and
grazing, tucked away as "wilderness" for the enjoyment of outsiders.
They abhorred the heavy hand of the federal government, particularly new Bureau of Land Management regulations that made grazing rights harder to come by and harder to keep. "Growth and use"
were the main objectives. In Nevada, where the federal government
controlled 87 percent of the land, Senator Paul Laxalt, a close ally to
the Gipper, admitted that the people "are tired of being ruled like
some faraway colony."[27]

Marvin Kammerer, too, warned that "the feudal system" was returning to South Dakota. Given their skepticism about outside, federal interference, both groups were in many ways the children of
the Missile Area Landowners Association, all rural Westerners interested in preserving their way of life and land. But beginning in the
late 1970s their paths clearly diverged over the solutions to the problems of the rural West. The sagebrush rebels wanted state control of
lands; the antimilitary activists wanted defense dollars reoriented to
agriculture—"farms not arms." The rebels wanted deregulation; activists sought greater attention to land stewardship.

Kammerer and others at the gathering had a political outlook akin
to what historian Catherine McNicol Stock has called left-wing producerism radicalism—a desire to be left alone to farm and produce,
to own land and have local control of important affairs. It was these
ideas that animated the Populist movement of the 1890s and the
Farmers' Holiday Associations and agricultural organizations of the
1930s. Historically the politics of radical producerism has been central

to successful agricultural organizing in the United States. And while vestiges of these ideas percolated in the American Agricultural Movement of the 1980s, it is generally understood that the ideas of left-wing producerism were no longer politically potent. They had been replaced with rural vigilantism or co-opted by interest-group politics. This displacement was underscored at the time by the growing power of the Sagebrush Rebellion and has since been reinforced by the electoral success of conservative candidates in the region.[28]

But the story of antimilitary activism in the missile fields suggests a more complicated outcome. Rural radical producerism was not eradicated, but instead proved adaptive. Kammerer and others joined forces with other marginal, grassroots efforts such as environmentalism, the American Indian movement, and local peace and justice communities. Through these combinations, the politics of producerism was reframed and given a powerful new impetus.[29]

On the plains, social justice activists began linking defense spending to the decimation of the farm; the military-industrial complex to the failure of agricultural policies; uranium mining to the destruction of regional water supplies and the desecration of sacred American Indian sites. Militarization tended to hurt the downtrodden, threatening the livelihoods of the vulnerable rural poor. These were important personal avenues into more abstract issues of nuclear energy and weapons. It was hard, as Sam Day well knew, to connect to the realm of experts and technicians—much easier to leave "thinking the unthinkable" to those trained to do so. But the incongruity of seeing $30-million B-52s roaring overhead while discussing federal policies that left farmers with 70 cents on the dollar for their produce was a stark reminder of the reality of the American farmer. Activists drew connections to sterile, useless pieces of silo land and what could be a thriving, complete ranch and then extended these connections out to the ruin of the farm and rural life. The issue of the family farm was taken up at a number of meetings during the Survival Gathering. "Agribusiness religiously destroys communities" was the matter-of-fact finale to a discussion of the land. Merle Hansen, of Nebraska, came to declare that the eradication of the small-time farmer and rancher was deliberate—part of a "planned genocide" that would leave production in the hands of huge conglomerates.[30]

The reality for small-time ranchers and farmers was certainly becoming dire in 1980. The 1970s had actually been a boom time for U.S. agriculture, but as was generally the case in the rural West, boom was followed by bust, and so began the 1980s. In South Dakota the farm crisis was spreading bile. It was hot and dry; another "drought cycle" was taking its toll. Grazing conditions were 25 to 60 percent of normal—grass and water were all but gone on some summer pastures. For the first time in thirty years the Oil Creek was dried up. South Dakota is "taking on [the] appearance of the desert Southwest," the *Rapid City Journal* moaned. Things would only get worse as the decade wore on. Cattle prices dropped to pre-1950s levels and Federal Land Bank interest rates soared to 18 percent. Many ranchers and farmers gave their land back, along with the work they had poured into it; rural communities shrank; towns disappeared.[31]

The connection between land use and nuclear weapons would become the most important justification for peace activism in the missile fields. By linking traditional ideas about rural production to the military and nuclear weapons, activists were able to build on the energy of the national and international peace movements and the growing farm movement and also garner local allies. In western South Dakota, Kammerer himself led the charge. "The arms race forces people to take every damn bit they can from the soil," he declared, just "to pay their bills." For such reasons, the South Dakota Peace and Justice Center wrote, "opposition to the nuclear arms race is a genuine *local issue*." The center announced that the U.S. government was "subsidizing certain silos" at the explicit expense of others: "the best kept secret of the gutting of American agriculture is the degree to which military spending is responsible." Up in Montana antinuclear activists were spinning the same story—noting that each year each Minuteman missile silo cost $500,000 to maintain. "With the money redirected from nuclear terrorism," the group Silence One Silo suggested, "Montana growers could get almost 30% closer to full parity" for their produce. "Agriculture is a more stable economic base than the military." Later investigative journalist and *New Yorker* correspondent Ian Frazier would make the stakes all the more graphic when writing about the Great Plains: in each county that housed the Minutemen, a single silo cost five years' worth of cattle, grain, and wheat.[32]

Within this context the proposed deployment of MX missiles was explosive. As the latest manifestation of the arms race, the MX was discussed during the Survival Gathering but truly became a local issue in 1982 when Reagan announced that forty to fifty of the new missiles would be implanted in rehabbed Minuteman silos. For a full year, until Wyoming was identified as the chosen site, residents of all of the Minuteman missile fields wondered if their state would be picked. "If [the MX] is not such a big deal," Kammerer fumed, we should "put an MX on Ronnie's ranch." South Dakotans joined with ranchers from Wyoming, Montana, Colorado, and Nebraska to form Western Solidarity and the Tri-State MX Coalition. The South Dakota Peace and Justice Center noted that given that the superpowers already had the power to blow the world up many times over, the MX was both unnecessary and too expensive—"the farm subsidy program costs less than the MX," the center argued. Yet farm subsidies would be cut rather than a weapon system. Montana governor Ted Schwinden declared that any plan to base the MX in Montana was "another incident of federalism being a one-way street. . . . With the growing Federal deficit approaching half a trillion dollars, military decisions of this magnitude have to be re-examined." Montanans agreed and took the issue to the November ballot—drafting Proposition 91, which called for both a nuclear freeze and a halt to MX deployment. On November 7, 1982, Montanans passed the proposition, a repudiation of the MX. Elsewhere the battle raged on.[33]

Lindi Kirkbride never thought much about nuclear missiles, despite the fact that in 1981 she had already been living next door to three of them for more than ten years. In 1970 she had moved with her new husband, Alan, to his family's ranch in Meridan, Wyoming (population thirty-seven). The Kirkbride ranch housed three Minuteman ICBMs. No one seemed to mind much. Lindi's father-in-law, Kenneth, a veteran of the war in the Pacific, believed both that the atomic bomb had saved his life and that the Soviets were a real threat. He believed in nuclear deterrence. In the early Cold War he felt it his patriotic duty to house the Minuteman missiles. And, like rural residents everywhere, he understood the road and infrastructure benefits. "I don't know anybody who said no to the missiles," he later recalled. Besides, he admitted, echoing many of his neighbors, "the Air Force was reasonable."[34]

For a decade Lindi had little quarrel with this logic. But that was before the MX. Shortly after Reagan announced his plans for the Peacemaker, Lindi and Alan Kirkbride became involved in Wyoming against the MX. While Lindi acknowledged that she was initially opposed to the MX because of the "land issue: I wanted to protect the land," eventually she realized the problem was deeper. In her own recounting she had a "spiritual awakening" that led her to a deeper commitment. While Alan drifted from the cause, Lindi dove in, becoming a lead spokeswoman for the No-MX campaign. She met with lawmakers, traveled to Washington, D.C., to testify before Congress, and appeared in local and national media outlets. In 1982 she met Marvin Kammerer when the two participated in the Ranchers for Peace people-to-people mission to the Soviet Union. Lindi's family did not agree with her cause but begrudgingly accepted her activism. The broader community was less forgiving. Lindi recounts that people treated her like a pariah for opposing the military.[35]

Despite opprobrium, a constellation of social justice activists in Wyoming, Colorado, and Nebraska surrounded Kirkbride in the No-MX fight. Sister Francis Russell founded the Tri-State MX Coalition. Margaret Laybourne, who had staged a lone protest against the deployment of Atlas missiles in 1958, actively participated in prayer vigils and protests at Warren Air Force Base. Cheyenne's Roman Catholic bishop, the Reverend Joseph Hart, called the MX system "morally indefensible." Others argued about the efficacy of ranching in Wyoming. "The stakes . . . are no less than the economic survival of the agricultural community as we know it," wrote Rod and Mae Kirkbride, relatives of Lindi, in a letter printed in the *New York Times*. We are "doing our patriotic duty now as hosts to the Minuteman silos," they continued. Please don't unsettle that with a new missile of dubious strategic value.[36]

Despite their efforts, the No-MX activists in Wyoming were ultimately unsuccessful. Residents of the "Cowboy State" generally supported the MX. A poll by the Cheyenne Chamber of Commerce found that three-quarters of business respondents welcomed the new missiles. Chamber president Bill Budd noted that the MX would be no different from the Minutemen. "It doesn't make any difference if they write on your tombstone if you were killed while they were shooting at a Minuteman or an MX," he told a visiting reporter. In December 1986, the first of fifty MX missiles were deployed to Wyoming. "I felt like I'd been kicked in the teeth. I wanted to throw up," Lindi Kirkbride later remembered.[37]

The Wyoming No-MX story points to one of the most intriguing features of the rural peace movement, a feature that also helps explain why—despite great odds and local condemnation—rural activists persisted for so long. Many activists understood their actions as part of a spiritual or religious calling. This was true across the missile fields, where, throughout the 1980s, antimissile protestors prayed, used religious imagery, and drew inspiration from worldwide spiritual leaders to justify their actions. In South Dakota the Reverend Carl Kline led annual Easter morning vigils to missile sites and to Ellsworth Air Force Base. Lindi Kirkbride offered prayers at the silos on her land. These spiritual connections were critical, though largely overlooked, an omission not unique to the peace movement. Religion is often absent from discussions of American political history, particularly the history of the Left. That story is generally one of increasing secularization. But in rural areas that lacked dedicated leftist traditions and organizations, religious rationales and institutions were critical in motivating protest. Antimissile activists understood their protest not as part of the progressive politics of American liberalism, but as an act of personal, redemptive suffering. These religious motivations in turn help explain one of the strange paradoxes of this antinuclear moment: many of the people involved identified themselves as conservative rural Americans, not secular radicals. In 1981, for example, Marvin Kammerer told a Rapid City reporter that he believes in "the Fort Laramie Treaty of 1868 [that gave the Black Hills to the Lakota], small farms, ranches and businesses, the Catholic Church, the Black Hills Alliance, the U.S. Constitution, Christianity, his family and community, and above all the land."[38]

Nationally the religious arm of the antinuclear movement was equally important, though also often marginalized. Drawing inspiration from the teachings and actions of Jesus, Gandhi, Martin Luther King Jr., and Dorothy Day (founder of the radical Catholic worker movement), by 1982 religious pacifists had already left a strong record of civil disobedience across nuclear America. Most famous was the Plowshares Movement, led by the Berrigan brothers, whose first antinuclear action was in September 1980. Eight activists (later known as the "Plowshares Eight") broke into a GE plant and hammered on the nose cones from Mark 12-A nuclear warheads that were destined for the Minuteman III. Their goal, based on the biblical prophecy of Isaiah, was literally to "beat swords into plowshares" (Isaiah 2:4). For the Berrigans—and many who followed—they were acting in the service of a higher calling, a great sense of self, a prophetic act. For their act of conscience and trespass the Berrigans and the other activists received five to ten years in prison. Their group made it onto the list of domestic terrorist organizations.[39]

While the Berrigan brothers sat in federal prison, hundreds of other nonviolent Christian pacifists took up their mantle. Despite the fact that the radical Catholic Left was marginalized by both the mainstream peace movement and the Church, it still managed to leave quite a dossier: between 1980 and 1989, twenty-five Plowshares actions, involving hundreds of people, were carried out in the United States and Europe. Many were held on religiously important days such as Easter, Good Friday, and Christmas. Eventually the Plowshares activists found their way to the missile fields in 1984 when the eleventh Plowshares action, by a group calling themselves the Silo Pruning Hooks, led to the arrest of four activists in Missouri: Helen Drye Woodson, the brothers (and priests) Paul and Carl Kabat, and Larry Cloud-Morgan. In later years more Plowshares actions were held in Missouri—including Plowshares Number 12 in 1985, and Silo Plowshares on Good Friday in 1986. Jean Gump was one of the Good Friday protestors. A suburban mother of twelve, grandmother, and devout Catholic, she had had enough of disarmament talks. She entered Missouri missile site M-10, poured blood from baby bottles, fashioned a cross to put on the silo lid, and spray painted "Disarm and Live" on the concrete top. The total damages to the site were $1,273.43; Gump was sentenced to eleven years in prison. For Gump and other Plowshares resisters, the goal was personal witness and acting in their faith. These were not political goals per se, though there were clearly broader political implications. A "prophetic act," according to activist Ann Morrissett Davidon, "is not based on calculations of risk or estimates of effectiveness but on the truth and rightness of the action itself as the actor perceives it."[40]

Reverend Carl Kline certainly shared this religious inspiration, as did many of the antimissile activists. Yet the Easter Lily Peace Project in South Dakota, as well as other forms of antimissile activism elsewhere, differed from the radical Catholic Left in important ways. The concerns of local missile protests were far more prosaic, rooted in the day to day. The South Dakota protests, for example, provided clear links to broader community issues. Nor did local activists intend to put themselves in prison for years. These activists did not deface government property as the Plowshares activists did. Their small acts of protest were generally treated as local affairs; local sentences were meted out, usually not more than six months. Kline connected the Easter protests to concerns about land and agriculture: "The arms race is beginning to have a visible and alarming impact on our South Dakota way of life," Kline argued, echoing the language of the Survival Gathering. "To a greater extent than is ever publicly acknowledged, farmers are watching their land slip away because our society is subsidizing the producers of weapons at the expense of the producers of food. We are converting butter into guns, we are choosing death over life." And death, according to Carl Kline, looked an awful lot like a Minuteman missile silo.[41]

At 6:15 PM on the evening of June 5, 1982, two young men approached the security fence at Montana's Minuteman R-29 silo, grabbed the chain links, and began to climb. It took just a few minutes for them to reach the top, where they threw a carpet over the barbed wire and swung over. Mark Anderlik, twenty-three, paused. Outside the fence thirteen supporters stood watching; behind them the Montana plains rolled on. The Rockies rose in the West. This was magnificent country, Anderlik thought. He took a deep breath. He was no longer nervous; he felt exhilarated. Anderlik dropped down inside the fence next to Karl Zanzig. The two got to work; they had no idea how much time they would have. They spread wheat seeds on the barren ground, seeds provided by David Hastings, the rancher whose land abutted the missile site. They sat on the concrete silo lid and broke the loaf of bread that LaVonne Hastings had given them. If they were quiet, they could hear the hum of the underground systems, whirring and ticking to check, cool, and monitor the Minuteman.[42]

They had 45 minutes to contemplate their trespass. The Air Force security crews did not arrive until 6:50 PM, at which point both men were cold. They had not planned on spending so much time in the missile site, and the sun was setting behind the mountains, leaving a chill. Zanzig and Anderlik were arrested and the observers ordered to leave. David Hastings was kicked off his own land at gunpoint. "We cross the fence not to foolishly risk our lives but to show that all of our lives are being foolishly risked," Anderlik and Zanzig declared. They were each sentenced to six months in federal prison. They served four and a half months, released early for good behavior.[43]

This was the first major protest of Silence One Silo, a Montana group that wanted to rid the state of a single Minuteman missile. This is "a project for Montanans," the group's information pamphlet asserted. "This [campaign] would show Montanans that we don't have to be chips in the gamble with our lives." Anderlik and Zanzig had come up with the idea for the project in 1980 after attending the International Survival Gathering. It was there, on the Kammerer ranch, that they began to plan a Montana-based antinuclear protest that could help people connect to the abstraction of nuclear weapons and war. Their first task had been to find area landowners willing to support their activities. They found David and LaVonne Hastings of Conrad, Montana.[44]

For nearly twenty years the Hastingses lived next door to a Minuteman missile. According to David, the Air Force had been a terrible neighbor. He recalled times his irrigation lines were torn up by careless crews and his property damaged, not to mention the general nuisance of having huge lumbering trucks block access to his own land and crops. "To the Air Force there is nothing out here but missiles," David spat. "They treat us like a bunch of Vietnam peasants." In 1982 the Hastingses permitted Silence One Silo to establish a peace camp on their property, about half a mile from the missile site R-29. For the next three years hundreds of activists from around the state and country would come to the Hastingses' ranch to protest. Most people came to observe the missile silos, to learn about peace and justice, to work with farmers, and to educate people about nuclear weapons. But others came to scale the fence, to place their bodies between missiles and their targets. From 1982 to 1985, more than a dozen people were arrested at silo R-29. Any and all tactics were welcome. Silence One Silo, in fact, hoped to purchase some of the Hastingses' land—the parcel adjacent to the missile silo—so that peace activists could have a permanent base camp that would not "tax the goodwill of the Hastings and other farm families." Neither of Silence One Silo's goals came to pass—the money couldn't be raised and the missiles wouldn't budge—but that did not stop the group from waging peace against the Minutemen.[45]

The example spread. Just over 30 miles to the north, ranchers Zane and Gloria Zell sponsored the "Little Peace Camp on the Prairie" in July of 1983 and 1985. In 1984 they planted a tree next to the silo, hoping to reclaim the land for productive purposes.[46]

On July 11, 1983, Sam Day saw his first Minuteman missile site. It was a "brief encounter," Day later wrote, almost an afterthought. The visit was simply "occasioned by a stopover during a get-acquainted tour of nuclear resistance groups." The real purpose of his visit was the small peace camp that had been set up on the Hastings ranch in Conrad, Montana. Day was astonished by what he found. He was inspired—even moved—by his experience at R-29 in Montana. He was awed by the dedication and conviction of individuals. When he stood at the missile silo fence, listening to the underground air conditioners hum, he knew he had found perhaps the most effective means of "getting people into close proximity" with nuclear weapons—better than the truck watch or divesting campaigns, better certainly than the Nuclear Freeze. If only people could gather at the fences and stare at the silo as he had done, feel the chill of terror that accompanies the realization that here lies a thermonuclear warhead with twenty times the power of the bomb that destroyed Hiroshima. For Day the missiles were both curse and opportunity—as long as people would heed the call and head out to the missile fields.[47]

Day wanted to somehow add to the efforts of the restless ranchers, to provide support for these courageous acts. He had to get people into the missile fields, get Americans to recognize the nuclear peril that had been buried in their heartland for decades. But first they had to know what to look for and where to look. For Day it was abundantly clear that the military necessity of missile dispersal had brilliantly doubled as a strategy for stymieing antinuclear activism. Not even the missile's neighbors always knew how to find the closest silo or launch center. With nothing more than a few loose guidelines such as "turn left at the big tree," "drive past the winter-wheat field," it could take hours to find something called "N-5." What if that spring the field had been sown instead with soybeans or corn? What if you didn't know the difference? It was easy to lose your bearings in the rolling grasses, the patchwork farmlands, the endless sky. And no map—not even the most detailed official variety—made note of the missiles. No, to find a launch site you had to know what to look for: well-graded and maintained gravel roads; triple transformers on commercial power lines; and, if you got lucky, a military vehicle parked at the edge of a gate.

So Day decided to map the Minuteman missile fields. The Strategic Air Command had never issued an official cartography of nuclear missiles, but Sam Day, Nukewatch, and scores of volunteers across the missile fields would. By pinpointing all Cold War missiles, Day hoped to force a national reckoning with the hidden geography of Armageddon. But more than that, Day realized, the maps and his organization, Nukewatch, could provide a service that would bring the various antimissile groups together; could perhaps collapse the boundaries between secular and religious resistance, between the national peace movement and local actions. The missile maps could be for everyone, radical activist and apolitical tourist alike. Whoever they were for, the maps would provide an invaluable service, since it was nearly impossible to find a missile silo otherwise.

The missile fields of Missouri were the first to be mapped, but the project quickly radiated out to all of the missile fields. In each case local activists were charged with finding silos and providing driving directions. After the local work was done, Nukewatch culled the information and created the maps, printing them on postcards, pamphlets, T-shirts, and finally, in 1988, gathering all of the information into *Nuclear Heartland: A Guide to the 1,000 Missile Silos of the United States*. Following the completion of each state's map, a rally and vigil was held, using the new maps so that activists could spread out and protest at multiple sites simultaneously. The effect was "stunning." Day reported that the maps of Missouri—titled " 'Show Me!'—A Citizens' Guide to the Missile Silos of Missouri"—"sold like hotcakes." Orders came in from all over the country as well as overseas. The Missouri launch took place on the weekend of November 9, 1985. In publicizing the event, local activists exhorted, "We want to encourage people from all over the 'show me state' and all over American to come . . . and see these 'gods of metal' for themselves." Hundreds of people did come, first for a gathering at Knob Noster State Park, and then using the maps they headed out into the missile fields. No one was arrested that day, but protestors held vigils at nearly forty different silos. According to Day, a "tradition" was born. A similar story was played out in the rest of the missile fields, where Nukewatch helped organize vigils to launch each map.[48]

Nukewatch also helped provide a vocabulary of the Minutemen, a language of resistance that would inscribe a new meaning for the missiles and onto the nuclear landscape. Local activists were allowed to name the silos—to give them extra weight, perhaps to make them into statements or memorials. In Montana, Minuteman silo R-29 became, appropriately enough, "David Hastings' Missile." A wing of missiles in South Dakota was named after figures in the Iran-Contra scandal—"Reagan Knew," "Ollie's Missile," and "North Forty." Many missiles evoked war-era terrors: "Auschwitz," "Blitzkrieg," "Dormann Dachau," and "Treblinka," all in North Dakota. Others were more tongue-in-cheek, reflecting the absurdity of the nuclear plains: "Moral Novocain" in Montana; "Star Wars Stiletto" in North Dakota; "Regretfully Yours" in South Dakota. Naming missiles helped make the nuclear realm less abstract.[49]

This reclaiming of the land and space was accentuated in small actions that missile activists took. In Missouri a Kansas City woman started an "adopt a missile program." Echoing the Air Force's attempts at missile adoption programs in the 1960s (aimed at fostering community support), activist individuals or groups would take ownership of one missile site, making it the focal point of protest.[50]

Little of this was illegal, of course, and the Air Force could do nothing about the mapping project. In fact a Malmstrom Air Force Base publicity officer noted that the location of the missiles themselves was actually no secret. "We can assume our enemies know where they are," he admitted. One retired Air Force security guard was less sanguine. "Maps like this," he spat, "draw the nuts and crazies like flies to sugar. Do you want to be responsible for causing an 'accident'?" Other Air Force officers were more philosophical about the protests, noting that the missiles were there precisely to protect the freedom to protest.[51]

For Day the culmination of these efforts was his own act of protest. The Missouri Peace Planters of 1988 was intended to be something of a "mass" protest—at least as far as missile activism was concerned. "We wanted to escalate the challenge to nuclear deterrence,"

Day wrote. "In the field and in the courts—by putting more people inside the fences of nuclear missile launch sites." Fourteen different individuals would cross the line that day, more than doubling the amount of arrests for one day in the missile fields to date.[52]

It was under these conditions that Day rented his clown suit and set off for Missouri in August 1988. To get to missile site K-8, dubbed "For the Rich," the map in *Nuclear Heartland* directed the protestors to drive 80 miles south to Rich Hill, where they would take County Road B east for six-tenths of a mile and then look for the telltale fence on the right. At precisely 7:00 AM, Day and Katie Willems took to the padlock with the bolt cutters. As they sliced away, their driver sped off. Sam Day would spend 40 minutes of his life on top of a nuclear missile silo; for that pleasure he would eventually receive the maximum sentence for his crime: six months in federal prison. In his sentencing hearing Day did not make religious arguments, but legal ones. Day told the judge that he acted "in the full knowledge that the law upholds the Government's right to be free of interference while preparing to blow up the world." And yet, Day added, "I also know that such laws are subject to judicial review." Day planned to give the court that option and to "strip away legal protection from nuclear genocide in the same ways courts in earlier times have struck down slavery, racial segregation, and similar practices once accepted but now repugnant to civilized people."[53]

But by the time Day crossed the line, he also knew that the broad antinuclear movement was waning. In part this had to do with the very real changes in U.S.-Soviet relations. Since his first term, Reagan had modified his position on nuclear arms negotiations. In 1987 he and Soviet leader Gorbachev had agreed on the historic Intermediate-Range Nuclear Forces Treaty, the elimination of all short- and intermediate-range missiles. The two leaders continued to discuss overall reductions, but the ultimate goal of abolishing all nuclear warheads remained elusive. The clear thawing in relations and progress on nuclear arms treaties weakened the peace movement.[54]

Yet in the missile fields protest continued. The final missile protest in South Dakota was in June 1989, just a year before residents learned that the Minuteman missiles would be deactivated, not because of Carl Kline, but because of the START I Treaty. In Missouri protests continued until the day the Minutemen came out of the ground. In October 1991, Knob Noster State Park was to be the site of another previgil rally as protestors went out into the missile fields. In North Dakota peace camps were called throughout the early 1990s. And in the Warren Air Force Base missile fields—eventually home to the MX—protests continued into the new millennium. On October 6, 2002, two Roman Catholic Dominican sisters were arrested for entering silo N-8, near Greeley, Colorado. They were each given nearly three years in federal prison.[55]

The longevity of protest in the missile fields paradoxically helps explain its general invisibility. Much of the protest remained local, deeply tied to community issues. In South Dakota, for example, Kline thought of the missile protests in terms of local issues—farms, equality, the environment. As those issues changed over time, missile activism could morph as well. In fact, in western South Dakota protest against the military continues. Marvin Kammerer never scaled a missile fence, but he was then, and remains today, central to social justice activism. People still gather at his ranch for meetings and to protest. Kammerer stays active in local politics, attending base and county planning meetings. According to Kammerer, the removal of the Minutemen would be just one small step in ridding the region of militarism. More important would be the unshackling of the local economy from its dependence on the Air Force—a proposition that, for a brief moment in 2005, was not as quixotic as it seemed.

7

Dismantling the Cold War

It started as a rumor. Pushed into the missile fields on the edge of winter. Casually thrown about in town. *Did you hear? The missiles are coming out.*

So? The missiles are often out—for maintenance, for repairs. Don't you remember when—

No, this time for real. Haven't you heard? The Cold War is over.

By the time the spring pastures were sown, the rumor had some substance. The Soviet Union was crumbling. Disarmament negotiations continued. Perhaps the missiles really would go.

The rumor was confirmed in the summer of 1991—yet reaction in South Dakota was mixed.

The Reverend Carl Kline celebrated. Though the last missile protest in South Dakota was in 1989, two years before, Kline felt a sense of satisfaction, as if his antinuclear actions and those of hundreds of thousands of people around the world had made an impression. "It was one of those times," Kline recalled, "when we felt like we actually had something to do with a foreign policy decision in this country."

Lyndy Ireland, living in the middle of Minuteman country, admitted that she was "sorry to see them leave," a sentiment echoed by other area residents. Would rural roads and power lines still be maintained to Air Force standards?

Gene Williams's initial relief was quickly overshadowed by a flash of pessimism: the missiles were coming out, but what of the land? Presumably he would get his 2 acres back, but after 30 years of dealing with the Air Force, he wasn't so sure.

Marvin Kammerer grumbled that the missiles should be crushed and a black flag flown "as a memento to our stupidity and arrogance."

Rancher William Bielmaier recalled an old promise made to his father: the land would be returned to the prairie.[1]

At Ellsworth Air Force Base, Tim Pavek found himself with a new job. For the past six years Pavek had been a missile-site facilities engineer, fixing things that went wrong at the launch sites and control centers. Now he had to take charge of getting rid of the things, dismantling the massive infrastructure, gutting the silos, and redistributing the land. When the Minutemen were taken out, that was when Pavek's real work began.[2]

It appeared that South Dakota's long, understated role in the Cold War was coming to an end. Yet for local landowners any sense of relief was premature. The announcement of missile deactivation was merely the beginning of a decades-long struggle to reclaim land long since taken. As was the case in the 1960s when the missiles were deployed, landowners who lived near the Minutemen again confronted tangled questions of land ownership, federal regulations, and a legacy of sacrifice that seemed to go unnoticed. The promise of redemption after decades of small injustices remained elusive; deactivation of the Minutemen did not undo years of harm. Rather, deactivation brought with it new insults and fresh problems. Once again for these landowners the question was not the stark either/or of supporting the Air Force or resisting. Instead the issue was confirming their own rights as property owners and citizens within the rubric of national security needs. For missile-field landowners, the two were pieces of the same puzzle—the implicit agreement between

citizen and state even when, on more than one occasion, that contract had been breached.

Yet that implicit contract within the missile fields was not the
only agreement made, nor would it prove the most decisive. The
arming of the missile fields was just a small part of a broader and
systemic process that made Rapid City and its environs dependent
on the flow of Pentagon dollars. While landowners carried on next
to the Minutemen, doing their time, as it were, their more metropolitan neighbors were reaping the rewards of that sacrifice. While
few dared phrase it as such, land had been traded not just for national security but also for a subtle economic dependency—a dependency that would become abundantly clear as the country tried,
without much success, to dismantle its Cold War national security
apparatus.

On the night of November 9, 1989, the Cold War was at last over.
With small hammers, chisels, and bare hands, Germans—from East
and West—began to dismantle one of the ugliest and harshest edi-
fices of the Cold War: the Berlin Wall. For twenty-eight years the
wall had stood as a physical reminder of the battle between the Soviets and the Americans. That night it came down, along with Communist regimes around the world. The Solidarity Movement in Poland
elected a new, non-Communist government; later that year Roma-
nians would violently depose their own Red legacy.

The United States, of course, had its own Cold War monuments,
though none as contentious or renowned as the wall. Most of these
monuments—the missiles—remained largely invisible. But still there
was a physical legacy with which the country would have to contend.
Scattered here and there were fences and no-man's-lands, parcels of
the nation made off-limits because of the imperatives of global Cold
War. Two-acre missile sites had not broken up families or divided a
country, but they did stand for something: the long-term sacrifices

made for an omnipresent war; the reach of international conflict into the most intimate of places. For residents of the missile fields, the stakes were most personal. The 8-foot fence was a barrier between productive land and nuclear wasteland. Just as the wall reminded Berliners of their perpetual separation, the missile fences reminded ranchers of the global implications for their seemingly remote fields. Even more critically, the barriers represented the arms race and the stupefying firepower each side had amassed and had aimed at each other, still, on the very day the wall came down.

The crumbling of the Cold War called into question the necessity of this nuclear landscape: if the wall could fall, perhaps so too could the missile fences. In fact their dismantling seemed inevitable, written into the very logic of nuclear deterrence. Missiles had been required to stymie a Soviet attack. If there was no Soviet Union, then there was no need for deterrence—or at least not for the massive forces built up over forty years of Cold War.

Yet the dramatic end to the Soviet Empire was not immediately met with equally dramatic arms reductions. Certainly there was talk—throughout the 1980s there had been much talk—but in 1991, even as the Soviet Union finally tottered, no firm agreements had been made. The Strategic Arms Reduction Treaty (START), initiated by President Reagan in 1983, went unsigned. START was an effort not simply to limit new weapons (as the SALT negotiations had been under Nixon and Carter), but actually to reduce the number of weapons on each side. Still, since the advent of the missile age in 1959, the number of long-range strategic weapons had only increased. In fact, in the fall of 1990, a full year after the Berlin Wall fell, the United States had 2,440 warheads deployed on 1,000 ICBMs, and the Soviets 6,547 warheads on 1,287 ICBMs; even more were carried on bombers and IRBMs and stored underwater on submarines. The end of the Cold War was the absolute pinnacle of the arms buildup. It was harder, it seemed, to rid the world of weapons of mass destruction than it had been to build them. It was more difficult to agree to step back from the brink than it had been to silently acquiesce to the possibility of global Armageddon.[3]

In this the United States held particular responsibility. Rather than move aggressively to dismantle weapons, the first Bush administration continued to propose new modernization programs and weapons systems as part of disarmament talks. It was a familiar refrain. Throughout the Cold War the United States had continually reached for the latest, most deadly weapons, further escalating the arms race while agreeing to scrap the oldest, most obsolete forces. It was not a particularly noble heritage, not for a country that publicly prided itself on its peaceful and defensive intent. Nor was it a particularly commendable position in 1989 and 1990 when the United States was the sole superpower, after the arms race had helped bankrupt the Soviet Empire. Yet the American government kept its missiles, and the Russians kept theirs.[4]

American citizens, too, were agitating for a "peace dividend." If the defense budget were sliced in half, they were told, $150 billion would be available for other purposes—bolstering social programs, improving schools, cutting taxes. Or, as a headline in the *Wall Street Journal* somberly reported, any such peace dividend would "Disappear into Sinkhole of U.S. Deficit," much of it the result of massive arms spending. But while Americans expected some sort of dividend, the Bush administration was not inclined to oblige. The president would not even utter the phrase "peace dividend." In keeping with the administration's rather sluggish response to the momentous events in the Eastern Bloc, Bush continued to move incrementally toward major strategic arms decisions. Rather than unilaterally take action, Secretary of Defense Dick Cheney assured Americans that any cuts would be tied closely to arms reduction talks, which meant no real cuts to the 1991 budget. In fact, instead of reductions, new weapons were to be considered: on the table was $2.8 billion to convert twelve MX missiles to mobile rail launchers and another $202 million to develop a new Midgetman ICBM. Thus, while the Cold

War was over, spending on new and existing Cold War–era weapons would persist.[5]

The glacial pace of disarmament discussions was reflected in the missile fields, where, in South Dakota, a Minuteman modernization program continued apace. As the Berlin Wall crumbled in Europe, missile facility engineers at Ellsworth Air Force Base solicited bids for fortifying the United States' own Cold War barriers. The Minuteman Integrated Life Expectancy Program was yet another round of upgrades. In 1990 the office of facilities engineers had some twenty-five programs on the books, many under bid, and ten men devoted full-time to upgrades, ten more to general maintenance. The end of the Cold War barely seemed to register in South Dakota, where the missile fields continued to be cultivated.[6]

This Cold War normalcy, the perpetual maintenance of the missile fields, was a costly facade. The fate of South Dakota's Minuteman II ICBMs had already been sealed. Arms-reduction experts knew that when START discussions were completed the missiles of South Dakota, Missouri, and Montana would go. Minuteman II was the nation's oldest and least destructive ICBM. Moreover, the Air Force was tired of maintaining such an expensive deterrent. The truth was that getting rid of the country's 450 Minuteman II missiles would barely dent the Air Force's nuclear deterrent capacity. It was part of the typical sleight of hand of arms-reduction talks that often made their public avowal more meaningful than actual cuts. START ended up being a case in point. The treaty itself did not specify that the Minuteman II missiles would be dismantled, only that certain limits be placed on the total number of missiles. By getting rid of the Minuteman IIs, the administration could boast that START would rid the United States of nearly one-half of its 1,000 ICBMs. While 450 missiles would be deactivated, the remaining missiles—500 Minuteman IIIs and 50 MXs—together carried 2,000 separately targeted warheads. This accounted for 80 percent of the nation's pre-START ICBM power, some 554 megatons, enough to destroy the world many times over, what journalist Strobe Talbott referred to as "a superfluity of death and destruction."[7]

START signaled the beginning of the end of South Dakota's missile fields, though nowhere in the treaty did it say just how fast that end would come. The rapid collapse of the Soviet Union and tumult behind the Iron Curtain accelerated that schedule. In September 1991, President Bush announced the drawing down of all Minuteman II missiles. South Dakota's Minutemen were taken off active alert. All of the missiles were "safed," so they could not be launched. This meant that missile crews had to travel to each individual launch site and manually deactivate the launch sequences. After thirty years of active, constant duty, the missiles would never again go back online.

The Air Force and Army Corps of Engineers turned to the task of taking the missiles out of the ground in the fall of 1991. Tim Pavek, a lifelong South Dakotan, had worked in the missile fields since 1984. Technically employed by the Army Corps of Engineers but working closely with the Air Force, Pavek was a facilities engineer. His job was to take care of the Minutemen's physical infrastructure, the silos and launch centers and nearly everything but the missiles themselves (that task fell to Air Force engineers). Jobs that aboveground seemed mundane—fixing a leaking toilet—took on added significance 32 feet below the earth's surface: "It was a serious business, you know," Pavek said, as water could flood a launch capsule and disable an entire wing of missiles. For Pavek and others, the job was a source of pride, a patriotic contribution.[8]

That fall Pavek's job was transformed from facilities engineer to Minuteman II deactivation program manager. The work was immediate and full-time. The central conundrum was how to dismantle a Cold War infrastructure that had been in place for three decades. Unlike in Berlin, citizens with hammers and pickaxes could not do this job (though certainly some protesters had tried and some land-owners would have relished the duty). The Minuteman missiles would have to come out nearly as precisely as they went in. There were few guidelines. Just as constructing the vast Minuteman fields had been a national first, taking them apart was unprecedented. In fact, South Dakota's deactivation would serve as something of a template for the missile fields in Missouri and North Dakota, also slated for deactivation. Simply ripping the missiles and silos from the ground or leaving them sealed in the plains was not possible. Instead, Pavek and the deactivation crews would have to navigate a tangled web of international and national protocols in order to dismantle 150 missiles, fifteen launch centers, and thousands of miles of underground cables.

So it was that once again South Dakotans found their lives intimately intertwined with global politics. Negotiations in far-off places like Moscow and Washington determined the first, broad guidelines for what would happen to South Dakota's missile sites. According to START the sites had to be destroyed and all missiles and warheads removed and dismantled. The missiles would have to be shipped off to Utah and the warheads transported to the Pantex plant in Texas, where all U.S. warheads are made and go to die. Back in South Dakota the silo head works had to be destroyed to a depth of 8 meters below ground level. The launch centers would then have to be filled with dirt after all sensitive materials were removed. All communication cables, that tangled web of wires that crisscrossed the plains, had to be spliced. Within these general guidelines it was up to the deactivation teams to fashion a more precise program. The Air Force took responsibility for removing the warheads and missiles and closing down the sites, which were then turned over to the Corps of Engineers for demolition. The first warhead was removed in December 1991, the final Minuteman missile taken from the field in 1994.[9]

The Corps of Engineers arguably had the more onerous task. They had to determine whether or not dangerous chemicals existed at the sites (lead paint, polychlorinated biphenyls, or PCBs, and asbestos were in wide use in the 1960s), figure out how to safely and efficiently destroy the silos, and deal with locals' concerns about the process. At the same time, the protocols followed in the 1960s— simply knocking on someone's door and telling them the government wanted some land for a missile site—were no longer acceptable. Federal environmental regulations enacted during the 1970s transformed how the military could dispose of its missile silos (just as they had transformed how the MX could be deployed). Because of the National Environmental Policy Act (NEPA), the Air Force and Corps of Engineers had to hold public meetings, issue press releases, and, perhaps most important, conduct an environmental impact review and issue a statement (EIS) about Minuteman II deactivation. The Deactivation EIS, started in 1991, detailed all possible contingencies and suggested best practices for silo demolition.[10]

After intensive study, the Corps' recommendation was to implode the missile silos once all sensitive materials were removed and salvaged. The imploded silo would be left "open" for a mandatory observation period, ninety days, so Russian satellites could confirm compliance with the START Treaty. Finally the silo would be filled in with rubble, leaving much of the old structure intact, underground. It was simply too expensive to remove all of the things buried underground. The chain-link fences would remain, enclosing a 2-acre gravel plain.[11]

In the missile fields, where landowners had long survived the era of Minutemen, the Deactivation EIS was a lightning rod. It was meant as a thorough account of all that hypothetically *could* go wrong, but missile-area landowners read it as a list of all the things that almost certainly *would* go wrong. Making matters worse, landowners felt they had not been properly consulted during the drafting of the EIS. Gene Williams, for example, and just about everyone else had missed the public meeting that federal agencies were required to hold during environmental impact reviews, because it was held in Rapid City, where no missile sites existed, and it was not well advertised in the missile fields themselves. (Only two members of the "public" attended.) When he got hold of the document, Williams was upset by what he found: the EIS noted that potential underground contaminants included not only asbestos and lead paint, but also sodium chromate liquid, PCBs, chromium, mercury, and a cadmium electroplating used to inhibit erosion. No mention was ever made of nuclear radiation. When Williams tried to find out more, he was directed to an anonymous office at the Strategic Air Command in Nebraska. In a letter to said office, Williams noted that it was not entirely clear which of these chemicals and materials were to remain permanently in the prairie. He understood that the Air Force was to destroy and bury the silos, but what of all the junk that was down in there? Williams had apt cause for concern. Missile silo E-6 sat in the middle of his wheat field. Sometime back he had noticed a dead spot creeping out from the silo fence and spreading across his field. The culprit was a sterilant used to kill the grass and weeds on the silo site, but it was leaching into the prairie. While that problem had been resolved, Williams was not entirely comfortable with what the Air Force would leave behind.[12]

Nor were landowners comfortable with the way that the Deactivation EIS recommended dismantling the missile silos. The government had determined that the cheapest and most effective way of riding the plains of their missile silos was by exploding them with TNT. For some landowners, this signified the ultimate insult: the U.S. military was going to terrorize its citizens with something that the Soviet Union had never dared do: "It's going to bomb us," declared missile-area landowner Clifford Fees.[13]

It was rumors about the EIS more than the general prospect of missile deactivation that mobilized South Dakota's landowners. In fact, without the EIS, landowners would have had very little information and very little to organize around. But in 1992 that is precisely what they did. In July, Gene Williams and his neighbor Wenzel

Kovarik called a meeting on local radio station KBHV. At 8:00 PM on
the seventh, fifty locals converged on the Wall Community Center.
For the second time a Missile Landowners Association was formed.
At the time Williams had no idea that thirty-one years before, his
father had taken the same route, also to Wall and also for a meeting
of landowners concerned with nuclear missiles. In 1961 the missiles
were coming in; now, in 1992, they were coming out.[14]

The Air Force and Corps of Engineers representatives involved
should not have been surprised when area landowners began to
make noise. A short history lesson would have disabused them of the
notion that deactivation would proceed without inquiry, that rural
agrarians would quietly let something happen to their land. What
these ranchers wanted was not continuation of the missile fields, but
consultation about their demise. The landowners quite simply wanted
to be made partners in decisions about their own livelihoods—
something that the national security state seemed incapable of providing. "I understand the need for world peace," Williams told a
Sioux Falls reporter. "But those of us living in the United States expect to be treated as important components of what happens. To not
be included kind of rubs a person the wrong way." For missile-area
landowners, decades of frustration funneled into this moment. "I
put up with them guys for 30 years and I've had it," Tom Davis spat.
"You can't imagine the things they've pulled."[15]

Williams and Kovarik understood what their fathers and grand-
fathers had known: working together they would have a better chance
of being heard. Taking advantage of small-state politics, the two ensured that representatives from the state's congressional delegation
would be present at the Wall meeting. That night a list of grievances
was drawn up and landowners agreed to canvass their neighbors in
advance of the next meeting, scheduled for August 10. Meanwhile
the state's congressional leaders set about trying to uncover the details of the Air Force deactivation plan. Senator Tom Daschle and
Congressman Tim Johnson dispatched a letter to the secretary of the

Air Force outlining landowner concerns: impact of detonation on basements and homes; responsibility of the Air Force for contamination; ownership of former missile properties; and better and ongoing communication with people in the field. While the Air Force seemed to be taking ranchers' outrage lightly, South Dakota's politicians knew that rural ire could be a powerful electoral force, particularly when aligned against you. Daschle and Johnson suggested the Air Force begin community outreach immediately.[16]

Despite official and unofficial pleas for information, there were few concrete answers available when seventy-five landowners met again in Wall in August 1992. Information coming from the Air Force seemed to be muddled and incomplete. This has all "been very frustrating," Paul Jensen wrote to Senator Daschle. Landowners were not out of line in their irritation. Answers to critical questions about ownership and missile disposal were couched in bureaucratic doublespeak—it was easy to read more than one message into official pronouncements about deactivation. For example, when asked if the missile silos *had* to be imploded, the Air Force responded with text from the START Treaty, which said nothing concrete about implosion. The START Treaty merely stipulated that "the silo door be removed, dismantled, or destroyed and the silo head works and the silo shall be destroyed by excavation to a depth of no less than eight meters, or by explosion to a depth of no less than six meters." Only when pressed was it revealed that the Strategic Air Command had decided explosive demolition would be the best route because of its "*cost effectiveness.*" The landowners now understood that other options could be on the table but that the Air Force had simply chosen the method of destruction least inconvenient to its bottom line without taking into account the needs of those Americans who had lived with the missiles for thirty years. Weren't they due *something?*, they wondered.[17]

Landowners pounced on the language of the treaty: "by excavation . . . *or* by explosion." The former certainly sounded less extreme and less potentially damaging. Moreover, excavation fit well with another deep-seated principle of rural living: why waste anything? In what sometimes amounted to near-sustenance agriculture, disposing of perfectly useful goods was tantamount to treason. Accordingly, area landowners had a host of suggestions for what could be done with decommissioned silos. A silo, it was suggested, would be "the best cyclone cellar around." Others saw the ranching benefits of such huge concrete cylinders: they would be great for underground storage of grain and water. "Speaking for only 3 neighbors and my business," Paul Jensen wrote to Daschle, "it is believed that the LF site B-9 could be used as a community water system . . . and solve our severe cattle and household watering problems." Jensen described the economic benefits of such a plan for an area susceptible to boom and bust cycles tied to water shortages. He also echoed Williams in his consternation over not being included in a planning process that showed little regard for "what we who live here consider to be important" and the intractability of the Air Force, whose "mission is implementation of policy rather than the making of that policy. I cannot spell out clearly enough," he concluded, "how important this water project would be to us."[18]

The landowners' demands were hardly unprecedented, nor their concerns unfounded. The military had a history of abandoning former missile sites, some for civilian use. In the 1960s, just as the Minutemen were being deployed, the first-generation Atlas missiles were deactivated. Unconstrained by international treaty obligations or national environmental regulations, the federal government either handed the silos over to local governments or sold them off to private parties. In Jackson County, Kansas, the local school board purchased an Atlas site for $1 and promptly transformed it into part of the Jackson Heights High School. Perhaps of more interest to South Dakota landowners was the story of Ed and Dianna Peden, who, in 1982, purchased an old Atlas silo near Topeka, Kansas, for $40,000 (it cost the government more than $4 million to build). It took more than a decade, but the Pedens eventually converted the concrete complex into a new age home replete with rattan rugs, tapestry-covered walls, the constant waft of incense, and a drum circle. They also began a business, the Twentieth Century Castle Company, aiding others interested in silo living. The Minuteman silos were not as large as the Titan and Atlas silos, but that did not make them seem any less useful.[19]

Landowners realized that while environmental regulations may keep them from using the old silos, those same regulations could perhaps also be used to safeguard their rights as property owners. Indeed, the EIS not only served to bring them together by providing a document of potential problems, but also played a role in getting their message heard. Arguments about the health of water and land resources garnered media and political attention. In the late summer of 1992, stories appeared in major American newspapers such as the *New York Times* and *USA Today*, as well as on *ABC Nightly News* and the *Today* show.[20]

In September, Republican senator Larry Pressler took the ranchers' concerns to heart and to Washington, D.C., where he introduced an amendment to the START I Treaty, which had yet to be ratified in the Senate. Amendment 3227 did not seek to keep the silos intact; instead, Pressler cited concerns about water safety and demanded that greater environmental reviews be written into START I compliance protocols. Echoing the ranchers' do-or-die language, Pressler warned his colleagues, "what we are talking about here are major underground supplies of water that make the difference between some of the finest range land in this country and the beautiful, but agriculturally useless, Badlands consisting of hard-packed clay, cactus and long dead river beds." The ranchers have done their duty of housing these missiles, Pressler reminded the Senate, and now they just want to protect their livelihoods, which "depend on a very basic commodity—water." The amendment quickly passed in the Senate, but it was a rather toothless political victory, since it required no real action and made no demands on the Air Force. It simply asked that the Compliance and Inspection Commissions "place on the agenda for discussion" ways to "minimize the impact [silo] elimination [could have] on the environment, including the impact on the water wells and aquifers."[21]

By linking their cause to arguments about environmental sustainability and water, these South Dakotans had learned an important lesson. They could not fight a large government bureaucracy without some sort of organized response, and in this case the environmental regulations of the previous decades came in handy. The new environmental regulations of NEPA provided effective tools for contesting the national security state as the No-MX coalitions did in the 1980s. First, environmental reviews served as a rallying point for communities. Without this public accounting, the landowners would not have had access to the information that encouraged them to get together. Moreover, using language that resonated with the growing national environmental consciousness was smart politics. The ranchers would play the abused, rural David against a huge, land-grabbing federal Goliath, a narrative that clearly also played well into the mythology of the antifederal, independent Westerner. "I think it comes down fundamentally to a lack of respect for those of us who live out here," Jensen fumed. "Those people live in the cities behind a desk and they think this is God forsaking nowhere. And what's that little piece [of land] in that huge expanse, you know."[22]

Though the South Dakota landowners and their spokesmen certainly built on the power and language of new environmental protocols, it would be erroneous to think of them as environmentalists. On the contrary, Kovarik echoed the fears that many rural Westerners had about the national environmental movement when they warned against the government turning the missile-area cable easements into a "rails-to-trails type deal . . . where you have every Tom, Dick and Harry being able to ride across your place because the cable easements have been turned over to the, you know, some biking group or whatever." No, most of these ranchers were not worried about the national environmental agenda. They did not want to see missile lands being turned over for wilderness areas. Instead these rural landowners were doing what their forefathers had done, which was to work within the system to get their point across. In this case they wanted to use and manage the lands they believed were rightly theirs. They knew what this land was supposed to look like, and now, as the end of the Cold War promised, what it could look like again. They also knew they would have an important role to play in making sure that happened. "There is a reason we live out here on the prairie in western South Dakota," Jensen argued. "And it has to do with the environment." Not, Jensen clarified, in the green, environmentalist sense of the term, but because of the love of the place and the land. "Leaving several hundred thousand tons of blown up concrete, lead paint, chain link fences, and roads, etc.," he said, was not in keeping with this ethos. And what of the long-term consequences? "What is the deterioration of all this material in that hole going to cost to the underground water system?," William Bielmaier wondered.[23]

Certainly there was ample precedent for military installations turned into disaster zones. Colorado's early Titan missile test area had been declared a Superfund site, and that state's missile sites were being evaluated for contaminants. In 1990 Ellsworth Air Force Base was put on the Environmental Protection Agency's National Priorities List. The EPA was concerned with jet fuel and other contaminants that were seeping into the groundwater and could "pose unacceptable health risks." And who in western South Dakota didn't know about the radiation problems associated with uranium mining in the Black Hills?[24]

Across the western plains it was not even contamination that provoked the biggest outcry. It was water. If there was one certainty in western South Dakota, it was that water would always be scarce. Nearly everything hinged on the precarious balance of that one resource. The problem for landowners was that the Air Force's chosen

method of silo demolition, TNT, threatened fragile wells and aquifers. Exploding silos raised profoundly uncomfortable questions:
Could sixty-year-old clay wells crumble? Would water sources be
disrupted? What was the risk of contamination? The Air Force and
Corps of Engineers dismissed these concerns and pointed to its detailed environmental studies, which determined that explosion of
the silos to a depth of 20.5 feet would be the most effective and efficient means of disposal. In addition, the blasts would be relatively
small and in short bursts—meant just to loosen the ground and silos,
not implode the entire structure. But this provided little assurance
to landowners, who noted that the documents themselves provided
that it was "possible, though unlikely, that the shock from the blast
could cause reservoirs to seep, and also influence shallow aquifer
recharge capability." Words like "slight" and "unlikely" are hardly
comforting to ranchers who lived in a region surviving only because
of lean, "slight" margins of grass, water, and cattle prices.[25]

Nor was the question of land ownership any less confusing. A
tangled web of national laws and statutes governed the distribution
of federal properties. Understanding who could own what and when
they could do so seemed to require an advanced degree in real estate
appraisal. And landowners had long understood that all missile sites
and launch centers were on *government-owned* lands—even if it was
just 2 acres in the middle of someone's wheat field. Disposal of that
land was thus entirely up to the U.S. government, regardless of what
may seem right or fair to those in South Dakota. The Air Force did
not attempt to make matters much easier. Queries about ownership
were generally answered in opaque legalese: "Disposal of Minuteman land will be controlled by the Property and Administrative Services Act of 1949, as amended, and Section 9781, title 10, United
States Code," seems to have been the favored response to the question "Who will get the land?" Through Senator Daschle, the Air
Force elaborated somewhat: previous landowners would have the
first option to reacquire missile sites *if and only if* three specific con-

ditions were met: (1) the original owner still owned the surrounding property; (2) that party was willing to pay fair market value for the land; and (3) that party would have to pay the cost of a land survey. If those conditions were not met—if there was more than one adjacent landowner or if the original land had been sold—then things got a lot more complicated. Standard government procedure required that the missile lands be offered initially to other governmental bodies— federal, state, county, township, down the line (thus Kovarik's fear of a "rails to trails-type deal")—and that eligible structures be made available as housing for the homeless, should it be needed. It seemed that right of first refusal would thus be granted to a host of faceless bureaucracies before local landowners would have a shot at what, in many cases, had once been their land. If no government agency wanted it, then the land would be opened for competitive bidding.[26]

It was clearly not what the landowners wanted to hear. Many recalled that their parents had been promised a return of their lands; many lamented that years of sacrifice would be compounded by yet another injury. Responding to this sense of injustice, Senator Daschle introduced a bill to amend property disposal rules so that the Air Force could offer missile lands to adjacent landowners in all cases. He added his personal plea that "the landowners of western South Dakota were forced to sell their land to the Air Force, and they did so for the defense of our country. They have sacrificed more than land during that time . . . they deserve the option of buying that land back." It was an option the landowners in South Dakota were ultimately given. So too were the landowners in North Dakota and Missouri, where the Minutemen were also dismantled. This grassroots mobilization was thus in some ways successful.[27]

The landowners were less successful in changing the way the missile silos were eliminated. They continued to press their case throughout 1993, but to little avail. All the while the Air Force and Corps of Engineers proceeded with their plans. The missiles were removed, leaving empty silos and demolition as the final act of deactivation.

The deactivation teams had little doubt that explosion would be the safest and best way to get rid of the silos, and they had little intention of changing that plan. Indeed, by the fall of 1993, M. A. Mortenson Company of Colorado Springs was awarded a $4.7 million contract to explode the missiles silos; it would ultimately cost $14 million. The first blast was scheduled for April 1994.[28]

It was eerily dark by 4:30 PM on April 5, 1994, when dozens of people gathered 13 miles outside of Union Center, South Dakota. It was an unlikely group of ranchers, Air Force personnel, Corps of Engineers representatives, and out-of-town journalists. The sun would not set for another few hours, but heavy black clouds hung low over the plains, giving the illusion of dusk. A hard rain began falling just before 5:00 PM.

At precisely 5:00 PM the signal was given and, a half mile away from the gathering, a plume of soil rose into the air, followed by a faint boom. Minuteman missile silo H-10, labeled "Son of Sam" by Nukewatch, was gone. There were no speeches, no cheers. Once the spectacle was over, the crowd took off for their vehicles to escape the downpour. Two years later, on September 13, 1996, the last silo was exploded. No one complained about the water.[29]

In South Dakota reaction was mixed. "Nuclear Missiles Will Be Missed," declared the *Sioux Falls Argus Leader* in its coverage of the first silo explosion. "I kind of hate to see 'em go," admitted Darrell Steffes, the owner of the land adjacent to H-1. "They contributed to our national security. And they've sure put a lot of money into the economy." Out in the missile fields small things reminded residents that the missiles may have had some positive influence. Don Paulsen, who had once watched Sputnik bleep overhead, knew that rural electricity and telephony would most likely not be as good without the Minutemen. From his own work with Golden West Telephone Company he had firsthand evidence of how the Air Force had needed local companies to provide advanced services at a time when few rural ranchers were willing to make such an investment. Similarly, many residents happy to wave good-bye to the missiles acknowledged that roads and power might not be well maintained without Air Force crews. National security had meant things would be taken care of. The Department of Defense subsidized road maintenance, particularly where the giant transporter-erector trucks would have to drive.[30]

Sentiment in Rapid City was similarly ambivalent. Surely most people agreed that getting rid of thermonuclear warheads was a good thing, but there were faint rumblings of concern: What did this mean for Ellsworth Air Force Base? What would this mean for the community? Jobs would be lost, families uprooted. In fact, in 1992 the base laid off 1,700 missile-maintenance personnel. Would Ellsworth need a replacement mission? The importance of Ellsworth Air Force Base to the region could hardly be overemphasized. In the early 1990s the base spent more than $60 million on housing, construction, and supplies and employed more than 7,000 people with a net payroll of $175 million. These hard numbers told only a fraction of the story, however. Indirect benefits were often more intimately felt: thousands employed in service and construction industries; dollars spent by airmen in the local communities; bowls of soup purchased at Wall Drug (coffee was free for missileers); relationships made; school rosters padded. By 1991 the national security state was deeply tied to the western plains.[31]

Fortunately for Rapid City, Ellsworth was considered a "super base"; it housed three alternate missions, including the B-1 Lancer. As a result, even after the missiles were deactivated, the base remained open. While expenditure and employment dipped in the early 1990s, by the end of the decade Ellsworth had regained its economic footing. In Missouri, where the Minutemen were also deactivated, the Air Force poured millions of dollars into upgrading roads and buildings to ensure the longevity of the B-2s there. "This place would be nothing without the base," a Missourian declared.[32]

In South Dakota, the dismantling of the missile fields was taken as an opportunity for celebration and reaffirmation of the region's role in national security, rather than dismal appraisal. Wing Commander Colonel Roscoe Moulthrop noted that deactivation represented "a Cold War victory that is yours [the people of the region] as well as ours." The Rapid City Chamber of Commerce concurred. "On behalf of the grateful citizens of the greater Rapid City area," the chamber wrote when the Minuteman Missile Wing was being deactivated in 1994, "We express our appreciation. . . . Without your valiant efforts, the dedicated powers of communism may have prevailed. . . . South Dakotans are privileged to have known you as friends, military professionals, and sentinels of our national security." The missiles were gone; the base remained; the missile plains were quiet again.[33]

But only for so long.

In the spring of 1999, before summer pastures were to be sown, Paul Jensen sat down to write an angry letter to his congressional representatives. Minuteman missile site B-9, on his family's land for thirty-five years, had not yet been returned. The missile and warhead were long gone, the site imploded in 1996. There seemed to be no practical reason for the delay in returning the land to its rightful owners. Nothing happened there other than the occasional Air Force crew sent to mow and tend to the fences. For Jensen it was a constant irritation, a continual reminder of his tenure housing the Minuteman. William Bielmaier declared the old missile site a "constant scar on our landscape." In fact housing the missiles may have been better. At least then there was a purpose, an explanation for his ire. Now there was just a blank hole in the middle of his field, a space that had been promised to his family but still sat idle.[34]

Senator Tom Daschle passed Jensen's concerns on to Secretary of Defense William Cohen, imploring him to accelerate the process.

Daschle was told that the Air Force's final "environmental documentation" would not be completed until the following year. At that point the Air Force would file the necessary paperwork on "excess" property and the whole process would be turned over to yet another bureaucracy—the Government Services Agency. The first flight of ten former missile sites—the "golf" flight near Red Owl—would be put up for sale sometime in the summer of 2001.[35]

It had taken just two years to put the Minutemen in, and it would take more than a decade to pull them out. For Jensen the process dragged on until 2003, when he received a copy of the "Quitclaim Deed" that gave him legal ownership to the small parcel that had once been his father's land. And there were caveats to the return. The 8-foot chain-link fence would remain. The Air Force would not pay to have it removed. Thanks to the presence of PCBs, landowners could not dig below 2 feet and the location of future wells would be restricted.[36]

It would be reasonable to assume that Jensen's tenure with the Minutemen—particularly the final convoluted decade of deactivation—would have made him forever wary of the U.S. Air Force. But this was not the case. Jensen, in fact, found himself caught in one of the strange paradoxes of the Cold War nuclear landscape. He resented the Air Force's insensitivity to his land but hardly rejected the Air Force in South Dakota. On the contrary, Jensen understood the importance of the military to western South Dakota and actively participated in its maintenance. Throughout the 1990s he was part of the base's honorary commanders program, which gets locals involved with Ellsworth. Jensen particularly enjoyed meeting and showing around Ellsworth's top brass. "They bring new things into our rather isolated community," he said enthusiastically. They are, according to Jensen, "one of the reasons we are kind of progressive around here. If not politically . . . in other areas."[37]

Jensen would know. In the early 1990s he followed the familiar exodus of people from farm to town by leaving his family's ranch house in favor of a perch in Rapid City. As a resident of Rapid City, Jensen came into increasing contact with the positive spillovers of Ellsworth—not just the economic benefits but those less measurable as well. The social, political, and cultural makeup of the region became deeply enmeshed with Air Force blue. Airmen and their families moved in, liked it, and stayed. Service retirees began to populate the area, providing closer and tighter links between base and city. An Ellsworth Air Force museum runs on their donated time. By the end of the Cold War, western South Dakota was deeply immersed in the national security apparatus. It was a story repeated across the country as military bases pumped money, jobs, people, and ideas into areas, transforming cities from agricultural outposts to modern, service-based economies.

It was a relationship that continued—in fact was in many ways heightened—when the Cold War came to an end. The end of the Minuteman era opened new vulnerabilities for Ellsworth Air Force Base. If the missiles had somehow served as stakes, holding the base to the prairie, now with them gone the military edge of western South Dakota had became a lot more precarious. In 2005, Rapid City found itself in a new and uncomfortable position when Ellsworth Air Force Base was placed on the top of the Pentagon's list of possible bases to close as part of the Base Realignment and Closure (BRAC) review.

The 2005 review was the fifth round of BRAC since the end of the Cold War. The collapse of the Soviet Union required a vast reconsideration of the American military behemoth. Not only would missile fields be dismantled, but the entire infrastructure of the Cold War had to be refigured to better cope with more diffuse, less easily defined threats. BRAC was first implemented in 1988 in recognition of both this practical need and the fact that communities and politicians would be reluctant to see their own military installations shuttered. Not a single military installation had been closed since 1977. Through BRAC it was hoped that deactivation could be made as transparent as possible, ridding militarization of its deep political ties. A redundant base in Texas would not, for example, be kept open simply because an important congressman called it home. Likewise a naval yard in Maine would not be shuttered simply because its congressional representative lacked the requisite clout. Demilitarization was to be made democratic, or at least less opaque.[38]

BRAC worked like this: The Pentagon first issued a list of superfluous bases—basically the installations it would not mind realigning or eliminating, bases with little or redundant national security value. This list was then passed on to an independent nine-member BRAC Commission, appointed by the president and approved by the Senate, that would evaluate said list, including holding public meetings and visits to potential sites. Final BRAC Commission recommendations were then sent to Congress for confirmation—in toto. Congress no longer had the option of picking and choosing its bases and installations; there were no closed-door negotiations on how to save such-and-such a base in a tough election year just because it would really help out Senator X. As a result of the 1988, 1991, 1993, and 1995 BRAC reviews, a total of 100 major military facilities were closed and another 145 realigned, for an estimated $16 billion in immediate savings, with an additional $7.3 billion annually. By 1997 the Department of Defense had reduced the number of total active-duty military personnel by 32 percent. As Representative Dick Armey of Texas proclaimed when BRAC was passed in 1988, Congress had finally "put the national interest ahead of parochial interests."[39]

The fifth round of base realignment suggested a different outcome: four previous rounds of BRAC had actually done more to sharpen and channel parochial desires than to elevate the national interest. In 2005, Secretary of Defense Donald Rumsfeld made much of trimming down the country's military infrastructure, of streamlining capabilities and making sure the armed forces could face "the new demands of war against extremists and other evolving 21st century challenges," particularly the costly wars in Afghanistan and

Iraq. Beginning in 2003, civilian and military leaders began evaluating the country's bases and military infrastructure to determine what was most expendable. At the same time, areas with bases of dubious value began working on their "why Base X is important" sales pitches. If history was any guide, these communities had to do all they could to stay *off* the BRAC list; once on, it was hard to be removed. In New London, Connecticut, home of the nuclear-powered submarine, the chamber of commerce mobilized. The state of Maine warned that if the Portsmouth Naval Shipyard were shuttered, the state would go into a recession. Statehouses hired Washington lobbyists to agitate on their behalf, adding yet another layer to the vast complex of regions, economies, and professions that made up the defense complex. Millions were spent, hundreds of phone calls made. The Columbia, South Carolina, Chamber of Commerce devoted $800,000 to the cause of keeping the state's bases around and hired the Rhodes Group, a defense lobbying firm complete with a former BRAC commissioner, to come to its aid. In Rapid City, South Dakota, the mayor's exhortations for maximum community effort to save Ellsworth were met with maximum response: local businesses, civic groups, and government agencies created a task force to respond to a potentially negative review from the BRAC Commission.[40]

The stakes were considerable. Previous base closures provided more than anecdotal evidence of what could become of areas abandoned by the military. The picture was particularly grim in rural areas where the local economy was less robust and diversified, thus less capable of sustaining even small economic shocks. Government studies confirmed this supposition. In previous base closings, rural counties lost twice as many jobs as metropolitan-based installations and did not recover them in the long run. As South Dakota governor Mike Rounds was quick to assert, western South Dakota was definitely a rural place. The loss of Ellsworth would devastate not merely the region's economy, but the entire state's, particularly given that the region lacked the real estate interests that could sop up the excess capacity. Rapid City Chamber of Commerce president and Ellsworth Air Force Base task force member Jim McKeon confirmed that Ellsworth contributed "about 9 percent of the Rapid City economy." [41]

So to the task of keeping their base off of the BRAC is to what these communities turned—the earlier the better. There were two main questions to consider: what made their base *appear* expendable, and how could they prove that it was, in fact, essential? For all of these communities, the goal was to effectively counter the Defense Department's arguments about redundancy and excessive costs. The BRAC Commission's priority considerations were, not surprisingly, categorized as "military value": how important is this installation for long-term security needs? It would have been instructive, at this point, for base advocates around the country to think about those bases that had avoided BRAC consideration over time— those considered essential to national security. What did they have? What made them different? In Rapid City such questions may have led to an uncomfortable lament: the loss of the Minutemen. Not a single base housing nuclear ICBMs was slated for review in 2005, nor in any year before, for that matter. Malmstrom, Minot, and Warren were "safe." The Minutemen kept them plugged to the ground. [42]

Without the Minutemen, residents interested in keeping Ellsworth around had to resort to the sorts of tactics other military communities used, namely, politics. In anticipation of the fifth round of BRAC, South Dakotans narrowly unseated their incumbent senator and the Democratic leader, Tom Daschle, in favor of upstart John Thune, largely because they thought a Republican could better ensure a continued military presence in the state. "A vote for Daschle is a vote against Ellsworth," one ad proposed. Not that Daschle had ever shirked his responsibility to Ellsworth, but, South Dakota residents surmised, perhaps a Republican would have better luck since the president and Congress were controlled by the GOP. [43]

In May 2005, just seven months after Thune beat Daschle, this seemed a strategy in need of revision. That month Ellsworth did, in fact, find its way onto the BRAC list. According to the Department of Defense, the B-1 bombers could be moved to Texas and Ellsworth Air Force Base shuttered for a net savings of $1.86 billion over twenty years. It was suggested that Thune's political fortunes were over. Reaction from his office—as well as from the entire Ellsworth community— was swift. South Dakota's congressional delegation and the Rapid City Chamber of Commerce swung into high gear. In Washington, D.C., the state's representatives staked out a suburban hotel where BRAC commissioners met, hoping to plead their case. When he was not allowed to speak, Thune stared down commissioners during Senate hearings. Closer to home, fliers and signs were pasted around town in advance of the BRAC commissioners' mandatory review trip to the city, encouraging locals to attend a rally at the city's Rushmore Plaza Civic Center on June 21: "Let's save Ellsworth. Attend the BRAC hearing." Nearly 8,000 people came— almost as many as had gathered on the Kammerer ranch in 1980 to protest uranium mining.[44]

Clearly there was more at stake than hard economic numbers. The *Rapid City Journal* reported that Big Brothers and Big Sisters would lose 20 percent of its volunteers if the base closed. The Box Elder Volunteer Fire Department would lose half its firefighters. Many local businesses worried about lost profits. The owner of Angelique's Custom Embroidery, for example, realized that much of her business was in custom work on military uniforms. Military retirees fretted about losing medications available at steep discounts on base. Those with a longer view realized that without an active military base, fewer people would realize the benefits of the city, and fewer military retirees would come back to the area. Chamber of Commerce president Jim McKeon warned, "A lot of people probably won't realize the impact until their soccer coach is gone and their Bible teacher is not here or their teacher's aide is gone."[45]

Nothing so aptly demonstrated the dependency of American municipalities on the military as the threat of its abandonment. The mere whiff of closure was enough to send fierce political rivals into a ferocious bipartisan embrace. Defense Secretary Rumsfeld, for example, received a letter signed by the entire California congressional delegation touting the Golden State's military virtues. It was the only time the entire delegation agreed on anything that year. The Cold War defense complex created strange bedfellows. The perceived necessity of Ellsworth could turn even the seemingly most devoted doves into hawks. Former senator and Democratic presidential nominee George McGovern, an avowed peacenik, lamented having to keep the base around. He would have preferred if the money had initially gone to public housing or agriculture, but since it had not, western South Dakota now needed that base. It is unlikely that any South Dakotan politician would disagree. The military had become so interlaced with perceptions of economic development and modernization that few residents were willing to try to go it alone.[46]

In the end, the art of *anticipating* closure, of being constantly ready to respond, had become something of a necessity around the country. The consequence was to wrap communities up even more tightly with their military installations. If you were told hundreds of times that you needed the defense complex, eventually you would believe it. Little energy would be expended to look for other options. In South Dakota the end of the Cold War and the loss of the Minutemen were greeted not with a widespread practical plan for an indigenous economic revival, but with greater attention to keeping Ellsworth around. In 2005 the state spent an estimated $12 million to keep the base. While a few fringe voices wondered if that money wouldn't be better spent on farm aid or local needs, maintaining Ellsworth easily overpowered those sentiments. Local politicians and business groups actively sought new missions, better land, and greater flexibility for the base. Of course Marvin Kammerer, whose own land was often part of such sacrifices, would hardly have agreed. But in general, the importance of Ellsworth had become nearly proverbial, making and breaking political fortunes. Few questions were

asked. It was easier to accept militarization than to confront its awkward realities.[47]

This is not, of course, how everyone chose to see the relationship.
While socioeconomic arguments about base closure were important,
many BRAC arguments justifiably centered on national security. Of
eight considerations the commission was to take into account, "economic impact on existing communities," was the sixth. In making
realignment recommendations, for example, the Department of
Defense weighed security and cost concerns to try to find the most
balanced fighting force. Strategic arguments were thus also mar-
shaled by opponents of base closure. In South Dakota, pro-Ellsworth
constituents argued that a base far inland and far removed was central to the War on Terror. Echoing concerns about vulnerability during the Cold War, South Dakotans proclaimed that putting all of the
B-1 bombers in one place (as the secretary of defense recommended)
would be unwise. What if they were all disabled by a storm or an
(unlikely) attack? While such arguments provided some cover for
bald parochial interests, they could barely disguise the horse-trading
that was quickly taking over the BRAC process. Rumsfeld ruefully
acknowledged that in making its final recommendations, the 2005
BRAC Commission had let economic considerations outweigh strategic ones.[48]

These tensions would not have surprised Kammerer. From his
perch on the northern edge of Ellsworth Air Force Base, the end of
the Cold War and community reaction merely confirmed his long-
held suspicions about militarism on the Great Plains. Kammerer
understood all too well the trade-off between the military and land,
between faith in the Pentagon and a willingness to produce. Over
the course of the Cold War his family's holdings had withered, con-
sumed by the voracious appetite of the national security apparatus.
When Ellsworth needed more land for a new runway, the Kammerer ranch had been the only place to put it. While Kammerer
accepted a nation's need for self-defense, he did not approve of the

Pentagon as a giant welfare program. Ellsworth, he argued, should never be used "as a jobs program"—which, at the end of the Cold War, was exactly what was happening. It was the "most wasteful form of welfare" cloaked "with a military blanket," he spat, noticing this irony.[49]

For Kammerer, the military presence in western South Dakota had turned ugly and unnecessary. It had created an unattractive dependency that empowered outsiders who did not understand the people and the land. In fact, they showed a fundamental lack of respect for the history of the plains and the work that had been done there. By the end of the Cold War, Kammerer knew that the national security state would not compromise; if you gave an inch, you would lose an acre. He thus had little patience for ranchers who sought solutions from within. You could fight power only from the outside, Kammerer would say, or be corrupted by it. You could not accept Air Force trips and then protest their treatment of your land.

In 2005, Ellsworth Air Force beat the odds and was taken off the BRAC list. Eight of the nine commissioners decided their initial decision was wrong and that Ellsworth was critical to the nation's force structure. Community impact was also important. According to one commissioner, closing Ellsworth would "dramatically impact" the region and "turn people's lives upside down and create a great deal of difficulty in the short-term." So to ensure social and economic continuity, a military installation the Department of Defense no longer wanted would remain open.[50]

Across South Dakota the response was euphoric. Local politicians were treated "like rock stars." More than once it was noted that the reversal saved the political fortunes of Senator Thune. It also created a new political force: statewide efforts to protect Ellsworth. In 2009, the state legislature created the South Dakota Ellsworth Development Authority with the explicit purpose of promoting and enhancing the military prospects of the region. The governor appoints seven commissioners who serve four-year terms. In 2009 Governor Rounds declared that the authority was created because "Ellsworth's current and future economic impact benefits the entire state and is something we cannot afford to lose."[51]

In 2010, the federal government—in the form of Ellsworth Air Force Base—was the largest employer in western South Dakota and the second-largest employer in the state, coming in only behind the state government. As the annual report on the base's economic impact noted, the contribution goes well beyond economic numbers. "Our Airmen volunteered more than 37,000 hours," the commander praised, specifically noting service as Little League coaches and with the Make-a-Wish Foundation. All the while, the airmen did their job: one-third of the active-duty personnel were "engaged in combat operations overseas." The mission of the 28th Bomb Wing: "to put bombs on target" with the B-1B Lancer aircraft.[52]

The relationship between military base and community is not isolated to the eastern edge of the Black Hills. Across the country Americans during the Cold War became inextricably and intimately bound to the subtle perpetuation of militarism. No one would argue directly that armaments and security risks and wars should be invented to prolong the Cold War infrastructure, but certainly the argument was suggested in the intense expectations people placed on military installations. By insisting that new missions be found for old bases, that more money be spent to upgrade facilities and fortify defenses, Americans had long since stopped resisting militarism and instead embraced it as an economic necessity. To be sure, they could still justify it in the name of national security. But under that veneer it was really just about butter. Indeed, across the country communities had traded in the American mythology of antimilitarism for one far more immediate and satisfying: militarism led to bounty, a myth from which the country still cannot wean itself.

The fences are the most visible reminders of South Dakota's scattered nuclear landscape. Chain-link government-issued barriers that once cordoned nuclear warheads off from the world now separate land from landowner. In keeping with the ethos of the plains that finds functionality in refuse, many landowners have opted to put their fences to use, using them to store hay and supplies. But others simply leave them idle. They do not want the fences, but they do not want to expend the energy to remove them either. The barriers are, after all, sunk some 8 feet into the ground. They cannot merely be rolled up and hauled away—perhaps the very reason the Air Force left them there in the end. It simply cost too much to remove them.

Here and there some of the missile fences have been removed, a task generally accomplished in anger. The landowner of former Minuteman site C-2 removed the fence and gravel, setting fire to the land. Charred grasses ring the area. But in the end that small plot of land has been recaptured, turned back over to the prairie, just as the Air Force once promised it would be.

Conclusion

Missiles and Memory

O n June 14, 2001, a few South Dakota landowners—having recently reacquired their land—may have been jolted from their nuclear-free bliss with an odd feeling of déjà vu. That morning a large white transporter-erector truck marked only with the large black block letters "US AIR FORCE" rumbled off I-90 at Exit 116. While trucks were a familiar site during the Cold War, no such truck had been seen in these parts since 1993. Transporter-erectors signaled one thing: missiles. For years it was these trucks that hauled missiles to and from their silos, reminding residents that things could go wrong, that the holes in their fields were not empty, and that the humming weapons under the plains could not be totally ignored.

But on this bright June morning the truck was only partially full. It was bringing a missile back to South Dakota, but one without warhead, fuel, and guidance systems—a mere shell. Dozens of airmen from Warren Air Force Base in Wyoming came to implant a dummy Minuteman into silo D-9 as part of the Minuteman Missile National Historic Site's static display. The missile itself was pumped full of concrete to keep it from collapsing under its own weight. In the fall of 2001 the Air Force officially turned the site over to the National

Park Service (NPS), which was charged with creating the first national park site that interprets the Cold War.[1]

"It's an honor to come back here," a former South Dakota missileer said. "This site pays tribute to the many men and women—the unsung warriors, who work with little recognition—for all of their hard work." Rancher Marvin Kammerer had something quite different to say. "It's plumb goofy," he sighed, yet another waste of taxpayer money. Perhaps the millions mandated for the park site should go into local agricultural needs rather than the commemoration of a weapon system.[2]

It was a visit to the historic site in 2004—when it was still in the planning stages—that initially piqued my interest in the Minutemen. Before then I knew about nuclear deterrence and the Cold War, but almost nothing about the country's ICBMs. South Dakota seemed the perfect place to run into this Cold War peculiarity. The haunting landscape of the western plains, the sparse population, the big sky, all lend themselves to surreal fantasies of things not being what they seem. Standing on the edge of former Minuteman missile site D-9, with the Badlands formations off in the distance, it was not difficult to imagine that the end of the world could begin here.

Of course, the world did not end. Not a single Minuteman was fired, precisely the reason there is now a historic site in the missiles' honor. This is not meant glibly, but rather to underscore the maxim that history is made—or at least written—by the victor. The Minuteman Missile National Historic Site exists because the United States "won" the Cold War. At the site the missiles are stand-ins for national and personal glory. There is nothing inherently wrong with preserving the Minuteman facilities, or in using them to interpret the past. Nor are the motives and intentions of the people and groups involved in the site's interpretive plan particularly biased. They intend the site to be as balanced as time and money will allow. Yet it is nearly impossible for the Minuteman Missile National Historic Site to be anything but a celebration of the American way of war.

The plaque near the viewing dome at D-9 reads, "This site was configured . . . as a lasting tribute to the Minuteman II weapon system and to all of the Warriors who maintained and operated it. Is standing proof that the Cold War did not just end, it was won!"[3]

The very nature of the Cold War conspires against a nuanced reading of the Minuteman missiles. This was a war that was never fought. The Minuteman missiles were never used. The historic site thus marks a sprawling complex of military installations—and personnel—that didn't do anything. "We were so well armed that we didn't have to do anything," admits former missileer Wendy McNeil. Missileers never actually did the things that become the stuff of monument. Most war commemoratives draw heavily on the fallen soldier: the ultimate sacrifice a citizen can give to home and nation. Such sacrifice becomes a touchstone for the patriotic obligation of the citizens who are left standing. But the domestic Cold War lacks such standard-bearers. Cold War sacrifice has a different meaning—a sacrifice of patience and vigilance, the tedium of waiting and watching. The personal side of the Minutemen then is a national story of how hundreds of men and women waited underground to keep watch over a weapon system that could destroy the world, and of how hundreds of others lived with these powerful neighbors. The Association of Air Force Missileers perhaps eulogized this best: "Only this new breed of warrior, missileers. . . . Instead of defending their land with bows and arrows as the Native American Indians did on the High Plains, these warriors defended and continue to defend America with wrenches and computer consoles." These do not, in our culture, seem heroic deeds. Indeed, men and women have sat at controls and monitored systems during every war and been honored only in the abstract through their fallen comrades. We can be certain that there will be no statues erected of a man sitting at the launch control facility.[4]

There are, however, statues and replicas of missiles scattered across the Cold War landscape, and these become the real objects of veneration. Indeed, the Minuteman Missile National Historic Site is not principally the story of American Cold War vigilance and victory, but more the story of the technologies that made that victory possible. While the local and personal certainly shape the direction of a larger national story, it is the national story—in this case of ICBMs, the Cold War, and nuclear deterrence—that dwarfs the mundane day to day of the missile fields.

And so our Cold War touchstones become the missiles and the guns and the guidance systems with which the Americans outpaced and outspent the Soviets. The physicality of these Cold War sites demands that it is the technology, not the people, that won the Cold War. As a result it seems to be the missiles themselves that we are commemorating. This sentiment can spill over to the scientists, engineers, and soldiers who developed, built, and maintained these weapons, the technowarriors of the age. But mostly it is the technology: the progress that reifies the narrative of national greatness. It is a seductive narrative: the nation has long looked in the mirror and seen progress and success smiling back. In the Cold War, the "we" who won is the system that created the bombs and the delivery mechanisms to destroy civilizations. Military hardware so easily becomes the stuff of monument because it reflects the confidence and progress we associate with national greatness.[5]

There is another level on which technological triumph is dangerous and disconcerting. This military-driven memory of the Cold War provides a teleology that clearly ignores the perils of the technology in question—not only the destructive potential of the weapons, but the costs and trade-offs undertaken in order to pay for such programs. Though secrecy and inconsistency make an accurate assessment of the Minutemen's costs elusive, it is clear that procuring, arming, and maintaining the missiles cost hundreds of billions of dollars. The Department of Defense estimates that today nearly $800 million is needed each year simply to maintain the remaining Minutemen. Those are dollars that could be spent elsewhere.[6]

The technological story also glosses over the violence of these weapons. The Minuteman was a weapon of mass destruction. Each of South Dakota's missiles was tipped with a 1.2-megaton warhead, large enough to destroy Seattle or Boston. And make no mistake, cities were prime targets—places like Kiev, Omsk, and Leningrad. While some of the Minutemen were aimed at military installations, population centers and industrial areas were considered fair game in maintaining the Cold War "balance of terror." The result would have been a carnage we cannot comprehend. Standing in front of a computer console or gazing down at a metal rocket is not likely to help us imagine or empathize with the intended victims. Nor does it help us understand the continued possibility of nuclear destruction. Today the Minuteman III missiles in Montana, North Dakota, Colorado, Wyoming, and Nebraska hold three separate warheads. Each warhead is capable of destroying a major metropolitan area, killing hundreds of thousands and leaving many more wounded.[7]

One certain target was Moscow, and there, too, enterprising Russians have tried to turn Cold War architecture into monument, or at least a tourist site. The privately run Confrontation Cold War Museum features a tour of an underground bomb shelter and command center deep under the capital city. American journalist David Holley visited the site and was struck by the "Soviet-era nostalgia" and the way that the tour guide emphasized American aggression. The United States, the guide told his audience, was "ready to use nuclear weapons against civilian populations." And so in Moscow, "it was life under gun sights. The threat was so imminent that our leadership could only have three or four minutes to make a decision."[8]

This is certainly not how Americans view their role in the Cold War. We chose not to think of our missiles as being aggressive or offensive, though clearly the Soviets did. In this way our understanding of the missiles has not changed much over time, but rather remains fixed in the expectations and presumptions of the people who built, maintained, and housed the system. What a visitor to the

Minuteman Missile National Historic Site learns today is remarkably similar to what the U.S. Air Force wanted people to know in the 1960s. A film at the site and available online recycles the idea that the missiles were built precisely as the "missile gap was widening." The consequences are far from immaterial. There was no missile gap. The United States built and maintained thousands of nuclear missiles even after learning that the Soviets were not doing the same thing. Indeed, at the time presidential advisers even recommended that the United States *limit* the production of missiles in order to signal restraint to the Soviets. In 1960 General Maxwell D. Taylor wrote that, in addition to bombers, the country would need at most "a few hundred reliable and accurate missiles." That, of course, did not happen, and so you will not learn of it at the historic site.[9]

The national myth of nonaggression has continued to mislead Americans in their relations with the rest of the world. Certainly during the Cold War, the Soviets did not find 1,000 ICBMs aimed at their cities particularly peaceful. Nor do the populations of countries currently under assault from American "drones." Nothing at the Minuteman Missile National Historic Site helps challenge this complacency.

The narrative of peaceful deterrence also bolsters the misconception that the United States avoided militarism during the Cold War. A full recounting of the missile fields, however, demonstrates how Americans were intimately integrated into the national security state, linking economic and political fates to the perpetuation of the military. Today in western South Dakota the quest for defense dollars seems neither terribly bizarre nor misguided. Ellsworth is a welcome and critical adjunct to the region's economic, social, and cultural life. It is expected that South Dakotans will lobby for their base. Only the most radical residents insist that the base should be closed. In fact, the Minuteman Missile National Historic Site now too has a stake in keeping Ellsworth around: airmen and base personnel have been strong supporters of and volunteers at the site.[10]

This story is not isolated to western South Dakota. The Cold War turned towns and communities across the country into defense dependencies, often in ways unseen. The result is a defense-based economy reliant on conflict, or the threat of conflict, for sustenance. Americans do not necessarily invent their enemies, but they are quick to embrace and amplify threats once identified. This is in part because there is a vested interest in doing so, precisely the sort of militarization of everyday life that Americans have so long claimed to abhor.

Understanding the nuances of these stories is all the more important and compelling given contemporary political debates about balanced budgets, populist anger, and the meaning of national security. The modern United States cannot deal with its budget problems without taking on the deep entanglements of the national security state. Just as residents of the missile fields want to hold on to their missiles, people all over the country are determined to enshrine their own Pentagon ties—not because of the national security imperative (though that provides nice cover), but because of the money. A frank discussion of how Americans have been "seduced by war" is in order.[11]

Abbreviations

Notes

Acknowledgments

Index

Abbreviations

ACE	Research Collection, Office of History, Headquarters, Army Corps of Engineers, Alexandria, Virginia
AFA	Air Force Association Archives, Arlington, Virginia
AFB	Air Force Base
AFHRA	Air Force Historical Research Agency
BAS	*Bulletin of the Atomic Scientists*
BMD	Ballistic Missile Division, U.S. Air Force
CEL	Papers of Curtis E. LeMay, Library of Congress, Manuscripts Division, Washington, D.C.
DNSA	Digital National Security Archive
EAFB	Ellsworth Air Force Base, South Dakota
FHC	Papers of Francis H. Case, Dakota Wesleyan University, Mitchell, South Dakota
FRUS	*Foreign Relations of the United States.* Washington, DC: U.S. Government Printing Office. Individual volumes titled topically and/or chronologically.
ICBM	Intercontinental ballistic missile

JCS	Records of the Joint Chiefs of Staff, Record Group 218, National Archives, College Park, Maryland
JFP	Jensen Family Papers, South Dakota State Historical Society, Pierre, South Dakota
KMP	Karl E. Mundt Papers
MIMI-NPS	Minuteman Missile National Historic Site, National Park Service, Cactus Flats, South Dakota
NACP	National Archives, College Park, Maryland
NASM	National Air and Space Museum, Archives Division, Washington, D.C.
NYT	*New York Times*
OSAF	Office of the Secretary of the Air Force, Record Group 340, National Archives, College Park, Maryland
SAC	Strategic Air Command, U.S. Air Force
SCP	Papers of Samuel C. Phillips, Library of Congress, Manuscripts Division, Washington, D.C.
SCPC	Swarthmore College Peace Collection, Swarthmore, Pennsylvania
SDOHP	South Dakota Oral History Project
SDPJC	Papers of the South Dakota Peace and Justice Center, Swarthmore College Peace Collection, Swarthmore, Pennsylvania
SDSHS	South Dakota State Historical Society, Pierre, South Dakota
SOS	Papers of Silence One Silo, Swarthmore College Peace Collection, Swarthmore, Pennsylvania
TDW	Papers of Thomas Dresser White, Library of Congress, Manuscripts Division, Washington, D.C.

Notes

1. Introduction

1. Paul Jensen, interview with the author, Rapid City, South Dakota, August 2008; Jensen, e-mail to the author, December 2010.

2. Jonathan Schell, *"The Fate of the Earth" and "The Abolition"* (Stanford, CA: Stanford University Press, 2000), 65.

3. E. P. Oliver, Secret Memorandum, "Two Months Later," January 14, 1958, DNSA, document number NH00408. All DNSA documents are available at www.gwu.edu/~nsarchiv/.

4. On the growth of the national security state see Michael J. Hogan, *A Cross of Iron: Harry S. Truman and the Origins of the National Security State, 1945–1954* (New York: Cambridge University Press, 1998); Michael S. Sherry, *In the Shadow of War: The United States since the 1930s* (New Haven, CT: Yale University Press, 1995); Charles E. Neu, "The Rise of the National Security Bureaucracy," in Louis Galambos, ed., *The New American State: Bureaucracies and Politics since World War II* (Baltimore: Johns Hopkins University Press, 1987), 85–108; and Aaron Friedberg, *In the Shadow of the Garrison State: America's Anti-Statism and Its Cold War Grand Strategy* (Princeton, NJ: Princeton University Press, 2000). For civilian-military relations see David S. Heidler and Jeanne T. Heidler, eds., *Daily Lives of Civilians in Wartime Modern America: From the Indian Wars to the Vietnam*

War (Westport, CT: Greenwood Press, 2007). Defense spending was as high as 37 percent of GDP during World War II, though by 1947 it was back down to 4 percent. Defense as a percentage of GDP started rising again in the early 1950s due to the Korean War and did not let up again until the 1970s. Defense outlays are currently around 3 percent of GDP. See "Table 3.1: Outlays by Superfunction and Function: 1940–2009," in Office of Management and Budget, *Historical Tables, Budget of the United States Government, Fiscal Year 2005* (Washington, DC, 2004), 45–52.

5. Catherine Lutz, "The Military Normal," in Network of Concerned Anthropologists Steering Committee, *The Counter-Counterinsurgency Manual* (Chicago: Prickly Paradigm Press, 2009).

6. The wars in Iraq and Afghanistan have, until recently, been administered with supplementary appropriations, not included in the defense budget. More consistently, Veterans Affairs, the Department of Homeland Security, and the maintenance of nuclear materials under the Department of Energy are not included in the defense budget. For example, see "Table 4.1: Outlays by Agency: 1940–2015," in Office of Management and Budget, *Historical Tables, Budget of the U.S. Government, Fiscal Year 2011*, www .whitehouse.gov.

7. On the dearth of scholarship on the military in the twentieth-century American West see William Deverell, "Politics in the 20th-Century West," in William Deverell, ed., *A Companion to the American West* (Malden, MA: Blackwell Publishing, 2004), 452. The economic literature on the Cold War is more significant. See, for example, Ann Markusen and Joel Yudken, *Dismantling the Cold War Economy* (New York: Basic Books, 1992); Ann Markusen, Peter Hall, Sabina Deitrich, and Scott Campbell, *The Rise of the Gunbelt* (New York: Oxford University Press, 1991); Roger Lotchin, ed., *Martial Metropolis: U.S. Cities in War and Peace* (New York: Praeger, 1984); Roger Lotchin, *Fortress California, 1910–1961: From Warfare to Welfare* (Lincoln: University of Nebraska Press, 1992); Paul A. C. Koisinen, *The Military-Industrial Complex: A Historical Perspective* (New York: Praeger, 1979); Roger Bolton, *Defense Purchases and Regional Growth* (Washington, DC: Brookings Institution, 1966); and Seymour Melman, *Pentagon Capitalism: The Political Economy of War* (New York: McGraw-Hill, 1970). On the environmental consequences of the Cold War see J. R. McNeill

and Corinna R. Unger, eds., *Environmental Histories of the Cold War* (New York: Cambridge University Press, 2010); Matthew Farrish, *The Contours of America's Cold War* (Minneapolis: University of Minnesota Press, 2010). For international relations see Andrew Bacevich, *The New American Militarism: How Americans Are Seduced by War* (New York: Oxford University Press, 2005) and *Washington Rules: America's Path to Permanent War* (New York: Macmillan, 2010). Two recent historical studies have highlighted the connections between domestic politics and the Cold War, linking the military-industrial complex to the perpetuation of the Cold War as well as showing the deep connections forged between defense dollars and political fortunes: Campbell Craig and Fredrik Logevall, *America's Cold War: The Politics of Insecurity* (Cambridge, MA: Belknap Press of Harvard University Press, 2009); Julian E. Zelizer, *Arsenal of Democracy: The Politics of National Security—From World War II to the War on Terrorism* (New York: Basic Books, 2010). More specific studies are cited in subsequent chapters.

   8. The literature on missile deployment is surprisingly thin. See Jeffrey Engel et al., *The Missile Plains: Frontline in America's Cold War* (Historic Resource Study, Minuteman Missile National Historic Site, South Dakota, 2003), http://www.nps.gov/mimi/historyculture/upload/Introduction-2.pdf; John Lonnquest and David Winkler, *To Defend and Deter: The Legacy of the United States Missile Program* (Rock Island, IL: Defense Publishing Services, 1996); Philip Glass, *Citizens against the MX: Public Language in the Nuclear Age* (Champaign: University of Illinois Press, 1993); and Catherine McNicol Stock, "Nuclear Country: The Militarization of the U.S. Northern Plains, 1954–1975," in Jeffrey A. Engel, ed., *Local Consequences of the Global Cold War* (Stanford, CA: Stanford University Press, 2008), 238–272.

   9. Catherine McNicol Stock and Robert Johnson highlight that rural areas are important in nineteenth-century U.S. historiography but tend to be left out of most twentieth-century work, particularly in the postwar period. See their introduction to *The Countryside in the Age of the Modern State: Political Histories of Rural America* (Ithaca, NY: Cornell University Press, 2001). There is a growing literature on the local impact of the Cold War. See especially Engel, *Local Consequences of the Global Cold War*. For the rural West see David M. Kennedy, "The Rural West Initiative," in

Visualizing the Rural West, Bill Lane Center for the American West, Stanford University, April 2010, http://www.stanford.edu/group/ruralwest/cgi-bin/drupal/introduction.

10. Though not the concern of this book, there is rich potential for studies on how the national security state transformed social relationships across the country. How, if at all, have the military and national security state—heavy with federal regulations and mandates—served as agents for change? For example, the desegregated armed services brought African American servicemen to places like South Dakota. See "Negro Airmen in a Northern Community: Discrimination in Rapid City, South Dakota" (Report of the South Dakota Advisory Committee to the U.S. Commission on Civil Rights, 1963), www.law.umaryland.edu. See also Catherine A. Lutz, *Homefront: A Military City and the American Twentieth Century* (Boston: Beacon Press, 2002), and Beth Bailey, *America's Army: Making the All Volunteer Force* (Cambridge, MA: Harvard University Press, 2009).

11. I draw on and expand upon scholarship explaining how the atomic bomb was both sold and presented to the American public, particularly in the late 1940s and 1950s. The mainstays remain Paul S. Boyer's *By the Bomb's Early Light: American Thought and Culture at the Dawn of the Atomic Age* (New York: Pantheon, 1985) and *Fallout: A Historian Reflects on America's Half Century with Nuclear Weapons* (Columbus: Ohio State University Press, 1998), and Allan M. Winkler's *Life under a Cloud: American Anxiety about the Atom* (Urbana: University of Illinois Press, 1993). On the cultural work of selling the bomb see Scott C. Zeman and Michael A. Amundson, introduction to Scott C. Zeman and Michael A. Amundson, eds., *Atomic Culture: How We Learned to Stop Worrying and Love the Bomb* (Boulder: University of Colorado Press, 2004), 1–8; A. Constandina Titus, "Selling the Bomb: Hollywood and the Government Join Forces at Ground Zero," *Halcyon* (1985): 17–30.

12. On the local implications of the military-industrial complex, Lotchin's *Martial Metropolis* and *Fortress California* are indispensable. Also of note is the work of economist Ann Markusen: see Markusen and Yudken, *Dismantling the Cold War Economy,* and Markusen et al., *Rise of the Gunbelt.*

13. The Third Amendment states, "No Soldier shall, in time of peace be quartered in any house, without the consent of the Owner, nor in time of war, but in a manner to be prescribed by law." Part of the Bill of Rights, the

Third Amendment was inspired by the Founding Fathers' deep aversion to militarism and standing armies. As James Madison wrote, "A standing military force, with an overgrown Executive will not long be safe companions to liberty."

14. Two different takes on this subject are Hogan, *Cross of Iron,* and Friedberg, *In the Shadow of the Garrison State.* Hogan shows how concerns with budgets, taxes, and spending placed significant curbs on the debate about the Cold War defense establishment—creating, in a sense, a need for nuclear weapons. Friedberg argues that a long-running popular fear of the garrison state acted as an important constraint on military spending during the Eisenhower administration. For American views on war see Adrian R. Lewis, *The American Culture of War: The History of American Military Force from World War II to Operation Iraqi Freedom* (New York: Routledge, 2006). For Cold War militarism in nontraditional forms see Laura McEnaney, *Civil Defense Begins at Home: Militarization Meets Everyday Life in the Fifties* (Princeton, NJ: Princeton University Press, 2000); Alan Nadel, *Containment Culture: American Narrative, Postmodernism, and the Atomic Age* (Durham, NC: Duke University Press, 1995); Stephen J. Whitefield, *The Culture of the Cold War* (Baltimore: Johns Hopkins University Press, 1997); and Kenneth D. Rose, *One Nation under Ground: The Fallout Shelter in American Culture* (New York: New York University Press, 2001).

15. Lewis, *American Culture of War,* 188. Sherry uses the term "militarization" rather than "militarism" to describe a process in the United States and to differentiate the United States from a more traditional view of militarism connected to German or Prussian militarism (Sherry, *In the Shadow of War,* ix–xii).

16. Fred Kaplan, *The Wizards of Armageddon* (New York: Simon and Schuster, 1983), 11.

17. John G. Norris, "Nike, Washington's Last-Ditch Defense," *Washington Post,* May 18, 1955, 23; Robert Elliot, "Beautiful, Deadly Nike Defends Chicago Area," *Chicago Defender,* September 24, 1955, 5. For locations of Nike sites see Mark Berhow, *US Strategic and Defense Missile Systems 1950–2004* (New York: Osprey Publishing, 2005), 18–36.

18. Valerie Kuletz, *The Tainted Desert: Environmental Ruin in the American West* (New York: Routledge, 1998), 6, 39. These huge sacrifice areas include the testing ranges of White Sands, New Mexico (3,200 square miles),

and the Nevada Test Site (1,375 square miles), along with dozens of re-
stricted Air Force test areas including the China Basin region of Southern
California. For western salience in this see Maria E. Montoya, "Land-
scapes of the Cold War West," in Fernlund, *Cold War American West*, 9–27.
On regionalism see Markusen et al., *Rise of the Gunbelt*; Markusen and
Yudken, *Dismantling the Cold War Economy*; Ric Dias, "The Great Can-
tonment: Cold War Cities and the American West," and Michael Welsh,
"The Legacy of Containment: The Military-Industrial Complex and the
New American West," in Kevin J. Fernlund, ed., *The Cold War American
West* (Albuquerque: University of New Mexico Press, 1998), 71–85 and 87–
100; Gerald Nash, *The American West in the Twentieth Century* (Engle-
wood Cliffs, NJ: Prentice-Hall, 1973) and "The West and the Military-
Industrial Complex," *Montana, the Magazine of Western History* 40, no. 1
(Winter 1990): 72–75; James L. Clayton, ed., *The Economic Impact of the
Cold War: Sources and Readings* (New York: Harcourt, Brace and World,
1970); and Clayton, "The Impact of the Cold War on the Economies of California and Utah," *Pacific Historical Review* 36 (November 1967): 449–473.

19. The best overview of this process is Gerald Nash, *The Federal Landscape: An Economic History of the Twentieth-Century West* (Tucson: University of Arizona Press, 1999), especially chapters 2 and 4.

20. Kaplan, *Wizards of Armageddon*, 10–11.

21. Other accounts of the Minuteman program—indeed of all Cold War
missile programs—are either more laudatory or do not directly address
these issues. Most recently Neil Sheehan's *A Fiery Peace in the Cold War:
Bernard Schriever and the Ultimate Weapon* (New York: Random House,
2009) does not adequately question the assumptions that went into making
missiles. While critical of the ultimate size of the arms race, Sheehan seems
to accept the necessity for massive missile programs. Even more laudatory
are earlier accounts of the Air Force missile programs, including Roy Neal,
Ace in the Hole: The Story of the Minuteman Missile (New York: Doubleday, 1962); F. Piper, *The Development of the SM-80 Minuteman* (Los Angeles: U.S. Air Force, Systems Command, Deputy Commander for Aerospace
Systems Historical Office, 1962); Jacob Neufeld, *Development of Ballistic
Missiles in the United States Air Force, 1945–1960* (Washington, DC: Office
of Air Force History, U.S. Air Force, 1990); Ethel M. DeHaven, *Aerospace:*

The Evolution of USAF Weapons Acquisition Policy, 1945–1961 (Los Angeles: U.S. Air Force, Systems Command, Historical Publication Series 62-24-6, 1962); G. Harry Stine, *ICBM: The Making of the Weapon That Changed the World* (New York: Orion Books, 1991); Lonnquest and Winkler, *To Defend and Deter*; David Stumpf, *Titan II: A History of a Cold War Missile Program* (Fayetteville: University of Arkansas Press, 2000).

1. Ace in the Hole

1. "Titan Missile Arrives," *San Francisco Chronicle*, September 18, 1960, 19 and Weather, 1.

2. Charles McCabe, "Fearless Critic at Opera Ringside," *San Francisco Chronicle*, September 17, 1960, 1. All six pages of the Women's World section were filled with opera news (p. 22). *Chronicle* staff members covered the opening. "Titan Missile Arrives," 19.

3. "Missile Wonders on Display Here," *San Francisco Chronicle*, September 23, 1960, 26.

4. "Minuteman Unveiling," AFA Press release, n.d.; "Minuteman ICBM Makes Its Debut Tonight," *The Booster*, September 22, 1960, 4; "Minuteman on the Move," *The Booster*, September 24, 1960, 2; "Deterrence on Display," *Air Force Magazine* 43, no. 11 (November 1960): 40–41; all in AFA.

5. Roy Neal's comments at the unveiling are reprinted, in part, in Roy Neal, *Ace in the Hole: The Story of the Minuteman Missile* (New York: Doubleday, 1962), 1–6.

6. "Talking Paper for Chief of Staff Bermuda Meeting," July 1960, Chief of Staff Files, 1960, Subject File 5-3, Commanders Conference, Box 36, TDW; Neal, *Ace in the Hole*, 96.

7. "Air Chief Predicts Big Missile Outlay," *NYT*, November 16, 1957, 2; Neal, *Ace in the Hole*, 41.

8. Herman Kahn, "We're Too Scared to Think," *Saturday Evening Post*, September 16, 1961, 12–14.

9. Standard accounts of the Minuteman program include F. Piper, *The Development of the SM-80 Minuteman* (Los Angeles: U.S. Air Force, Systems Command, Deputy Commander for Aerospace Systems Historical Office, 1962); Jacob Neufeld, *Development of Ballistic Missiles in the United*

States Air Force, 1945–1960 (Washington, DC: Office of Air Force History, U.S. Air Force, 1990); G. Harry Stine, *ICBM: The Making of the Weapon That Changed the World* (New York: Orion Books, 1991). Neal's *Ace in the Hole* deals more with cultural and political aspects of the weapon but is hagiography.

10. On JCS wariness see Herbert York, Memo for the Chairman, Air Force Ballistic Missile Committee, November 5, 1959, "Minuteman Weapon System Program," Box 62, Central Decimal Files 1959, JCS. In 1961 the Air Force was still requesting "several thousand" Minutemen. See Ralph W. E. Reid, Memo to Executive Office of the Bureau and Budget, "Discussion Notes for NSC Meeting, February 1," January 30, 1961, DNSA document number NH00423. Both Desmond Ball and George Reed have examined the problem of force levels for the Minuteman. Reed asserts that political bargaining was responsible for the final number deployed. See Reed, "US Defense Policy, US Air Force Doctrine, and Strategic Nuclear Weapon Systems, 1958–1964: The Case of the Minuteman ICBM" (PhD diss., Duke University, 1986), 184–189. Ball argues that it was bureaucratic politics that led to missile numbers. McNamara said that huge ICBM numbers were due to inaccurate Soviet estimates; Arthur M. Schlesinger has said it was because of political factors—i.e., quid pro quo with the Air Force and Congress. See Ball, *Politics and Force Levels: The Strategic Missile Program in the Kennedy Administration* (Berkeley: University of California Press, 1980), xxv. Ball writes that Minuteman force levels were the result not of careful analysis but of "arbitrary judgment and visceral feelings" (p. 275). David Rosenberg's seminal essay, "The Origins of Overkill," provides a view of force levels that takes into account faulty intelligence estimates, interservice rivalry, and the propensity of the Strategic Air Command to base force levels on redundant targets in the Soviet Union. David Alan Rosenberg, "The Origins of Overkill: Nuclear Weapons and American Strategy, 1945–1960," in Steven Miller, ed., *Strategy and Nuclear Deterrence* (Princeton, NJ: Princeton University Press, 1984), 113–182. All agree that there was a general failure of the JCS and those in charge to take appropriate control of this situation; all agree that too many missiles were built. For McNamara's decision see Stephen Schwartz, ed., *Atomic Audit: The Costs and Consequences of U.S. Nuclear Weapons since 1940* (Wash-

ington, DC: Brookings Institution Press, 1998), 185. The popular monikers for the Minuteman come from "Minuteman: The Missile That Closed the Gap," *Reader's Digest,* October 1962, 167–168; "Minuteman in Modern Dress," *Life,* August 18, 1958, 36; and Neal, *Ace in the Hole.* In 1960 Senator John F. Kennedy argued both that there was a missile gap and that the Minuteman was an "ultimate weapon." See John F. Kennedy, Speech, American Legion Convention, Miami Beach, FL, October 18, 1960, www .presidency.ucsb.edu.

11. Background on Hall and Q from Stine, *ICBM,* 232; John Lonnquest and David Winkler, *To Defend and Deter: The Legacy of the United States Missile Program* (Rock Island, IL: Defense Publishing Services, 1996), 73; and Neal, *Ace in the Hole,* 83–85. "[Hall] had the personality of a fish," according to Lt. Gen. Otto J. Glasser in his interview with Lt. Col. John J. Allen, January 5, 1984, AFHRA, 67.

12. Notes on a Meeting with the President, President's Office, White House, March 19, 1956, 2:30 PM, 278; Diary Entry by the President, March 30, 1956, *FRUS 1955–1957,* National Security Policy, vol. 19, 275–276. For more on Eisenhower's long view of the nation's defenses and his refusal to build weapons based on fear see Fred Kaplan, *The Wizards of Armageddon* (New York: Simon and Schuster, 1983), 145–147; John Lewis Gaddis, *Strategies of Containment: A Critical Appraisal of Postwar American National Security Policy* (New York: Oxford University Press, 1982), 127–163.

13. On the number of missiles under development see "The Bird and the Watcher," *Time,* April 1, 1957. This number included ballistic and guided missiles in the Army, Navy, and Air Force. Some $6 billion was to be spent on missiles in 1958—about 20 percent more than was spent in 1957. On fiscal prudence and redundant missiles see "The History of the Strategic Air Command: SAC Participation in the Missile Program from March 1957 through December 1957," U.S. Air Force, SAC, Historical Division, January 1, 1958, 63, DNSA document number NH00007 (hereafter cited as "History of SAC: 1957"); "Memorandum of Discussion at the 309th Meeting of the NSC," January 11, 1957, *FRUS, 1955–1957,* vol. 19, 402. Specifically it was hoped that a decision would be made regarding the intermediate-range ballistic missiles Thor (Air Force) and Jupiter (Army), one of which was to be canceled by the end of the year after review, though

due to Sputnik both ultimately went forward. Neufeld, *Development of Bal-listic Missiles*, 166–168. On Eisenhower's ideas about missile numbers see Lonnquest and Winkler, *To Defend and Deter*, 77; for Eisenhower's 150 missiles see Rosenberg, "Origins of Overkill," 46. Jerome Weisner, scientific adviser to Eisenhower and later to Kennedy and Johnson, wrote that people within both the Eisenhower and Kennedy administrations believed that in the early 1960s the United States had enough missiles to deter the Soviets and that perhaps limiting the number of missiles and "showing restraint" could persuade the Soviets to do the same, thus limiting the arms race. That did not happen. See Jerome Weisner, "Arms Control: Current Prospects and Problems," *BAS*, May 1970, 6–7. In 1960 General Maxwell Taylor wrote that the country would need at most a "few hundred reliable and accurate missiles" for deterrence to be effective. See Maxwell D. Taylor, *The Uncertain Trumpet* (New York: Harper, 1960), 148, 158.

14. "Bird and the Watcher"; Gardner quoted in Neufeld, *Development of Ballistic Missiles*, 149; "Consensus Missing in Missile Views," *Washington Post*, October 20, 1957, E5. The story quotes Gardner from 1956.

15. On concerns with Minuteman and Polaris see Neal, *Ace in the Hole*, 94–95; Col. Edward Hall, interview with Air Force History Branch, Washington, DC, July 1989, AFHRA, 19–20.

16. Information gathered from Neal, *Ace in the Hole*, 49–51; Douglas Martin, "Edward Hall, Developer of Missile Programs, Dies at 91," *NYT*, January 18, 2006, C15; Neil Sheehan, *A Fiery Peace in the Cold War: Bernard Schriever and the Ultimate Weapon* (New York: Random House, 2009), 236–249.

17. Neal, *Ace in the Hole*, 51–52; Martin, "Edward Hall." On Operation Paper Clip see Linda Hunt, "U.S. Cover-Up of Nazi Scientists," *BAS*, April 1985. Sheehan, *A Fiery Peace*, 243, is skeptical of Hall's retelling of this story.

18. For Hall's statement "we can design a weapon system" see Neal, *Ace in the Hole*, 82–33. For Hall's faking of an intelligence report see Neal, *Ace in the Hole*, 61. For Sheehan's assessment see *A Fiery Peace*, 246.

19. On Hall's instructions see Piper, *Development of the SM-80 Minuteman*, 17–19. On Hall's work habits see Neal, *Ace in the Hole*, 85. On the missile's design see Col. Hall, Assistant for Weapon System "Q," Memo to Col. Terhune, Dep. Commander, Weapon Systems, January 23, 1958, "Q"

program schedules, in the appendix to Piper, *Development of the SM-80 Minuteman*, Document 44 (hereafter all documents found in Piper are cited as "Piper Documents"). Minuteman financials are detailed in Charles H. Eger, "Minuteman Financial History 1955–63," Ballistic Systems Division, Minuteman Costs, Box 11, SCP; Piper discusses cost comparisons in early program development. These numbers are just missile costs and do not take into consideration construction and maintenance costs. It was estimated that Minuteman ground/maintenance would cost 30 percent less than that for Titan and Atlas. See Piper, *Development of the SM-80 Minuteman*, 20–22. Titan, for example, cost $49 million for facilities and $53 million for grounds support; numbers come from Ballistic Missile Panel, "Progress Report" to Dr. Killian, April 22, 1959, DNSA document number NH00658. For Hall's thoughts on simplicity see Reed, "US Defense Policy," 58–60. The best overview of nuclear weapons costs is Schwartz, *Atomic Audit*.

20. See, for example, "Minute-Miser" program materials from Boeing, n.d., Ballistic Systems Division, Minuteman ICBM, Press, Box 16, SCP. "Minuteman Cost-Cutting Aims Outlined," *Missiles and Rockets*, June 24, 1963, 40–42; and Eger, "Minuteman Financial History 1955–1963." Neal's speech is pieced together from Neal, *Ace in the Hole*, 8–9; "Deterrence on Display," 41; and *The Booster* coverage of the event. Cost estimates are from Stephen Schwartz, "Nuclear Weapons Delivery System Cost Analysis," May 9, 2009, paper in possession of the author. Primary Minuteman contractors, not including the subcontractors as well as the hundreds of smaller firms that were involved in construction and maintenance of the sites, were based in Washington, California, Utah, Colorado, and Maryland.

21. Eisenhower expressed many of these sentiments in an account of a conversation he had with Bernard Baruch, "Diary Entry, March 30, 1956," *FRUS 1955–1957*, National Security Policy, vol. 19, 275–276. On Eisenhower's strategic goals and fiscal restraint see Gaddis, *Strategies of Containment*, 127–163; Kaplan, *Wizards of Armageddon*, 145–147; and Campbell Craig, *Destroying the Village: Eisenhower and Thermonuclear War* (New York: Columbia University Press, 1998).

22. "Soviet Satellite Visible with Binoculars," *NYT*, October 5, 1957, 2; Don Paulsen, interview with Stephen Bucklin, Wall Community Center,

South Dakota, August 25, 2005, 14, South Dakota Oral History Project, 3189, Oral Histories, MIMI-NPS.

23. Lyndon B. Johnson quoted in Yanek Mieczkowski, "Ike's Wise Restrained Response to Sputnik," History News Network, October 1, 2007, http://hnn.us/articles/43173.html; Paul Dickson, *Sputnik: The Shock of a Century* (New York: Walker and Co., 2007), 117; Edgar M. Bottome, *The Missile Gap: A Study of the Formulation of Military and Political Policy* (Rutherford, NJ: Fairleigh Dickinson University Press, 1971).

24. "History of SAC: 1957," 63; Glasser interview, 61; Reed, "US Defense Policy," 76. Department of Defense ballistic missile tsar William Holaday approved Minuteman for research and development only on February 27, 1958. See Piper, *Development of the SM-80 Minuteman*, 31–33.

25. "Missiles You'll Hear of in '58," *US News and World Report*, January 3, 1958, 58–59.

26. Hall interview, 2; Glasser interview, 67. For background on Glasser and Phillips see Sheehan, *A Fiery Peace*, 66–67.

27. Only 47 Minuteman missiles were approved in 1958; they were to be operational in 1963, with an additional 100 to be ready for fiscal year 1964. Air Force Ballistic Missile Division HQ, Memo to Chief of Staff, USAF, "Ballistic Missile Program Planning Information," August 29, 1958, Piper Document 88. For the 10,000 estimate see Ball, *Politics and Force Levels*, 69–70. For an overall view see Piper, *Development of the SM-80 Minuteman*, 47. For a summary of the numbers see Lonnquest and Winkler, *To Defend and Deter*, 77.

2. Selling Deterrence

1. Hall was using "Sentinel" as late as January 29, 1958. Memorandum for Colonel Terhune, "Sentinel Force Requirements," appendix to F. Piper, *The Development of the SM-80 Minuteman* (Los Angeles: U.S. Air Force, Systems Command, Deputy Commander for Aerospace Systems Historical Office, 1962), Document 46 (hereafter all documents found in Piper are cited as "Piper Documents"); Roy Neal, *Ace in the Hole: The Story of the Minuteman Missile* (New York: Doubleday, 1962), 89–90; Col. Edward Hall, interview with Air Force History Branch, Washington, DC, July 1989, AFHRA, 21.

2. For an example of an internal BMD report see the cover of "Chronology of Minuteman Report," Ballistic Systems Division, Minuteman Costs Reports and Other Documents 1963, Folder 6, U.S. Air Force, 1942–1989, Ballistic Systems Division, Minuteman ICBM, Box 11, SCP. Other examples include Boeing press materials, also in SCP; "Facts for Missile Areas Landowners," Jensen Family Correspondence, 1960–1962, JFP; and "Minuteman in Modern Dress," *Life*, August 18, 1958, 36. "Minuteman: The Missile That Closed the Gap," *Reader's Digest*, October 1962, 167–175, uses "the shot heard around the world" to describe its first successful test flight (p. 174). For the NAA ad see *Aviation Week*, July 12, 1965. American Machine and Foundry Company's (AMF) ad in *Ordnance* magazines from November–December 1960 features little minuteman action figures on the backs of train cars. Both are clips from "OM-48500-01 Minuteman Missile (SM-80, LGM-30)" NASM. See also BF Goodrich advertisement, *Time*, August 10, 1962. For an overview and more examples of space race imagery in the popular press see Megan Prelinger, *Another Science Fiction: Advertising the Space Race, 1957–1962* (New York: Blast Books, 2010).

3. Ernst Lehner, *American Symbols: A Pictorial History*, 2nd ed. (New York: William Penn Publishing Corp., 1957), 7, 9, 17. Contrary to this account, the minutemen of Concord did not turn back the troops. In fact the minutemen in Lexington were unable to hold back the advance, which is why the Brits moved into Concord. It was on their way back to Boston that the British suffered heavy losses from militiamen and farmers who lined the roads.

4. "Minuteman in Modern Dress," 36.

5. Jack Foisie, "A Stalemate Means War, General Says," *San Francisco Chronicle*, September 23, 1960, 4. In *The Pentagon Propaganda Machine* (New York: Liveright, 1969), J. William Fulbright has particular contempt for Air Force public relations. On Air Force public relations also see Spencer Weart, *Nuclear Fear: A History of Images* (Cambridge, MA: Harvard University Press, 1988), 145–150. For the importance of cultural images and representations in the making of American air power see Steven Charles Call, "A People's Air Force: Air Power and American Popular Culture" (PhD diss., Ohio State University, 1997); Eisenhower, quoted in Michael S. Sherry, *In the Shadow of War: The United States since the 1930s* (New Haven, CT: Yale University Press, 1995), 235. Eisenhower was referring

to the prevalence of publicity about all missiles. Corporations often used pictures of missiles or references to the systems they were designing in promoting their own role in Cold War defenses and linking patriotism to products for domestic consumption.

6. The *San Francisco Chronicle* provided complete coverage of the event. See "How Companies Operate at the AFA Convention," *San Francisco Chronicle*, September 24, 1960, 2; "Air Force Association Opens Convention Here," *San Francisco Chronicle*, September 22, 1960, 4; "AF Association Meets Today," *San Francisco Chronicle*, September 21, 1960, 3.

7. "How Companies Operate at the AFA Convention." "Deterrence on Display," *Air Force Magazine* 43, no. 11 (November 1960): 123; and "1960 AFA Convention Is Biggest Ever," *Convention Booster*, September 22, 1960, 1, both in AFA.

8. General Thomas White's papers are replete with concerns about Air Force publicity, especially regarding missiles. An apt example is, S. E. Anderson, Letter to Gen. Thomas White, February 9, 1959, Chief of Staff Files, 1959, Subject Files: Command Files, Air Research and Development Command, Box 26, TDW. On Sam Phillips briefing reporters see Olivia Browne, *Aviation Magazine*, Letter to Bagby, June 28, 1960, Box 10, Folder, SCP. For turnover ceremonies see Montana turnover public relations documents from November 1962 in Box 12, Folder 7, SCP; and for TV interview in Wyoming see Box 19, Folder 4, SCP. The issue of military public relations and the Air Force's early predilection in this direction has been noted by scholars, though not specifically relating to the Minuteman or deterrence. See Weart, *Nuclear Fear*, 145–150. For internal admission of public relations issues see Malcolm A. MacIntyre, interview with George M. Watson Jr., September 6, 1985, U.S. Air Force Collection K239.0512-1683, AFHRA and MIMI-NPS, 22. MacIntyre admits that as undersecretary of the Air Force in 1957–1959 he dealt with Hanson Baldwin of the *New York Times* and a half dozen others. The reporters were amenable to keeping certain things from the public eye. The Aviation Writers Association (AWA) was organized in 1938 as reporters and editors, public relations representatives, and other writers associated with aviation. The AWA had close connections to other industry groups. See Karen Miller, "'Air Power Is Peace Power': The Aircraft Industry's Campaign for Public and Political Support,

1943–1949," *Business History Review* 70 (Autumn 1996): 311; Hall interview, 1. On cooperation Neal received see Neal, *Ace in the Hole,* 8–12, 14–15.

9. William Safire has identified "bang for the buck" as originating with Secretary of Defense Charles E. Wilson in 1954. See Safire's *New Language of Politics: A Dictionary of Catchwords, Slogans, and Political Usage* (New York: Collier Books, 1968). "Minuteman: The Missile That Closed the Gap," 167–168. For "most important weapon" see also "Minuteman/ America's Hidden Sentinel," *Steel Horizons* 25, no. 3 (1963): 26, NASM.

10. Maj. Gen. O. J. Ritland, Commander, Air Force BMD, "Deterrence in the Aerospace Age," address delivered before the Aviation Writers Association, May 2, 1960, Ballistic Systems Division, Minuteman ICBM, Press, Box 16, SCP; "Minuteman: The Missile That Closed the Gap."

11. Ballistic Systems Division Press Release, November 11, 1962, Malmstrom AFB, MT, 1962–1964, Ballistic Systems Division, Minuteman, U.S. Air Force 1942–1989, Box 12, SCP. For Phillips's handwritten notes regarding the February 1961 Vandenberg AFB test launch see Ballistic Systems Division, Minuteman ICBM, Press, Box 16, SCP. For similar comments see Jack Blades of AMF in "'Father' of Minuteman-on-Rails," *Missiles and Rockets,* October 17, 1960, 17. This narrative is also central to Neal's *Ace in the Hole,* which goes into great depth on the role of Boeing in creating the Minuteman. "Ace in the Hole," *Time,* December 29, 1961, 12.

12. A. J. Muste, "Our Pro-Russian H-Bombs," *The Progressive,* January 1955, 17. On the rise of the defense bureaucracy see Michael J. Hogan, *A Cross of Iron: Harry S. Truman and the Origins of the National Security State, 1945–1954* (New York: Cambridge University Press, 1998); Aaron Friedberg, *In the Shadow of the Garrison State: America's Anti-Statism and Its Cold War Grand Strategy* (Princeton, NJ: Princeton University Press, 2000); and Charles E. Neu, "The Rise of the National Security Bureaucracy," in Louis Galambos, ed., *The New American State: Bureaucracies and Politics since World War II* (Baltimore: Johns Hopkins University Press, 1987), 85–108.

13. Eisenhower was not the only one worried about creeping militarism. See John M. Swomley Jr., "The Growing Power of the Military," *The Progressive,* January 1959, 24–28.

14. Michael Sherry shows this for the airplane, which first allowed the abstract, distant sense of war to permeate American ideas of fighting. See Sherry, *The Rise of American Air Power: The Creation of Armageddon* (New Haven, CT: Yale University Press, 1989); Walter Lippmann, "Why Are We Disarming Ourselves?," *Redbook,* September 1946, 106. Lippmann was hardly the only critic of the "technocracy" of the Cold War. See also the editorials of Manhattan Project physicist Eugene Rabinowitch in *BAS,* cited in note 15. Rancher quoted in Peter T. Kilborn, "Ranchers Wary of Plan to Wreck Missile Silos," *NYT,* August 17, 1992, A12.

15. Eugene Rabinowitch, "Avengers Who Work in the Missile Fields," *BAS,* November 1960, 355–357. Perhaps these technowarriors would have been William Whyte's ultimate horror. See Whyte, *The Organization Man* (New York: Simon and Schuster, 1956). For the missileers see "Minuteman's New Home on the Montana Range," *Fortune,* August 1963, 53. Missileers themselves have long lamented what they see as their second-class status in the Air Force. See Gretchen Heefner, "Missiles and Memory: Dismantling South Dakota's Cold War," *Western Historical Quarterly* 38, no. 2 (Summer 2007): 181–203. Henry Adams quoted in Editorial, *BAS,* January 1956, 2.

16. "Defense: The Missile Gap Flap," *Time,* February 17, 1961; Fred Kaplan, *The Wizards of Armageddon* (New York: Simon and Schuster, 1983), 286–288. On concerns with vulnerability see Kaplan, *Wizards of Armageddon,* 85–173. On different derivations of the Minuteman see Jeffrey Engel et al., *The Missile Plains: Frontline in America's Cold War* (Historic Resource Study, Minuteman Missile National Historic Site, South Dakota, 2003), 26–33.

17. *Time* magazine erroneously assured its readers that the Minuteman cost just $3 million each in 1961, including ground equipment and installation costs. See "Defense: Ace in the Hole," *Time,* December 29, 1961, 12. For complete financial breakdown, including spiraling costs, see Charles H. Egers Jr., "Minuteman Financial History, 1955–1963," 109, Minuteman, Costs, Box 11, U.S. Air Force, 1942–1989, SCP. For a summary of problems see Frank G. McGuire, "Air Force Defends Minuteman Program," *Missiles and Rockets,* May 13, 1963, 18.

18. All documents pertaining to this interview are found in "TV Interview with WY Senator Gale McGee," Folder 4, U.S. Air Force, 1942–1989,

Ballistic Systems Division, Minuteman Intercontinental Ballistic Missile, Box 19, SCP. Newspaper coverage of Minuteman deployment to Wyoming does not mention the issues of targeting.

19. "TV Interview with WY Senator Gale McGee."

20. On "tidal wave" see Neal, *Ace in the Hole*, 21. See also "Hinds, John: Ace in the Hole, draft, n.d.," Folder 1, U.S. Air Force, 1942–1989, Ballistic Systems Division, Minuteman Intercontinental Ballistic Missile, Box 26, SCP. The manuscript is marked with at least four different people's writing and initialed in many places, especially those where declassification is being considered or approved. The four individuals who reviewed the text seem to be Sam Phillips, Col. R. W. Barnes (initialed remarks "B"), John Hind, and an unidentified individual with the initials "C. A." My analysis of the edits comes from a review of the marked-up manuscript against the final, published version, *Ace in the Hole*. Specific citations are as follows: "Destroy enemies" to "defeat" was not changed: original draft, 1; Neal, *Ace in the Hole*, 7. "Destroy nations" was changed to "destroy enemy targets": original draft, 6; Neal, *Ace in the Hole*, 12. The "reality of the terrible power of the national defense" was changed to "the reality of the national defense": original draft, 6; Neal, *Ace in the Hole*, 12. Finally, on "nuclear impasse" concerns see original draft, 18, and Neal, *Ace in the Hole*, 95.

21. On drawing fire away from the population see U.S. Congress, House, Committee on Government Operations, Published Hearing, *Civil Defense*, 86th Cong., 2nd sess., March 28–31, 1960, 137 (hereafter cited as Holifield Committee Hearing 1960). The assumption here was that there would be 700 Minuteman missiles. For the estimate of 900 missiles see Col. Robert Bowers, Memo to Gen. Terhune, January 29, 1958, Sentinel Force Requirements, Piper Document 46. The assumption was that Soviet missiles would have Circular Error Probability (CEP) of 2 miles. See, for example, "Presentation by the Director, WSEG, to the NSC on the Subject of Offensive and Defensive Weapons," October 13, 1958, 21, DNSA document number NH00411. For the rationale on silo hardening see specifically the appendix to Secret, Minutes, August 19, 1958, DNSA document number NH00632. Memorandum of Conference with the President, March 17, 1959, 4, DNSA document number NH01354. Weapons System Evaluation Group quoted in "Presentation by the Director, WSEG, to NSC," 18.

22. "Facts of Attack," *Time*, July 6, 1959. This information comes from the U.S. Congress, Joint Committee on Atomic Energy, Special Subcommittee on Radiation, *Hearing on Biological and Environmental Effects of Nuclear War*, 86th Cong., 1st sess., June 22–26, 1959, which is much more detailed.

23. Col. Robert Bowers, Memo to Terhune, January 29, 1958, Sentinel Force Requirements, Piper Document 46.

24. See Chapter 5 for a discussion of rising awareness of nuclear secrecy.

25. Paul S. Boyer notes the contradictory fears and desires of the population relating to things atomic in the early atomic age in *By the Bomb's Early Light: American Thought and Culture at the Dawn of the Atomic Age* (New York: Pantheon, 1985). Weart goes into great detail on the various ways and agencies that were concerned with the public perception of nuclear weapons and fallout. He makes a convincing case that these efforts in conjunction with the secrecy that quickly descended on all things nuclear (under the mantle of national security) served to help numb the American public to nuclear realities (Weart, *Nuclear Fear*, 160–169). Many historians have noted Eisenhower's tendency to remain upbeat and optimistic even about the grimmest possibilities; it was a tendency he exhibited both in his own speeches as well as in his comments on the statements of those in his administration. See Robert Divine's exploration of the test ban debate, *Blowing on the Wind: The Nuclear Test Ban Debate, 1954–1960* (New York: Oxford University Press, 1978), 9 and 23. A more recent account is Dee Garrison's, where the expression "Alert, not alarm" appears; see *Bracing for Armageddon: Why Civil Defense Never Worked* (New York: Oxford University Press, 2006). McGeorge Bundy says that efforts to use atomic power in constructive ways were in earnest but had zero effect on the arms race. See his *Danger and Survival: Choices about the Bomb in the First Fifty Years* (New York: Random House, 1988), 287–288. In publicizing peaceful uses of the atom, Eisenhower and his administration were also considering world opinion and the impact of nuclear testing and weapons on the nation's alliances. This was particularly true after the Bravo tests in 1954. This first test of a thermonuclear device caused an international uproar when it became clear that fallout was far more dangerous than previously thought. See John Lewis Gaddis, *We Now Know: Rethinking Cold War History* (New

York: Oxford University Press, 1997), 227–228. JoAnne Brown, "'A Is for Atom, B Is for Bomb': Civil Defense in American Public Education, 1948–1963," *Journal of American History* 75, no. 1 (June 1988): 79. *Duck and Cover*, Archer Productions, 1951, available through the Prelinger Archives, http://www.archive.org/details/DuckandC1951. *Life* survival guide, author's possession. Weart, *Nuclear Fear*, 157. Boyer demonstrates that early concern with atomic weapons in the 1940s gave way to general complacency in the 1950s, in part because of government efforts. See *By the Bomb's Early Light*. Chet Holifield quoted in Holifield Committee Hearing 1960, 232.

26. The most comprehensive looks at peace movements and disarmament efforts are Lawrence Wittner, *Resisting the Bomb: A History of the World Nuclear Disarmament Movement, 1954–1970*, vol. 2 of *The Struggle Against the Bomb* (Stanford, CA: Stanford University Press, 1997); Milton S. Katz, *Ban the Bomb: A History of SANE, the Committee for a SANE Nuclear Policy, 1957–1985* (Westport, CT: Greenwood Press, 1986); and Amy Swerdlow, *Women Strike for Peace: Traditional Motherhood and Radical Politics in the 1960s* (Chicago: University of Chicago Press, 1993). The Dr. Spock ad was commissioned by SANE and created by Leonard Sirowitz, 1963. According to Peace Action, the ad first appeared in the *New York Times* and was reprinted in 700 other papers around the world. See "Peace Action Accomplishments," www.peaceactionwest.org.

27. *Them!*, directed by Gordon Douglas (Warner Bros., 1954); *Gojira (Godzilla)*, directed by Ishiro Honda (Toho Film Co., 1954); *Attack of the 50 Foot Woman*, directed by Nathan Juran (Woolner Brothers Pictures, 1958). For *On the Beach* see Weart, *Nuclear Fear*, 218; *On the Beach*, directed by Stanley Kramer (Stanley Kramer Production Company, 1959). The film opened on December 17, 1959, in eighteen capitals of the world. "Review" from *New York Times*, January 17, 1960, notes that the "acerbity with which some authorities have lashed out at this film is, indeed, uncommonly surprising and hard to understand." On Cold War films see Margot A. Henrikson, *Dr. Strangelove's America: Society and Culture in the Atomic Age* (Berkeley: University of California Press, 1997); Thomas Doherty, *Cold War, Cool Medium: Television, McCarthyism, and American Culture* (New York: Columbia University Press, 2003).

28. Quoted in Weart, *Nuclear Fear*, 218. "'On the Beach' Scored," *NYT*, January 6, 1960, 24; "'On the Beach' Scored by Civil Defense Head," *NYT*, December 18, 1959, 34.

29. Weart, *Nuclear Fear*, 150. The public presentation of air power has been covered by historians, though no one has extended this discussion to missiles. For the 1930s and 1940s see Sherry, *Rise of American Air Power*; for the early Cold War see Call, "A People's Air Force."

30. Sherry, *In the Shadow of War*, argues that the nation did become militarized. I depart from his analysis somewhat in that I argue that there were small sections of the country that were sacrificed—that became militarized—so that the rest of the country could avoid that fate.

3. The Mapmakers

1. Gene S. Williams, telephone interview with Erin Pogany, January 7, 2003, Oral Histories, MIMI-NPS. Gene S. Williams's father is Gene E. Williams.

2. Peter Braestrup, "More ICBMs to Be Ready in April," *NYT*, March 25, 1961, 11. The ICBM program won the 1962 American Society of Civil Engineers Outstanding Civil Engineering Achievement award, as indicated in "Minuteman Directorate History," Army Corps of Engineers, Ballistic Missile Construction Office, Air Force Systems Command, 2, Military Files XVIII-9-2, ACE. See also President Science Advisory Committee, Memorandum of Conference with the President, March 4, 1959, DNSA document number NH01354.

3. Ed Hall, Interoffice Letter to General Charles Terhune, October 7, 1957, New Ballistic Missile Office, in appendix to F. Piper, *The Development of the SM-80 Minuteman* (Los Angeles: U.S. Air Force, Systems Command, Deputy Commander for Aerospace Systems Historical Office, 1962), Document 31 (hereafter all documents found in Piper are cited as "Piper Documents"); Charles H. Egers Jr., "Minuteman Financial History, 1955–1963," 8 and 9, Minuteman, Costs, Box 11, U.S. Air Force, 1942–1989, SCP. Neal notes that the original plan called for 1,000–1,500 missiles. Neal, *Ace in the Hole: The Story of the Minuteman Missile* (New York: Doubleday, 1962), 93; Piper, *Development of the SM-80 Minuteman*, 21. Curtis LeMay,

Memo, "Vice Chief of Staff Meeting," December 22, 1959, Piper Document 128. In this LeMay notes that one of the reasons Minuteman costs have gone up so much is that the original plan of siting 600 missiles together in a relatively open and easy-to-access location had given way to a plan that sited the missiles in smaller squadrons in remote and hard-to-access areas. The number of people required to maintain the system across many different missile fields would also increase.

4. On the national security "blank spots" across the country—and, indeed, the world—see Trevor Paglen, *Blank Spots on the Map: The Dark Geography of the Pentagon's Secret World* (New York: Dutton, 2009); Valerie Kuletz, *Tainted Desert: Environmental and Social Ruin in the American West* (New York: Routledge, 1998). For the built Cold War environment see Tom Vanderbilt, *Survival City: Adventures among the Ruins of Atomic America* (Princeton, NJ: Princeton Architectural Press, 2002). For more culturally driven tourist views of defense-related spaces see Sharon Weinberger, *A Nuclear Family Vacation: Travels in the World of Atomic Weaponry* (New York: Bloomsbury USA, 2008); the most recent addition is the more sensational Annie Jacobson, *Area 51: An Uncensored History of America's Top Secret Military Base* (Boston: Little, Brown and Company, 2011).

5. Frederick J. Shaw, ed., "Locating Air Force Base Sites: History's Legacy," AFHRA, 2004, www.scribd.com/doc/50159327/27/Table-2-1-New-Air-Force-Bases-1950s. See especially the essays in Kevin Fernlund, ed., *The Cold War American West, 1945–1989* (Albuquerque: University of New Mexico Press, 1998).

6. Joint Chiefs of Staff, Memorandum to the Weapon Systems Evaluation Group, "ICBM and IRBM Siting and Deployment," May 16, 1957, DNSA document number NH00577; Memorandum for the Director, WSEG, "Future Deployment of IRBMs," January 31, 1958, 471.6 Guided Missiles, Warheads, ICBMS, Central Decimal Files 1958, JCS. I do not have documentation from the April 9, 1957, meeting, but follow-on memos about WSEG Report No. 26 indicate that it was at that meeting that the "relative merits" of overseas versus domestic siting were taken up. See Memorandum to the JCS, "WSEG Report No. 26," October 23, 1957, DNSA document number NH00590.

7. Lapp quoted in U.S. Congress, House, Committee on Government Operations, Published Hearing, *Civil Defense*, 86th Cong., 2nd sess., March 28–31, 1960, 237–238 (hereafter cited as Holifield Committee Hearing 1960). See also Memorandum to the JCS, "WSEG Report No. 26." The 1960 House Military Operations Subcommittee dealt with the location of ICBMs and potential danger to civilian populations from attacks at these sites. See House Military Operations Subcommittee Report, March 25, 1960, 2, copy found in 65–60 Guided Missile Base Sites Correspondence, Box 457, Security Classified General Correspondence, 1956–1965, OSAF, NACP (hereafter cited as House Military Operations Subcommittee Report, 25 March 1960). The subject of siting was also taken up during the October 13, 1958, Presentation by the Director, WSEG, to the National Security Council on the Subject of Offensive and Defensive Weapons Systems, DNSA document number NH00411, 21. For IRBM deployment in Europe see Philip Nash, *The Other Missiles of October: Eisenhower, Kennedy and the Jupiters, 1957–1963* (Chapel Hill: University of North Carolina Press, 1997).

8. No more specific information was given on locations, perhaps because the issue was quickly dropped. See "House Military Operations Subcommittee Report, 25 March 1960," 33. Canada was also briefly considered by the Air Force, likely dropped for the same reasons. See "History of the Strategic Air Command: Strategic Air Command Participation in the Missile Program from March 1957 through December 1957," USAF, SAC Historical Division, January 1958, DNSA document number NH00007 (hereafter cited as "SAC History 1957"); and "Strategic Air Command Participation in the Missile Program, 1 January 1958–30 June 1958," USAF, SAC Historical Division, November 1958, DNSA document number NH00009 (hereafter cited as "SAC History 1958"). The U.S. Air Force and the Royal Canadian Air Force did have conversations about overflight issues and consequences. See USAF/RCAF Discussions on the ICBM Program, Secret, Memorandum, August 22, 1957, 6 pp., DNSA document number NH00585. For ongoing consideration of Hawaii and Alaska see "Air Force Surveying New Minuteman Sites," *NYT*, August 26, 1962, 17.

9. On IRBMs see Nash, *Other Missiles of October*. See also General Thomas White, Memo for Director of Information Services, November 13,

1958, and Memo for DCS/Operations, March 18, 1958, both in Chief of Staff memos, January 1958–December 1958, Box 15, TDW. For more on IRBMs and problems of deployment to Europe see Joint Chiefs of Staff Central Decimal File 1958, Box 82, Folder, Guided Missiles, JCS. See also "SAC History 1958," 36–40, for background on diplomatic negotiations with NATO over IRBM deployment, especially "IRBM Program, Secret Memo," September 17, 1957, DNSA document number NH01060; and "Conversation on IRBM arrangements with UK, November 23, 1957," Memo from John Guthrie, DNSA document number NH01067. Italian defense minister quoted in Memorandum for the record, "Possible Deployment of IRBMs to Italy," December 26, 1957, DNSA document number NH01070. On control of weapons see "House Military Operations Subcommittee 25 March 1960," 33; for similar sentiments see Presentation by the Director, WSEG, to the National Security Council on the Subject of Offensive and Defensive Weapons Systems; and U.S. Senate, Hearing, Subcommittee on Military Construction, 85th Cong., 2nd sess., May 19 through July 10, 1959, 333–334. LeMay was copied on WSEG Report No. 26, so he knew of it.

10. Director, Joint Staff, "Memo on WSEG Report No. 26," to Joint Chiefs of Staff, October 23, 1957, DNSA document number NH00590, 4.

11. The secretary of the Air Force was chairman of the Ballistic Missile Committee. Complicating any clear chain of command, management of nearly all Air Force procurement, research and development, and operational programs was being studied and reorganized throughout the late 1950s and early 1960s. See Ethel M. DeHaven, *Aerospace: The Evolution of USAF Weapons Acquisition Policy, 1945–1961* (Los Angeles: U.S. Air Force, Systems Command, Historical Publication Series 62-24-6, 1962). A note on usage: "Air Force" refers to no particular branch or division—in other words, I use "Air Force" when a particular division is not specified or when the sentiment or idea under discussion seemed so ubiquitous within the Air Force that specification is misleading or unnecessary. SAC was responsible for the nation's nuclear arsenal and also targeting. See David Alan Rosenberg, "The Origins of Overkill Nuclear Weapons and American Strategy, 1945–1960," in Steven Miller, ed., *Strategy and Nuclear Deterrence* (Princeton, NJ: Princeton University Press, 1984), 113–182. It was SAC's job to figure

out the operational specifications of the Minuteman. See "Proposed Pre-liminary Operational Concept for the Minuteman," April 8, 1958, Piper Document 76, 2. In 1957, before the BMD was established, the Air Research and Development Command (ARDC) was responsible for siting. See Jacob Neufeld, *Development of Ballistic Missiles in the United States Air Force, 1945–1960* (Washington, DC: Office of Air Force History, U.S. Air Force, 1990), 178–184, 201.

12. The first time this list appears in the document is the appendix to Memo, "Announcement of Additional Minuteman Bases," August 11, 1960, Guided Missile Base Sites Correspondence 60–65, Security Classified General Correspondence 1956–1965, OSAF, NACP. See also "SAC History 1957" and "SAC History 1958."

13. "SAC History 1957," 71; Neufeld, *Development of Ballistic Missiles*, 159. Between August and November the planned Initial Operating Capability for Atlas changed from July 1959 to October 1960. The reasons were budget cuts, concerns with production, and the ability to build a long-term rather than temporary system. Sputnik pushed it forward again to July 1959. See Neufeld, *Development of Ballistic Missiles*, 175.

14. Fred Kaplan, *The Wizards of Armageddon* (New York: Simon and Schuster, 1983), 111–154. This was the Gaither Committee, and their November 1957 report specifies that the Air Force should "increase our ICBMs from 80 to 600." See "Deterrence and Survival in the Nuclear Age," DNSA document number 01329, 6.

15. The Air Force refers to it as "aggressive" and the National Intelligence Estimates as a "high priority" "crash" program. For estimates see Peter J. Roman, *Eisenhower and the Missile Gap* (Ithaca, NY: Cornell University Press, 1995), 34–35; and Kaplan, *Wizards of Armageddon*, 155–161. For National Intelligence Estimates and Circular Error Probability estimations see Special National Intelligence Estimate Number 11-10-57, "The Soviet ICBM Program" (Director of Central Intelligence, December 10, 1957), http://www.foia.cia.gov; Kaplan, *Wizards of Armageddon*, 156–160. On Air Force estimates of Soviet capabilities in the early 1960s see March 1960 Memorandum to the Chief of Staff, USAF Thomas D. White, "The Threat," Subject Files: Air Staff Decisions, Chief of Staff Files, 1960, TDW. Holifield Committee Hearing 1960, 241, and Desmond Ball, *Politics and*

Force Levels: The Strategic Missile Program in the Kennedy Administration (Berkeley: University of California Press, 1980), 50.

16. "Table of USSR/Russian ICBM Forces," Archive of Nuclear Data, NRDC Nuclear Weapon Program, http://www.nrdc.org/nuclear/nudb/datainx.asp.

17. "SAC History 1958," 39–40. Atlas missiles were eventually deployed in California, Kansas, Nebraska, New Mexico, New York, Oklahoma, Washington, and Wyoming. Titans were deployed in Arizona, Arkansas, California, Colorado, South Dakota, and Washington.

18. Air Force Headquarters informed the BMD of this requirement in July 1959. Andrew S. Low, Secret Memo to Thomas D. White, October 27, 1959, USAF, Directorate R&D, "Minuteman Program Summary," DNSA document number NH00677. See also "SAC History 1957"; Piper, *Development of the SM-80*, 68–69; and President's Science Advisory Committee, Ballistic Missiles Panel, "The Minuteman Program," Secret Report, May 16, 1960, 9, DNSA document number NH00704.

19. John Lonnquest and David Winkler, *To Defend and Deter: The Legacy of the United States Missile Program* (Rock Island, IL: Defense Publishing Services, 1996), 241 and 243.

20. Joseph Kingsley Jr., AF Legislative Liaison, Letter to Senator Michael Mansfield, February 4, 1960, with attached "Memo for the Record" and attached Memorandum of the "briefing for Senator Mansfield Concerning Minuteman program for Malmstrom AFB," 65–60 Guided Missile Base Sites correspondence, Box 457, Security Classified General Correspondence, 1956–1965, OSAF.

21. Vernon Taylor, Letter to Senator Mike Mansfield, May 9, 1960, Military Files XVIII-8-10, Corps of Engineers Research Collection, ACE. Woodrow Berge, Acting Assistant Chief of Engineers for Real Estate, Army Corps, Letter to Mike Mansfield, June 10, 1960, Military Files XVIII-8-10, ACE.

22. Berge, Letter to Mansfield. While there is no central narrative of how the land acquisition process took place, its general contours can be inferred. It is Taylor's refusal that allows us to retell his story today, since records of this were kept. Taylor, Letter to Mansfield.

23. Dick Rebbeck, "Land Owners May Take Problems to Washington," *Rapid City Daily Journal*, April 7, 1961.

24. Marvin Miles, "Vast Complex to Hide Forest of Missiles," *Los Angeles Times*, October 23, 1960, F3; Memo from Gen. White to ARDC, Air Mobility Command, SAC, "Policy Concerning Release of Information on Minuteman," November 4, 1960, Box 36, Missiles/Space, TDW.

25. "Deterrence on Display," *Air Force Magazine*, November 1960, 40.

26. Philip Dodd, "1st War-Ready Crew to Have 55 Minutemen," *Chicago Daily Tribune*, June 2, 1960, C24; "55 Minutemen Set in First Squadron," *NYT*, June 2, 1960, 3.

27. Max Freedman, "How Important Is Symington?," *Washington Post*, November 7, 1959, A8; "A Dark Horse in the Spotlight: Stuart Symington," *NYT*, April 16, 1956, 22; "Defense His Specialty: William Stuart Symington," *NYT*, August 8, 1960, 10; Richard Novak, "Steady Stu," *Wall Street Journal*, March 25, 1959, 12; Symington speech in the Senate on July 21, 1954, quoted in Paul I. Wellman, *Stuart Symington: Portrait of a Man with a Mission* (New York: Doubleday, 1960), 199–201.

28. Linda McFarland, *Cold War Strategist: Stuart Symington and the Search for National Security* (Westport, CT: Praeger, 2001), 78–96; "Defense His Specialty." Symington, quoted in McFarland, *Cold War Strategist*, 89; "Ike Losing Cold War, Symington Warns," *Washington Post*, April 29, 1959, A9.

29. James C. Olson, *Stuart Symington: A Life* (Columbia: University of Missouri Press, 2003); Thomas S. Power, SAC Commander in Chief, Letter to Maj. Gen. William P. Fischer, Director of Legislative Liaison, Office of Secretary of the Air Force, February 11, 1959, including a copy of Symington, Letter to Power, February 2, 1959, Confidential and Secret, Security Classified General Correspondence, 1956–1965, OSAF. For more on Symington's role in defense and the Air Force in particular see Kaplan, *Wizards of Armageddon*, 163; McFarland, *Cold War Strategist*.

30. "A Dark Horse."

31. Ibid.; McFarland, *Cold War Strategist*, 129.

32. The most extensive treatments on the West's relationship with military spending remain Gerald Nash, *The Federal Landscape: An Economic History of the Twentieth Century West* (Tucson: University of Arizona Press, 1999), 42; and Gerald Nash, *The American West Transformed: The Impact of the Second World War* (Bloomington: Indiana University Press, 1985).

More specific studies on the relationship between the West and the war include Marilynn Johnson, *The Second Gold Rush: Oakland and the East Bay in World War II* (Berkeley: University of California Press, 1996); and essays in Roger Lotchin, ed., *The Martial Metropolis: U.S. Cities in War and Peace* (New York: Praeger, 1984). On Cold War and the West see Fernlund, *The Cold War American West, 1945–1989*. On aerospace see Nash, *Federal Landscape*, 44–51. The story of the South cannot be told without the military either. See Bruce Schulman, *From Cotton Belt to Sunbelt: Federal Policy, Economic Development, and the Transformation of the South 1938–1980* (Durham, NC: Duke University Press, 1994).

33. Roger W. Lotchin uses "arsenal of democracy"—borrowed from Franklin Delano Roosevelt—in the introduction to the volume he edited, *Martial Metropolis*, x. Lotchin and the authors of the essays that follow rightly point out the intimate relationship between military spending and urban growth in the West—paying particular attention to some overlooked cities in the interior. Lotchin's *Fortress California* remains a crucial text for understanding the importance of World War II in California's growth. See Lotchin, *Fortress California, 1910–1961: From Warfare to Welfare* (Lincoln: University of Nebraska Press, 1992). For the West in general see Richard White, *"It's Your Misfortune and None of My Own": A New History of The American West* (Norman: University of Oklahoma Press, 1993), 496–531. Markusen et al. have also written on the importance of World War II: "during and after World War II, in a way that was never before true, defense spending became a major determinant of economic prosperity and decay." See Ann Markusen, Peter Hall, Scott Campbell, and Sabina Deitrick, *The Rise of the Gunbelt: The Military Remapping of Industrial America* (New York: Oxford University Press, 1991), 3. For South Dakota specifically see Scott Heidepreim, *A Fair Chance for a Free People: A Biography of Karl E. Mundt* (Madison, SD: Leader Printing Co., 1988), 52.

34. Nash, *American West Transformed*, 19, 23.

35. Michael S. Sherry, *In the Shadow of War: The United States since the 1930s* (New Haven, CT: Yale University Press, 1995), 139.

36. On Case's personality see John R. Milton, *South Dakota: A Bicentennial History* (New York: Norton, 1977), 124 and 145; Richard Rollin Chenoweth, "Francis Case: A Political Biography" (PhD diss., University of

Nebraska, Lincoln, 1977), 59–61, www.digitalcommons.unl.edu/disserta tions/AAI7718722/.

37. Julius Duscha, "The Pentagon's Wasted Billions," *The Progressive,* October 1961, 13. See also "Table 3.1: Outlays by Superfunction and Function: 1940–2009," in Office of Management and Budget, *Historical Tables, Budget of the United States Government, Fiscal Year 2005* (Washington, DC, 2004), 45–52. In the 1960s Clayton wrote that "defense spending will loom as the single most important economic and demographic factor in the history of the Far West during the past two decades," James L. Clayton, "The Impact of the Cold War on the Economies of California and Utah," *Pacific Historical Review* 36 (November 1967): 473. Of course as Karen Merrill has pointed out, federal spending was significant everywhere in the country, not just in the West. See Karen R. Merrill, "In Search of the 'Federal Presence' in the American West," *Western Historical Quarterly* 30 (Winter 1999): 449–473.

38. Kenneth T. Jackson, "The City Loses the Sword," in Lotchin, *Martial Metropolis,* 151–162. For more on unequal patterns of Cold War spending see essays in Fernlund, *Cold War American West,* especially Michael Welsh, "The Legacy of Containment," 87–100, and Timothy Chambless, "Pro-Defense, Pro-Growth, and Anti-Communism," 101–118. There were numerous congressional inquiries into defense procurement, contracting, and spending that all point to a growing preoccupation with how and where defense monies were being spent. A contemporaneous account is Roger E. Bolton, *Defense Purchases and Regional Growth,* Studies in Government Finance (Washington, DC: Brookings Institution, 1966).

39. Ed Niciejewski, "Titan Work Leaves Definite Stamp on City Economy," *Rapid City Daily Journal,* January 31, 1961, 1.

40. Of the Air Force Nash writes, "scores of new air bases quickly became significant local adjuncts to local western economies. . . . Such a military presence was especially important in areas whose economies were not diversified." See Nash, *Federal Landscape,* 51. Darwin Daicoff shows that for areas with less economically diverse cities, base closure can be particularly devastating. See Daicoff's *Economic Impact of Military Base Closings* (Washington, DC: U.S. Arms Control and Disarmament Agency, 1970). See also Ric Dias, "The Great Cantonment: Cold War Cities and

the American West," in Fernlund, *Cold War American West*, 81. Memo, "Announcement of Additional Minuteman Bases," August 11, 1960, Guided Missile Base Sites correspondence 60–65, Security Classified General Correspondence 1956–1965, OSAF, NACP.

41. Background on Whiteman comes from "Whiteman Air Force Base," history memorandum, www.whiteman.af.mil/. Olson writes that Symington's influence was important in getting the ICBMs to Whiteman. See Olson, *Stuart Symington*, 421.

42. Howard James, "Grim Picture of Bomb Hit in Loop Is Given," *Chicago Tribune*, August 23, 1961, 1. During 1961 a host of newspapers ran their own stories on the blast effects. See Lapp testimony during the Holifield Committee Hearing 1960, 219.

43. "Minuteman Chronology, December 1955–30 June 1960," Air Force BMD, Historical Divisions, DNSA document number NH00021, 43–44 (hereafter cited as "Minuteman Chronology"). The original source is "Deputy Commander Ballistic Missiles, Weekly Report," September 17, 1959, Memorandum for the Chief of Staff, Thomas D. White from the Directorate of Research and Development, "Minuteman Program Summary," October 27, 1959, DNSA document number NH00677.

44. "Minuteman Program Summary"; and November 5, 1959, Memorandum from Herbert F. York to Air Force BMC, "Minuteman Weapon System Program," DNSA document number NH00680. White's comments are found in Chief's Staff Meeting Memo, November 10, 1959, Chief of Staff Meetings, Box 25, TDW. Douglas quoted in Neal, *Ace in the Hole*, 132. SAC and the Air Staff had long had a contentious relationship—while a command of the Air Force, SAC was actually responsible to the Joint Chiefs of Staff. This also helps explain SAC's resistance to most RAND briefings and studies, since RAND came out of the Air Staff as well. SAC, and particularly LeMay while the head (Powers was his deputy at the time), were "fiercely jealous of any trespassing." See Kaplan, *Wizards of Armageddon*, 104. See also House Military Operations Subcommittee Report, March 25, 1960, 5, copy found in 65–60 Guided Missile Base Sites correspondence, Box 457, Security Classified General Correspondence, 1956–1965, OSAF; also see Telex number AFCVC-85836, Hq USAF, to Hq SAC, Info AFBMD, April 13, 1960, Piper Document 138; and "Minuteman Chronology," 25.

45. "Gruesome" is relative here because the Holifield Committee was actually accused of trying to be "too objective" and therefore mitigating the horrors of nuclear war. They specifically did not call many vocal antinuclear advocates or scientists.

46. Holifield Committee Hearing 1960, 138.

47. Telex number AFCVC-85836, Hq USAF, to Hq SAC, Info AFBMD.

48. Curtis LeMay, Memo to Air Force BMC, November 14, 1960, "Minuteman Site Selection," Box 457, Security Classified General Correspondence, 1956–1965, OSAF; "Minuteman Chronology," 92–99.

49. "AF to Establish 150 ICBM Sites in N.E.," *Boston Globe*, January 6, 1961, 23.

50. Sec. Sharp, Memo to Chairman, Office of Secretary of Defense, BMC, November 17, 1960, 65–60 Guided Missile Base Sites Correspondence, Box 457, Security Classified General Correspondence, 1956–1965, OSAF. See also "Minuteman Chronology," 99. SANE Flyer, Folder 3, Ballistic System Division, Minuteman Chronological File, January–February 1961, Box 9, U.S. Air Force, 1942–1989, SCP.

51. For more on the antinuclear movement see Chapter 5. Senator Bridges wrote to Air Force chief of staff Tommy White in June 1960 inquiring about whether or not Pease AFB could host the Minuteman. White replied on June 14 informing Bridges that no decisions had been made. See Thomas White, Letter to Senator Styles Bridges, June 14, 1960, Subject Files: Missiles/Space, Box 36, 1960 Chief of Staff Files, TDW. Conversations with Bridges are also alluded to in Memorandum, "(UNCL) Announcement of Additional Minuteman Bases," August 11, 1960, which notes that Bridges wanted to be consulted before any basing decisions were made public, especially if they were related to New England; 65–60 Guided Missile Base Sites Correspondence, Box 457, Security Classified General Correspondence, 1956–1965, OSAF.

52. See Polaris Action files as well as *The Strange Case of the Missing Woodlands*, August 1961, Committee for Nonviolent Action, New England Branch, Box 33, the Records of the Committee for Nonviolent Action (DG 017), SCPC.

53. For example, see Memo, "Questions about Missiles," March 5, 1959, Box 24, Series B, Correspondence, 1957–1966, Records of the National Office of SANE, New York, NY (DG 58), SCPC.

54. Arthur Springer, Letter to Lawrence Scott, Bob Pinkus, and others, June 26, 1958, "Cheyenne Appeal—Draft Memos," Box 11, Committee for Nonviolent Action (DG 17), SCPC.

55. The evidence in the Minuteman case supports what Markusen et al. found in their broad study of Cold War defense spending: "while a few singular cases of the exercise of political muscle can be cited, empirical studies show a remarkable lack of evidence." They go on to say rather emphatically that "congressional influence, then, is limited." See Markusen et al., *Rise of the Gunbelt*, 40. While congressional interest was minimal in missile spotting, it was perhaps more important later on when upgrades and changes were made to the Minuteman. Indeed, Markusen et al. suggest that Congress has a more important role to play in follow-on military decisions (though those can also often be overplayed). Memorandum on missile base siting for Maj. Gen. Montgomery from Theodore Runyon, Colonel, Air Force BMC, November 16, 1960, Guided Missile Base Sites Correspondence, Box 457, Security Classified General Correspondence, 1956–65, OSAF.

4. Cold War on the Range

1. "Minutes from Wall Meeting," April 6, 1961, "Minuteman Unit EAFB General Projects, 1961," FHC.

2. Ibid.; Harold Schuler handwritten notes, April 6, 1961; both in "Minuteman Unit EAFB General Projects, 1961," FHC.

3. Schuler handwritten notes; "Minutes from Wall Meeting."

4. "Minutes from Wall Meeting"; Harold Schuler, Letter to Francis Case, April 12, 1961, "Minuteman Unit EAFB General Projects, 1961," FHC.

5. "Minutes from Wall Meeting," 21. See "'Little People' Seem 10 Feet Tall to Engineers at Meeting," *Pierre State News*, October 13, 1961. Also see "Minutes from Wall Meeting" and "Minutes from Rapid City Meeting," April 4, 1961, and "Minutes from Union Center Meeting," April 5, 1961, all in "Minuteman Unit EAFB General Projects, 1961," FHC.

6. "Missile Area Landowners Association, Articles of Association," "Minuteman Unit EAFB General Projects, 1961," FHC.

7. Leonel Jensen, Letter to Case, November 16, 1960, and Jensen, Letter to Case, March 25, 1961, both in Jensen Family Correspondence 1960–1962, JFP.

8. Jensen did not know it at the time, but the visitor was an Army Corps of Engineers real estate agent. Jensen, Letter to Case, November 16, 1960, Jensen Family Correspondence 1960–1962, JFP.

9. Leonel Jensen, Speech at Rapid City meeting, February 1961; Jensen, Letter to Case, November 16, 1960; Case, Letter to Jensen, November 18, 1960; all in Jensen Family Correspondence 1960–1962, JFP.

10. Siting began in the last few weeks of October 1960, when Corps of Engineers personnel went out to survey land. Rights of Entry for Survey and Exploration began on November 2, 1960. While the Minuteman wing at Ellsworth was slated for only 150 missiles and fifteen launch control centers, clearly more sites were surveyed than were needed. According to the Real Estate Office at Ellsworth, 198 sites were surveyed in 1960; Real Estate Office, Ellsworth AFB, Legal Documents file, MIMI-NPS.

11. Jensen, Letter to Case, November 16, 1960; Case, Letter to Jensen, November 18, 1960; all in Jensen Family Correspondence 1960–1962, JFP.

12. "Missile Site Deals Not Fair," *Aberdeen Paper*, March 10, 1961, "Minuteman Unit EAFB General Projects, 1961," FHC; Pellegrin, Letter to MALA Directors, March 27, 1961, "Jensen Family Correspondence 1960–62," JFP.

13. Wallace Stegner, *Wolf Willow*, excerpt in Tony Hillerman, ed., *The Best of the West: An Anthology of Classic Writing from the American West* (New York: HarperCollins, 1991), 144; Wallace Stegner, *Wolf Willow: A History, a Story, and a Memory of the Last Plains Frontier* (New York: Viking Press, 1962).

14. For the first "land boom" see Paula M. Nelson, *Prairie Winnows Out Its Own: The West River Country of South Dakota in the Years of the Depression and Dust* (Iowa City: University of Iowa Press, 1996), 207. Background on South Dakota comes from Nelson, *Prairie Winnows Out Its Own*; John R. Milton, *South Dakota: A Bicentennial History* (New York: Norton, 1977); and Herbert Samuel Schell, *History of South Dakota* (Lincoln: University of Nebraska Press, 1968). Milton's is the more literary—and biased—account. Schell provides specifics and apt overviews of South Dakota agriculture, politics, and transitions. See also Mary W. M. Hargreaves, *Dry Farming on the Great Plains, 1900–1925* (Cambridge, MA: Harvard

University Press, 1957), 1–2. For Teddy Roosevelt and Hamlin Garlan's use of "sterile poverty" see Milton, *South Dakota*, 8. For "desert" see Schell, *History of South Dakota*, 13. Kathleen Norris notes that the novelist Ole Rolvaag first used "Great Desolation" and *Newsweek* called the region the "American Outback" in the 1980s. See Norris's *Dakota: A Spiritual Geography* (New York: Ticknor and Fields, 1993), 7. In 1936 South Dakota recorded its highest and lowest temperatures: −58 degrees Fahrenheit and 120 degrees Fahrenheit. See National Oceanic and Atmospheric Administration, Satellite and Information Service, "All-Time Climate Extremes for South Dakota," http://www.ncdc.noaa.gov/extremes/scec/getextreme.php?forwhat=st&elem=ALL&state=SD. Schell, *History of South Dakota*, 11, provides rainfall information but only from the first half of the twentieth century. Stegner's quote is from *Wolf Willow*, 7.

15. Virtually all texts on South Dakota mention these extremes; perhaps, as Milton writes in *South Dakota*, they go back to Lewis and Clarke. See Schell, *South Dakota History*, for Buffalo chips (p. 178) and general information on South Dakota's "natural setting" (pp. 3–14).

16. Nelson, *Prairie Winnows Out Its Own*, xxxiii and 188; Catherine Mc-Nicol Stock, *Main Street in Crisis: The Great Depression and the Old Middle Class on the Northern Plains* (Chapel Hill: University of North Carolina Press, 1992).

17. David Fauske, interview with Steven Bucklin, Wall, South Dakota, August 22, 2005, SDOHP 3186, 3–4, MIMI-NPS. On the type of farming see Nelson, *Prairie Winnows Out Its Own*, 20. Paul Jensen, interview with the author, Rapid City, South Dakota, August 2006. Other families have similar stories: Lyndy Ireland, interview with the author, Philip, South Dakota, August 2006.

18. On the type of farming see Hargreaves, *Dry Farming*, 1–2, 12–16; Schell, *History of South Dakota*, 353–355. For information on South Dakota's soil see Schell, *History of South Dakota*, 9–11. On the Great Depression and New Deal programs in South Dakota see Stock, *Main Street in Crisis*; Nelson, *Prairie Winnows Out Its Own*.

19. William Bielmaier, interview with Robert Hilderbrand, Wall, South Dakota, August 22, 2005, 3, MIMI-NPS. For information on general acreage see Hargreaves, *Dry Farming*, 187. Ireland interview; Jensen interview.

20. South Dakota was the first state to adopt the initiative and referendum (1898). On South Dakota politics see Daniel J. Elazar, "Political Culture on the Great Plains," *Western Historical Quarterly* 11 (July 1980): 261–283; Alan L. Clem, *Prairie State Politics: Popular Democracy in South Dakota* (Washington, DC: Public Affairs Press, 1967); Clem, *Government by the People? South Dakota Politics in the Last Third of the Twentieth Century* (Rapid City, SD: Chiesman Foundation for Democracy, 2002). Jefferson is quoted in Catherine McNicol Stock, *Rural Radicals: Righteous Rage in the American Grain* (Ithaca, NY: Cornell University Press, 1996), 18. It is here that she outlines the idea of "producerism." R. Douglas Hurt, "Agricultural Politics in the Twentieth-Century West," in Jeff Roche, ed., *Political Culture of the New West* (Lawrence: University of Kansas Press, 2008), 52–53.

21. On the broad story of the relationship between the federal government and the American West see Gerald Nash, *The American West in the Twentieth Century: A Short History of an Urban Oasis* (Albuquerque: University of New Mexico Press, 1977); Nash, *The American West Transformed: The Impact of the Second World War* (Bloomington: Indiana University Press, 1985); Richard White, *"It's Your Misfortune and None of My Own": A New History of the American West* (Norman: University of Oklahoma Press, 1993), 520–531. On South Dakota and ranchers' experience managing the federal government see Schell, *History of South Dakota*, 353–354; Christopher McGrory Klyza, *Who Controls Public Lands? Mining, Forestry, and Grazing Policies, 1870–1990* (Chapel Hill: University of North Carolina Press, 1996), 113–115 and 127–128; Stock, *Main Street in Crisis*, 14; Elazar, "Political Culture on the Great Plains," 274. For a contemporary account of the relationship between landowners and the BLM see *Daily Belle Fourche Post*, March 13, 1961. On Forest Service rangeland policies and local and federal management issues see Charles F. Wilkinson and H. Michael Anderson, *Land and Resource Planning in the National Forests* (Washington, DC: Island Press, 1987), 78. On the idea of compromise see, specifically, Elazar, "Political Culture on the Great Plains," 274; Jon Lauck, John E. Miller, and Edward Hogan, "Historical Musings: Contours of South Dakota Political Culture," *South Dakota History* 34 (Summer 2004): 157–178. For broader trends of federal involvement being a compromise with locals see White, *"It's Your Misfortune,"* 473.

22. The description of South Dakota terrain as "ideal" is from "History of the Minuteman Construction Wing II," Ellsworth Area Engineer Office, U.S. Army Corps of Engineers, August 1961–August 1963, 3, Military Files XVIII-9-3, ACE. Information about the Parsons-Saven firm is from Jeffrey Engel et al., *The Missile Plains: Frontline in America's Cold War* (Historic Resource Study, Minuteman Missile National Historic Site, South Dakota, 2003), 65.

23. "US Steel Ad," *Illinois Technolograph* 76 (October 1960): 2, http://www.ideals.illinois.edu/bitstream/handle/2142/9393/IlTech761.pdf?sequence=2; T. J. Hayes III, "ICBM Site Construction," *Military Engineer* (November–December 1962): 399–403; Engel et al., *Missile Plains*, 65; "History of Minuteman Construction Wing II," 6 and 131.

24. "Rocket Warning Issued in Moscow," *NYT*, April 22, 1961, 9.

25. Jacob Neufeld, *Development of Ballistic Missiles in the United States Air Force, 1945–1960* (Washington, DC: Office of Air Force History, United States Air Force, 1990), 217. Bernard Schriever, Telex to Air Force BMD Los Angeles, February 11, 1961, Subject Files: Commands and Schools, Box 43, Chief of Staff Files, 1961, TDW.

26. "Progress Report to Dr. J. R. Killian, Jr. from the Ballistic Missile Panel," April 22, 1959, DNSA document number NH00658; Peter Braestrup, "Congress Plans Three Studies in Lag at Missile Sites," *NYT*, February 27, 1961, 1; U.S. House Committee on Appropriations, *Air Force Intercontinental Ballistic Missile Base Construction Program*, 87th Cong., 1st sess., 13–15, February 1961 (hereafter cited as Sheppard Committee). For more on problems see Lt. Gen. Otto J. Glasser, interview with Lt. Col. John J. Allen, January 5, 1984, AFHRA, 59; Neufeld, *Development of Ballistic Missiles*, 209. Problems with missile site construction were covered extensively by the Army Corps of Engineers. See T. J. Hayes, Letter to Lt. Gen. E. C. Itschner, Chief of Engineers, January 11, 1961, "Military— Missiles and Space," Military Files XVIII-5-1, ACE; Hayes, Letter to Lt. Gen. Walter K. Wilson, Chief of Engineers, September 12, 1961, Military Files XVIII-5-1, ACE; Hayes, Memorandum, January 26, 1960, "ICBM Real Estate Requirements"; "Draft: Air Force-Corps of Engineers Conference, Lowry Hill Air Force Base," July 5, 1960, Diary Folder January–June 1960, Box 3; both in Papers of Colonel T. J. Hayes, Vice Commander of the

Army Corps of Engineers, ACE. In June 1960 the Army Corps of Engineers held a conference on construction to determine what was needed in the field to make the program go smoothly. Reasons for slowdowns included changes to the design of sites and missiles, labor issues, and contractor issues. The story of labor at missile sites has yet to be told, though it was often contentious. A Missile Site Labor Commission was established in 1961 to deal with disputes; see Secretary of Defense to Army, Navy and Air Force, "Memorandum: Missile Sites Labor Commission," June 16, 1961, Military Files XVIII-5-1, ACE. See also the files from the commission, Records of the Federal Mediation and Conciliation Service, RG 280, NACP.

27. Neufeld, *Development of Ballistic Missiles*, 209.

28. Stanley T. B. Johnson, Corps of Engineers, Chief, Technical Liaison Office, Letter to Gen. A. C. Welling, Commanding General, CEBMCO, September 30, 1960, CEBMCO Correspondence" 285/53, Military Construction Files, ACE.

29. On the public relations campaign see Johnson, Letter to Welling. This concern is obvious throughout the ACE files.

30. Braestrup, "Congress Plans Three Studies." See also Glasser interview, 59. The Sheppard Committee is discussed briefly in Neufeld, *Development of Ballistic Missiles*, 219.

31. Martin is quoted in "History of Minuteman Construction Wing II," 7; "ICBM Site Construction," 403. Dick Rebbeck, "Missiles Can't Wait," *Rapid City Daily Journal*, April 4, 1961, 1.

32. Jensen, Speech at Rapid City meeting.

33. Hayes, Letter to Jensen, June 26, 1961; Case, Letter to Jensen, June 21, 1961; both in Jensen Family Correspondence 1960–1962, JFP.

34. "Minutes from Wall Meeting," 11 and 16. Virgil M. Horton, Letter to Case, March 14, 1961; Raymond Neascher, Letter to Case, March 18, 1961; both in "Minuteman Unit EAFB General Projects, 1961," FHC. Gene Williams, interview with the author, August 31, 2006.

35. "Minutes from Union Center Meeting," 12; "Minutes from the Wall Meeting," 11 and 16. In the transcripts to these meetings, the Air Force officer is identified alternately as part of the 120th Strategic Air Force, or as part of the 850th Strategic Missile Squadron.

36. Jensen, Letter to Case, November 16, 1960, Jensen Family Correspondence 1960–1962, JFP; see also Case's handwritten note dated Novem-

ber 23, 1960, "Minuteman Unit EAFB General Projects, 8-20-1960"; FHC. Gen. Tommy Power, Letter to Case, December 8, 1960, Jensen Family Correspondence 1960–1962, JFP; also in "Minuteman Unit EAFB General Projects, 8-20-1960," FHC.

37. Karen R. Merrill, *Public Lands and Political Meaning: Ranchers, the Government, and the Property between Them* (Berkeley: University of California Press, 2002), 6; Williams interview; Schell, *History of South Dakota*, 354. Particularly appalled were Senators Thurmond and Cannon: U.S. Senate, Committee on Armed Services, Unpublished Hearings, *Military Construction Authorization for 1962*, 87th Cong., 1st sess., April 1961, 235. The lesson appears to have been learned to some degree by the Air Force because by the time of the MX deployment they were initially interested in Nevada and Utah precisely because of the large swaths of public lands. "History of the Real Estate Branch July 1952-Dec 1962," 8, Missiles and Space CEBCMO-ICBM, Military Files XVIII-4-4, ACE.

38. Hayes, Letter to Jensen, May 6, 1961, Jensen Family Correspondence 1960–1962, JFP.

39. Information about ranchers' expectations is from Air Force, Letter to Case, February 16, 1961; Case then passed the information on to Leonel Jensen; see Case, Letter to Jensen, February 25, 1961; both in Jensen Family Correspondence 1960–1962, JFP. Section 301 of Public Law 86-645 (July 1960) made land acquisition a product of negotiations between a willing seller and buyer. "Missile Area Land Owners Meeting Held Here March 11," *Philip Pioneer Review*, March 23, 1961. The meeting is recounted in Louis K. Freiberg, Letter to Gene Pellegrin, March 17, 1961, Jensen Family Correspondence 1960–1962, JFP.

40. Pellegrin, Letter to Case, March 28, 1961, "Minuteman Unit EAFB General Projects, 1961," FHC. Pellegrin, Letter to MALA Directors, March 27, 1961, "Jensen Family Correspondence 1960-62," JFP. Apparently the Corps of Engineers also changed the terms of rights of ingress and egress; see Case, Letter to Ohmer Cook, rancher in Cottonwood, South Dakota, and Leonel Jensen, April 11, 1961; Pellegrin, Letter to MALA, March 27, 1961. Survey results are in Hayes, Letter to Jensen, May 6, 1961. To account for these concerns a "right of entry & appraisal committee" was set up during the March 22 directors meeting; see Pellegrin, Letter to MALA, March 24, 1961, and March 27, 1961; all in Jensen Family Correspondence

1960–1962, JFP. "Land Owners Talk Missile Site Values," *Rapid City Daily Journal*, March 23, 1961, 1. For depreciation values see Jensen, Letter to Case, March 25, 1961, Jensen Family Correspondence 1960–1962, JFP; "Missile Site Land Owners Appoint Committee," *Rapid City Daily Journal*, March 30, 1961, 1. Values come from Pellegrin, Letter to MALA Directors, June 13, 1961, Jensen Family Correspondence 1960–1962, JFP. "Land Owners Talk Missile Site Values."

41. Case, Letter to Pellegrin, April 25, 1961; Case, telegram to Jensen, April 3, 1961; both in Jensen Family Correspondence 1960–1962, JFP. For Case's own account and comments, refer to his statements in Senate, Committee on Armed Services, Unpublished Hearings, *Military Construction Authorization for 1962*, 215–222. On comments to McNamara see Senate Appropriations Hearing on the FY62 Department of Defense Budget, U.S. Congress, Senate, Committee on Appropriations, *Department of Defense Appropriations for 1962*, 87th Cong., 1st sess., April 1961, 12.

42. Case, Letter to Pellegrin, April 25, 1961, Jensen Family Correspondence 1960–1962, JFP. For similar sentiments see Senate Unpublished Hearing on Military Construction Authorization, April 1961. "History of Minuteman Construction Wing II." This figure is for *construction* only and does not take into consideration the cost of the Corps of Engineers and Air Force personnel involved, materials used, the missiles and their development, transport, or equipment and housing. The total cost of each missile *silo*, as Schwartz has shown, was $3.8 million, which included all materials, manpower, etc. Stephen Schwartz, ed., *Atomic Audit: The Costs and Consequences of U.S. Nuclear Weapons since 1940* (Washington, DC: Brookings Institution Press, 1998).

43. Hayes also notes that he spoke with a Sturgis lawyer, Dale Morman, who told him, "don't sign till the price is right!" Hayes, Letter to Jensen, June 11, 1961; Freiberg, Letter to Jensen, May 24, 1961; both in Jensen Family Correspondence 1960–1962, JFP. Jensen, Speech at Rapid City meeting; "Federal Land-Buying Hindered by Property Owners' Lawsuits," *NYT*, May 19, 1962, 39.

44. See U.S. Congress, Senate, Committee on Appropriations, *Department of Defense Appropriations for 1962*, 87th Cong., 1st sess., Apr. 1961, 12; "Minuteman Site Problem Reaches McNamara's Desk," *Rapid City Daily*

Journal, April 21, 1961, 1; Case testimony during Senate Unpublished Hearing on Military Construction Authorization, April 1961.

45. Values come from Pellegrin, Letter to MALA Directors, June 13, 1961, Jensen Family Correspondence 1960–1962, JFP. For concerns about potential damages and compenstation see Jensen, Speech at Rapid City meeting. Senate Unpublished Hearing on Military Construction Authorization, April 1961, 218.

46. Jensen, interview with the author; Jensen, Speech at Rapid City meeting. The hardship cases were: Naescher, Horton, Dartt, Niederwerder, Topinka, Simpfendorfer, and Hicks, according to a file in "Minuteman Unit EAFB General Projects, 1961," FHC. Air Force, Letter to Case, received June 6, 1961, Jensen Family Correspondence 1960–1962, JFP. I have found that regulations stipulated that a dwelling had to be at least 1,200 feet from a silo; however, the Corps of Engineers amended some of those regulations eventually.

47. The Air Force used the Army Corps of Engineers table on explosives when determining safe distances: "Minutes of 10–11 Sept. 1962 Meeting of the Advisory Committee to the Secretary of the Air Force on Minuteman Safety Distances," September 11, 1962, Subject File: Missiles, United States Air Force, 1942–1989, Box 13; "Memo on Minuteman Problems," May 5, 1962, Subject File: Problems, 1962, United States Air Force, 1942–1989, Box 16; handwritten note, May 1963, in Subject Files: Correspondence, Minuteman 1960–1963, United States Air Force, 1942–1989, Box 10; all in SCP. "Landowners Will Be Offered Definitive Agreements on Land for Minuteman," *Rapid City Daily Journal*, May 20, 1961; see also "History of the Real Estate Branch July 1952–Dec 1962," Missiles and Space CEBMCO-ICBM, Military Files XVIII-4-4, ACE. Information about what *might* happen is inferred from a few sources: Don Paulson, interview with Steven Bucklin, August 25, 2005, 12, MIMI-NPS; Joseph T. Kingsley Jr., Deputy Director Legislative Liaison, USAF, Letter to Case, June 5, 1961, Jensen Family Correspondence 1960–1962, JFP. Bielmaier, interview, 3.

48. Quoted in Army Corps of Engineers, "Facts for the Landowner," pamphlet, Jensen Family Correspondence 1960–1962, JFP.

49. Herman Kahn, testimony, U.S. Congress, House, Committee on Government Operations, Published Hearing, *Civil Defense*, 86th Cong., 2nd sess., March 28–31, 1960, 883.

50. On concern with accidental launch see Department of State, Policy Planning Staff, Memorandum of Conversation, December 11, 1959, "Bernard Schriever Comments on Intermediate-Range Ballistic Missiles in Europe, Tactical Missiles, Anti-Ballistic Missiles, and Strategic Balance," DNSA document number NH00683, 2. See also "Abstract of Minuteman History," Subject Files: Ballistic Systems Division, Minuteman History 1962–1967, 1983–1987, U.S. Air Force, 1942–1989, Box 12, SCP (hereafter cited as "Abstract of Minuteman History"). On fail-safe measures see "Progress Report to Dr. J. R. Killian, Jr. from the Ballistic Missile Panel," April 22, 1959, 1. The report specifically talks about the Titan's new system but compares it to information already known about the Minuteman. See also "Abstract of Minuteman History." Charles H. Egers Jr., "Minuteman Financial History, 1955–1963," 109; "Minuteman, Costs," Box 11, United States Air Force, 1942–1989, SCP.

51. "Lauritsen Committee Report to Lt. General Bernard Schriever Concerning the United States Air Force Minuteman Program," June 15, 1961, Air Staff Actions, Missiles 1961–1964, Official Correspondence, Chief of Staff, USAF 1961–1965, Command Assignment Papers, 1928–1965, CEL. The Air Force thought enough had been done—indeed they were already deploying extant missiles to Montana and did not intend to slow down for fail-safe upgrades. I have found no direct evidence of accidental launches in any unclassified material; however, there are certainly suggestions of such accidents—alluded to as well in the Phillips collection (SCP); There was also an accident at Malmstrom that involved an explosion of the first stage, though this was contained within the silo.

52. Egers, "Minuteman Financial History"; "Lauritsen Committee Report."

53. F. Piper, *The Development of the SM-80 Minuteman* (Los Angeles: U.S. Air Force, Systems Command, Deputy Commander for Aerospace Systems Historical Office, 1962), 69, 70–73. Delivery of actual missiles was delayed from February 1962 to May 1962.

54. Desmond Ball, *Politics and Force Levels: The Strategic Missile Program in the Kennedy Administration* (Berkeley: University of California Press, 1980), especially 189–195. Herman Kahn, *On Thermonuclear War*

(Princeton, NJ: Princeton University Press, 1960), 10–11; Henry Kissinger, *Nuclear Weapons and Foreign Policy* (New York: Norton, 1958).

55. On McNamara see Ball, *Politics and Force Levels*; Campbell Craig, *Destroying the Village: Eisenhower and Thermonuclear War* (New York: Columbia University Press, 1998). Kennedy was also an early convert: in 1959 he warned that Ike had driven the United States "into a corner where the only choice is all or nothing at all, world devastation or submission"; quoted in Ball, *Politics and Force Levels*, 187.

56. "Abstract of Minuteman History."

57. Jensen, Letter to Pellegrin, May 5, 1961; Hayes, Letter to Jensen, May 6, 1961; both in Jensen Family Correspondence, 1960–1962, JFP. The issue of patriotism comes up repeatedly in the Jensen correspondence and is noted by Case in Senate, Committee on Armed Services, Unpublished Hearings, *Military Construction Authorization for 1962*, 222. On Jensen's condition see "Right of Entry Addendum," 1961; Jensen, Letter to Bergum, May 31, 1961; all in Jensen Family Correspondence 1960–1962, JFP. Jensen's right of entry was actually signed on June 9, 1961.

58. Dick Rebbeck, "Ranchers Figure Loses in Cattle," *Rapid City Daily Journal*, August 13, 1962. Meade County Stockgrowers, Letter to Case, March 1962; Western South Dakota Farm Bureau, Letter to Case, March 1962; both in "Minuteman Unit EAFB General Projects, 1962," FHC.

59. For the June meeting see Jensen, Letter to Bergum, June 10, 1961; for the "false statements" the landowners claimed the Corps was making see Pellegrin, Letter to MALA Directors, June 20, 1961; both in Jensen Family Correspondence 1960–1962, JFP. Williams interview, 3. Also see Williams correspondence with Case, November 1961, "Minuteman Unit EAFB General Projects, 1961," FHC.

60. Case, Letter to Alan McCone, Special Assistant for Installations, USAF, June 20, 1961; Hayes, Letter to Case, September 8, 1961; both in "Minuteman Unit EAFB General Projects, 1961," FHC. Land condemnation proceedings were filed in Deadwood, South Dakota. Unfortunately neither the National Archives and Records Administration in Kansas City nor the U.S. District Court in South Dakota can find the records from 1961. Hayes, Letter to Jensen, June 11, 1961, Jensen Family Correspondence 1960–1962, JFP. Hayes was right—the Corps offered $700 and then

quickly ramped it up to $1,000. Hayes told them to speak with his lawyer, and he was pretty sure $2,500 was his minimum. Hayes, Letter to Jensen, June 26, 1961. Holdouts were given a boost in October when a settlement between ranchers and the Corps of Engineers was delivered just east of the missile fields. Landowners on the edge of the Missouri River were being told that they had to move to make way for the flood—the intended consequence of a series of dams being constructed to tame the mighty river. Missouri River landowners weren't happy for reasons that would have resonated with MALA: dishonest Corps of Engineers real estate agents, ridiculously low appraisals, and inconsistent information. But one thing was promising: a Missouri River landowner who refused to sell his land had just received $94,000 from a jury—nearly double what the Corps of Engineers had offered, as reported to MALA in Pellegrin, Letter to MALA, October 31, 1961, Jensen Family Correspondence 1960–1962, JFP. Pellegrin enclosed an article from the *Pierre State News*, October 13, 1961: "'Little People' Seem 10 Feet Tall to Engineers at Meeting." See also "Missouri's Dams Stir Big Battles," *NYT*, May 29, 1960, 42. Gene S. Williams, interview with Erin Pogany, January 7, 2003, Oral Histories, MIMI-NPS, 3. Also see Williams correspondence with Case, November 1961, "Minuteman Unit EAFB General Projects, 1961," FHC.

61. Harvey Haidle, Letter to Case, July 28 1961, "Minuteman Unit EAFB General Projects, 1961," FHC. Cecil Hayes, Letter to Jensen, May 6, 1961, Jensen Family Correspondence 1960–1962, JFP. Case, Letter to Major General Keith Barney, September 18, 1961, "Minuteman Unit EAFB General Projects, 1961," FHC. On a military reservation see Secretary of the Air Force Eugene Zuckert, Letter to Case, September 11, 1961, "Minuteman Unit EAFB General Projects, 1961," FHC.

62. Engel et al., *Missile Plains*, 65.

63. "The Inconvenience of Missile Sites," *Sioux Falls Argus Leader*, May 1961, 4, "Minuteman Unit EAFB General Projects, 1961," FHC.

64. Bruce Schulman, *From Cotton Belt to Sunbelt: Federal Policy, Economic Development, and the Transformation of the South, 1938–1980* (Durham, NC: Duke University Press, 1994), 151. See also Catherine A. Lutz, *Homefront: A Military City and the American Twentieth Century* (New York: Beacon Press, 2002).

5. Nuclear Heartland

1. "Minuteman's New Home on the Montana Range," *Fortune*, August 1963, 124–129; "Minuteman: The Missile That Closed the Gap," *Reader's Digest*, October 1962, 167–175. On the daily life and jobs of a missileer and other missile-field workers see Jeffrey Engel et al., *The Missile Plains: Frontline in America's Cold War* (Historic Resource Study, Minuteman Missile National Historic Site, South Dakota, 2003), 113–117. More detail can be found in the interviews of various airmen (and eventually women) who worked in the missile fields; see, for example, Alonzo Hall, interview with Robert Hilderbrand, Rapid City, South Dakota, May 18, 1999; Andy Knight, interview with Steven Bucklin, May 19, 1999; Ken Bush, interview with Steven Bucklin, Rapid City, South Dakota, May 17, 1999; Wendy McNeil, interview with Erin Pogany, Waco, Texas, February 3, 2003; all at MIMI-NPS. I also learned a great deal about the missileers from talking with Colonel (Retired) Charles G. Simpson, Executive Director of the Association of Air Force Missileers (telephone interview with author, July 2006).

2. In thinking about how the missiles were incorporated into American life relatively easily, I draw on scholarship about how the Cold War was normalized. See, for example, Stephen J. Witfield, *The Culture of the Cold War* (Baltimore: Johns Hopkins University Press, 1996); Laura Belmonte, *Selling the American Way: U.S. Propaganda and the Cold War* (Philadelphia: University of Pennsylvania Press, 2010); Elaine Tyler May, *Homeward Bound: American Families in the Cold War Era*, rev ed. (New York: Basic Books, 2008); Margot A. Henriksen, *Dr. Strangelove's America: Society and Culture in the Atomic Age* (Berkeley: University of California Press, 1997); Kenneth D. Rose, *One Nation Underground: The Fallout Shelter in American Culture* (New York: New York University Press, 2001); Lisle A. Rose, *Cold War Comes to Main Street: America in 1950* (Lawrence: University Press of Kansas, 1999).

3. Roger Lotchin, ed., *Martial Metropolis: U.S. Cities in War and Peace* (New York: Praeger, 1984), 223. According to Lotchin these relationships were not new, but the military-civilian courtship was amplified during the Cold War. For an in-depth study of the military in Fayetteville, North Carolina, see Catherine Lutz, *Homefront: A Military City and the American*

20th Century (New York: Beacon Press, 2002). "The Inconvenience of Missile Sites," *Sioux Falls Argus Leader,* May 16, 1961, in Jensen Family Correspondence 1960–62, JFC, and in "Minuteman Unit EAFB General Projects, 1961," FHC.

4. Hoadley Dean, Letter to Karl Mundt, January 17, 1966; "Memo, Mc-Call from Madison," December 8, 1965; both in KMP, microfilm reel 72. On the transformative potential of military funds see Bruce Schulman, *From Cotton Belt to Sunbelt: Federal Policy, Economic Development, and the Transformation of the South, 1938–1980* (Durham, NC: Duke University Press, 1994), 150–151. For Hayes's concerns see Cecil Hayes, Letter to Francis Case, September 8, 1961, and Secretary of the Air Force Eugene Zuckert, Letter to Case, September 11, 1961, both in "Minuteman Unit EAFB General Projects, 1961," FHC.

5. Almon "Hoadley" Dean, South Dakota Hall of Fame Inductee, http://www.sdhalloffame.com; Dean, Letter to Mundt, January 17, 1966, KMP, microfilm reel 72.

6. "Summary of Operational Program for South Dakota," Musgrave, Memorandum for the Chief of Staff, Curtis LeMay, October 13, 1961. Contemporaneous information on Ellsworth comes from a briefing file that was given to Gen. Curtis LeMay before his October 1961 meeting with Senator Case: Musgrave, Memo to LeMay, "Congressional Background," October 13, 1961, Tab A-1, 3, Congressional, 1961–1964, Official Correspondence, CEL. Chief of Staff, USAF 1961–1965; Command Assignment Papers, 1958–1965; both in CEL. For explicit linking of the population explosion to Ellsworth Air Force Base see South Dakota Advisory Committee on the U.S. Commission on Civil Rights, "Negro Airmen in a Northern Community," *Report on Rapid City* (March 1963), 6. Tim Pavek, interview with Steven Bucklin, May 22, 1999, 2, MIMI-NPS. Larry Owen, Rapid City Chamber of Commerce Manager, Letter to Case, December 22, 1960; Owen, Letter to Case, January 10, 1961; William H. Coacher, Lawyer in Sturgis, South Dakota, Letter to Case, January 25, 1961, all in "Minuteman Unit EAFB General Projects, 1961," FHC. "EAFB's Contribution," *Rapid City Daily Journal,* July 17, 1962, 1.

7. "SD into the Space Age," *Senator Francis Case Reports,* March 23, 1959, "Newsletters," FHC.

8. Owen, Letter to Case, January 10, 1961, "Minuteman Unit EAFB General Projects, 1961," FHC. "Minuteman Promises Economic Lift," *Rapid City Daily Journal*, January 17, 1961, 1; "Minuteman Will Require Supplies, Equipment, Housing," *Rapid City Daily Journal*, January 18, 1961; "Minuteman Will Affect Region's Schools, Power, Transportation," *Rapid City Daily Journal*, January 10, 1961. "Minuteman Locations Still Just Guess Says EAFB Official," *Daily Belle Fourche Post*, January 11, 1961, 1 and 6.

9. Owen, Letter to Case, December 22, 1960; Owen, Letter to Case, January 10, 1961; both in "Minuteman Unit EAFB General Projects, 1961," FHC.

10. B. B. Hodson, Letter to Case, October 17, 1960; B. B. Hodson, Letter to Case, January 7, 1961; Donald L. Cammack, Letter to Case, February 7, 1961; Doyle Grossman, Letter to Case, February 18, 1961; all in "Minuteman Unit EAFB General Projects, 8-20-1960," FHC.

11. For the Depression-era $55 million disbursement see Herbert S. Schell, *History of South Dakota* (Lincoln: University of Nebraska Press, 1975), 354–355. "Butte Soil Conservation District Annual Report Highlights Success during 1960," *Daily Belle Fourche Post*, March 18, 1961. The Missouri River Dam project was a result of the 1944 Flood Control Act, which requested the construction of dams and reservoirs to employ veterans and the unemployed to avoid layoffs like those that hit after World War I. Along with the GI Bill, this legislation was intended to smooth the postwar economic transition; see Michael Welsh, "The Legacy of Containment," in Kevin J. Fernlund, ed., *The Cold War American West* (Albuquerque: University of New Mexico Press, 1998), 89. Shorty Ireland, lifelong plains resident and rancher, married to Lyndy Ireland, interview with the author, Philip, South Dakota, August 27, 2006.

12. For South Dakota's political culture see Daniel J. Elazar, "Political Culture on the Great Plains," *Western Historical Quarterly* 11 (July 1980): 261–283; Jon Lauck, John E. Miller, and Edward Hogan, "Historical Musings: Contours of South Dakota Political Culture," *South Dakota History* 34 (Summer 2004): 157–178; Alan Clem, *Government by the People? South Dakota Politics in the Last Third of the Twentieth Century* (Rapid City, SD: Chiesman Foundation for Democracy, 2002). On Karl Mundt see Scott

Heidepreim, *A Fair Chance for a Free People: A Biography of Karl E. Mundt* (Madison, SD: Leader Printing Co., 1988), 36–37. Mundt said this of himself in a January 30, 1945, news release, quoted in Heidepreim, *A Fair Chance for a Free People*, 67.

13. On South Dakotans' feelings on foreign aid see Alan L. Clem, *Prairie State Politics: Popular Democracy in South Dakota* (Washington, DC: Public Affairs Press, 1967), 61, 83.

14. In 1960 34 percent of the state's men aged fourteen and older were classified as veterans; see Table D-1, "Selected Characteristics of Population, South Dakota," in *Census of Population and Housing*, vol. 1: *Characteristics of the Population, South Dakota* (Washington, DC: U.S. Census Bureau, 1960), 43–339. For "moderate conservatism" see Clem, *Government by the People?*, 140. On Case see Richard Rollin Chenoweth, "Francis Case: A Political Biography" (PhD diss., University of Nebraska, Lincoln, 1977), 118 and 139, www.digitalcommons.unl.edu/dissertations /AAI7718722/. For Case's support of Eisenhower see *Congressional Record*, February 8, 1960, 1971; Musgrave, Memo to LeMay, "Congressional Background."

15. Paul Jensen, interview with the author, Rapid City, South Dakota, August 29, 2006, 7 and 9.

16. Pamphlets in Jensen Family Correspondence 1960–62, JFP; Jensen interview, 7 and 9. On civil defense programs and efforts in the rural United States see Jenny Barker-Devine, "'Mightier than Missiles': The Rhetoric of Civil Defense for Rural American Families, 1950–1970," *Agricultural History* 80, no. 4 (2006): 415–435.

17. "Shelter Skelter," *Time*, September 1, 1961, www.time.com. For the national program see Rose, *One Nation Underground*.

18. President John F. Kennedy, "Radio and Television Report to the American People on the Berlin Crisis," July 25, 1961, the White House, www.jfklibrary.org.

19. Cost of silos is from Stephen Schwartz, ed., *Atomic Audit: The Costs and Consequences of U.S. Nuclear Weapons Since 1940* (Washington, DC: Brookings Institution Press, 1998), 132. On shelter spaces in South Dakota see Stuart Pittman, Assistant Secretary of Defense, Letter to Karl Mundt, January 2, 1963, and attachments, KMP, microfilm reel 13.

20. Lawrence Freedman notes that Kennedy's nuclear strategies were "not effectively explained to the public"; *The Evolution of Nuclear Strategy* (New York: St. Martin's Press, 1989), 237. "Minuteman, Real Estate Handbook," pamphlet, Boeing Airplane Company, News Bureau, n.d., Maps and Missile Sites, JFP.

21. On the sense of fatalism in the plains see David Fauske, interview with Steven Bucklin, Wall, South Dakota, August 22, 2005, SDOHP 3186, 11, MIMI-PS. Herman Kahn, "We're Too Scared to Think," *Saturday Evening Post*, September 16, 1961, 12–14.

22. William Bielmaier, interview with Robert Hilderbrand, August 22, 2005, 9, MIMI-NPS; Lyndy Ireland, interview with the author, August 27, 2006.

23. For Kennedy's "ace in the hole" comment see Engel et al., *Missile Plains*, 25. This was also the title of Roy Neal's book about the missiles. Following Kennedy's declaration, it also became the slogan for the first missile flight to be on active duty at Malmstrom AFB.

24. Report cited in "Chance of War in '60s Reported," *NYT*, July 4, 1960, 28; "Red China Tagged as Top Menace in Starting an Accidental War," *Washington Post*, July 5, 1960, A2; "Researchers Cite Danger," *Los Angeles Times*, July 4, 1960, 2. For "fictional portrayals" see "Minuteman's New Home on the Montana Range."

25. On the accident see "Moon Stirs Scare of Missile Attack," *NYT*, December 8, 1960, 71. Criticism is found in "End of the World (Almost)," *The Progressive*, February 1961, 8.

26. Donald Robinson, "How Safe Is Fail Safe?," *Los Angeles Times*, January 27, 1963, L4. In 1968 the Department of Defense released a list of thirteen serious nuclear weapons accidents between 1950 and 1968. In 1980 that number (through 1980) was revised to thirty-two; see Jaya Tiwari and Cleve J. Gray, "U.S. Nuclear Weapons Accidents," Center for Defense Information, www.cdi.org/Issues/NukeAccidents/Accidents.htm.

27. Chuck Raasch, "Nuclear Accident Near Black Hills among Worst," *Sioux Falls Argus Leader*, November 22, 1993, 1; "U.S. Nuclear Weapons Accidents: Danger in Our Midst," *Defense Monitor* 10, no. 8 (1981), Center for Defense Information, Washington, DC, http://docs.nrdc.org/nuclear/files /nuc_81010001a_n22.pdf.

28. See, for example, Jack Raymond, "Pentagon Backs 'Fail-Safe' Set Up," *NYT*, October 21, 1962, 69; Art Buchwald, "Button Plan Sews Up Prevention of A-War," *Washington Post*, January 27, 1963, E7; "Precautions to Avert Accidental War Cited," *Washington Post*, February 5, 1963, A6.

29. Robinson, "How Safe Is Fail Safe?"; William F. Buckley Jr., "A Self-Starter for Nuclear War?," *Los Angeles Times*, February 18, 1963, A5.

30. Buckley, "A Self-Starter for Nuclear War?"

31. "Minuteman's New Home on the Montana Range"; "Minuteman: The Missile That Closed the Gap."

32. "The Missileers," *Time*, July 6, 1962. The *BAS* recognized this effort; see Eugene Rabinowitch, "Avengers or Revengers?," *BAS* (November 1960): 355–357; "Minuteman U," *Time*, January 8, 1965, 47. See also Douglas Diltz, "New Military Breed—The US Missileman: Training Rocketeers a Crucial Task," *Chicago Tribune*, February 19, 1963, 8.

33. Robinson, "How Safe Is Fail Safe?"; Engel et al., *Missile Plains*, 113–117.

34. Robinson, "How Safe Is Fail Safe?"

35. Lt. Col. Gene R. Smith, Commander, 821st Transportation Squadron, EAFB, Letter to Jensen, n.d.; Brig. Gen. Richard C. Neeley, U.S. Air Force Commander, Letter to Jensen, October 1966; both in Correspondence and Reports, 1965–1993, JFP.

36. Jensen interview, 15 and 16. Gene Williams, interview with the author, Kadoka, South Dakota, August 2006; Tad Bartimus and Scott McCartney, *Trinity's Children: Living Along America's Nuclear Highway* (Boston: Harcourt, 1992), 227.

37. John Lonnquest and David Winkler, *To Defend and Deter: The Legacy of the United States Missile Program* (Rock Island, IL: Defense Publishing Services, 1996), 94; Engel et al., *Missile Plains*, 67–69. Pavek interview, 20. Norman Fauske, interview with Steven Bucklin, Wall, South Dakota, August 2005, 13; see also David Fauske interview, both in MIMI-NPS. Kenneth Kirkbride, quoted in Bartimus and McCartney, *Trinity's Children*, 226.

38. Don Paulsen, interview with Stephen Bucklin, Wall Community Center, South Dakota, August 25, 2005, SDOHP 3189, 24 and 20, MIMI-NPS.

39. "History of Minuteman Construction Wing II, Ellsworth Area Engineer Office, US Army, Corps of Engineers, 1 August 1961–31 August

1963," 171, Military Files XVIII-9-3, ACE. For economic effects elsewhere see "The Minuteman Missile Gives a Boost to the Economy in North Dakota," *NYT*, February 4, 1963, 14. For a broader view of the economic impact on South Dakota see Engel et al., *Missile Plains*, 67–68. "Letters to Senator Case Explain Local Labor Procurement Policies for Minuteman Projects," *Pioneer Review*, October 12, 1961, 1. Senate Unpublished Hearing on *Military Construction Authorization for 1962*, April 1961, 218. For overview of the type of work needed see "History of Minuteman Construction Wing II, Ellsworth Area Engineer Office." William Cissell, interview with Robert Hilderbrand, Wall Community Center, South Dakota, August 25, 2005, SDOHP 3184, 2–3, MIMI-NPS. For similar sentiments see Engel et al., *Missile Plains*, 67–68.

40. House of Representatives, Hearings before the Military Operations Subcommittee of the Committee on Government Operations, 86th Cong., 2nd sess., March 28–31, 1960, 236. Lonnquest and Winkler, *To Defend and Deter*, 122, 241–242; Boeing press release, February 28, 1969, Minuteman Missiles, NASM. Schwartz, *Atomic Audit*, 107. This figure *does not* include research and development, testing, or operation and support.

41. Dean, Letter to Mundt, January 17, 1966, KMP, microfilm reel 72. Engel et al., *Missile Plains*, 90–91.

42. For South Dakota dates see Lonnquest and Winkler, *To Defend and Deter*, 414–416, Minuteman development timeline, 241–251. For the Air Force boast see U.S. Air Force news release, "Minuteman Is 'Big Stick,'" February 1, 1971, Minuteman Missiles, NASM.

43. Lonnquest and Winkler, *To Defend and Deter*, 120, 244; Schwartz, *Atomic Audit*, 131. Freedman, *Evolution of Nuclear Strategy*, 336–337. On anti-ballistic missile measures for the Minuteman see Mark Berhow, *US Strategic and Defensive Missile Systems, 1950–2004* (New York: Osprey Publishing, 2005), 18–36; "Stanley R. Mickelson Safeguard Complex," February 2004, preservation fact sheet, in possession of the author; Sid Moody, "One of Our Missile Sites Is Missing," *Alton Telegraph*, January 24, 1981.

44. William Beecher, "Pentagon Is Studying Mobile 'Garage' for the Minuteman," *NYT*, January 7, 1970, 10.

45. In the early 1970s, the Soviets had 1,299 missiles, the United States 1,054; Lonnquest and Winkler, *To Defend and Deter*, 119. On echoes see Fred Kaplan, *The Wizards of Armageddon* (New York: Simon and Schuster,

1983), 356–391. "No Time for Hide-and-Seek Missiles," *NYT*, July 31, 1978, A14.

46. On fears of vulnerability see "Big Missile, Little Security," *NYT*, June 13, 1979, A24; "Toward SALT: America the Vulnerable," *NYT*, April 1, 1979, E18; James Kelly, "Debating the Debate," *Time*, October 19, 1981.

47. *MX Deployment Management Plan*, A-1, Military Files XVIII-38-1, ACE. Other strategies to deal with the vulnerability/first-strike issue included a trigger response protocol for the ICBMs, by which any sign of attack would be met with a before-hit launch of them all. This was seen as cheap but dangerous. The other option was to abandon the idea of the land-based ICBM force and concentrate on air- and seaborne deterrence.

48. Support is mentioned in William E. Schmidt, "MX Opposition Gaining in Utah and Nevada," *NYT*, June 8, 1981, B11; Erica Shoenberger and Amy K. Glasmeier, "Selling the MX: The Air Force Asks Nevada to Move Over," *The Progressive*, May 1980, 17.

49. On western wariness of environmental rules see James Morton Turner, "'The Specter of Environmentalism': Wilderness, Environmental Politics, and the Evolution of the New Right," *Journal of American History* (June 2009): 123–149. On public meetings see Glasmeier, "Selling the MX"; Philip Glass, *Citizens against the MX: Public Language in the Nuclear Age* (Champagne: University of Illinois Press, 1993). For general anti-MX sentiment see Tom Wicker, "An MX in the Backyard?," *NYT*, December 21, 1980, E17. On coalitions and groups opposed to the MX see Schmidt, "MX Opposition Gaining"; "MX in Search of a Home and Mission," *NYT*, March 31, 1980, A22; "2 Key Senators Oppose Missiles for Their State," *NYT*, June 26, 1981, A1. The most detailed accounting is in Glass, *Citizens against the MX*.

50. For a good overview of the issues and people involved see Paul J. Culhane, "MX and the Public Lands Subgovernment," in Phillip O. Foss, ed., *Federal Lands Policy* (Westport, CT: Greenwood Press, 1987). For political opposition see "2 Key Senators."

51. For Laxalt's thoughts see "2 Key Senators"; for general boom-bust concerns see Glasmeier, "Selling the MX."

6. The Radical Plains

1. Samuel H. Day Jr., *Crossing the Line: From Editor to Activist to Inmate—A Writer's Journey* (Baltimore: Fortkamp Publishing Co., 1991), 197–205; Day, *Prisoners on Purpose: A Peacemaker's Guide to Jails and Prisons* (Madison, WI: Nukewatch, 1989).

2. David Blackhurst, interview with Steven Bucklin, typed transcript, May 19, 1999, 5, MIMI-NPS. On what the missileers did see Jeffrey Engel et al., *The Missile Plains: Frontline in America's Cold War* (Historic Resource Study, Minuteman Missile National Historic Site, South Dakota, 2003), 108–117.

3. Engel et al., *Missile Plains*, 111.

4. Also breached: K-11, K-10, and G-11. Bonnie Urfer and Sam Day, Letter to "The Dirty Two Dozen," June 27, 1988; "Reclaiming the Land," statement of the Missouri Peace Planters, http://no-nukes.org/mpp88/. The Peace Planters were Sam Day, Katie Willem, Gail Beyer, Bonne Urfer, Dorothy Eber, Katy Feit, Sam Guardino, Kathy Kelly, Dan McGuire, Mile Stanek, Paul Foley, Ariel Glenn, and the Reverend Jerry Zawada.

5. Day, *Prisoners on Purpose*; Day, *Crossing the Line*. Randell Beck, "14 Arrested at Missouri Missile Silos," *Kansas City Star*, August 15, 1988, 1.

6. On conservative capture see Michael Kazin, *The Populist Persuasion: An American History* (New York: Basic Books, 1998); the title of chapter 10 is "The Conservative Capture." Catherine McNicol Stock, too, sees a rightward tilt in rural Populist politics in the latter half of the twentieth century; see her *Rural Radicals: Righteous Rage in the American Grain* (Ithaca, NY: Cornell University Press, 1996), part 3. On "red state," see especially the writing of Timothy Egan, such as "Red State Home Companion," *Opinionator* (blog), *NYT*, April 14, 2011, www.opinionator.blogs .nytimes.com. As McGreggor Cawley reminds his readers, "generalizations about Western political patterns are usually tenuous at best," though that has not seemed to stop most people from making them; see Cawley's *Federal Land, Western Anger: The Sagebrush Rebellion and Environmental Politics* (Lawrence: University of Kansas Press, 1993), 5. On similar challenges see Mary Summers, "From Heartland to Seattle: The Family Farm Movement of the 1980s and the Legacy of Agrarian State Building," in

Catherine McNicol Stock and Robert D. Johnston, eds., *The Countryside in the Age of the Modern State: Political Histories of Rural America* (Ithaca, NY: Cornell University Press, 2001), 304–325. Summers also points out the erasures of the agrarian state-building movement from U.S. history, something that has allowed a right-wing appropriation of rural radicalism. The comment regarding there being "more to our rural conservative state" is quoted in *SD Peace and Justice Center* [newsletter], February 1985, SDPJC.

7. Samuel H. Day Jr., "The Restless Ranchers of Missile Country," *The Progressive*, October 1983.

8. Marvin Kammerer, interview with the author, August 2006; Kammerer interview with the author, February 2007; Michael Crater, "Kammerer: Farmer Who Hates the Bomb," newspaper clipping, n.d.; Marian Eatherton, "Convinced Ordinary People against War," newspaper clipping, n.d.; all in Kammerer papers, Kammerer Ranch, Elk Vale, South Dakota (hereafter cited as Kammerer papers). Unless otherwise noted, all documents from the Kammerer Ranch were copied and are now on file with the author.

9. I have not been able to receive confirmation of this incident from the U.S. Air Force. There were, however, a number of documented "broken arrows" during the Cold War, including bomber scrambling. Crater, "Kammerer: Farmer Who Hates the Bomb."

10. The Cheyenne Appeal is generally erased from most histories of the CNVA at this time, but there is ample documentary record of it in the CNVA files. See especially Tatum O'Neill, Letter to Olson, July 22, 1958; Lawrence Scott, Letter to O'Neill, July 18, 1958; both in Cheyenne Appeal, Correspondence, CNVA-projects, Cheyenne Memo Drafts, Series VI, Box 11, Committee for Nonviolent Action, DG 17, SCPC. One local woman, Margaret Laybourne, protested the Atlas sites in 1958. She would later protest the MX and Minuteman; Margaret Laybourne, e-mail to the author, August 2011.

11. Kammerer interview, February 2007. Bob McBride, "The Cowboy Populists of Meade County," unpublished paper, 1988, Kammerer papers.

12. Kammerer interview, August 2006. Crater, "Kammerer: Farmer Who Hates the Bomb"; Eatherton, "Convinced Ordinary People against War."

13. Quoted in Eatherton, "Convinced Ordinary People against War"; Crater, "Kammerer: Farmer Who Hates the Bomb."

14. On the Black Hills Alliance and how its interracial connections and cooperation were novel see Zoltan Grossman, "Cowboy and Indian Alliances in the Northern Plains," *Agricultural History* (Spring 2003): 355–389.

15. Examples of journalists and publications that tried to pierce the veil of silence around nuclear materials include L. W. Nordheim, "Fear and Information," *BAS*, November 1954, 342; Ralph Lapp, "Atomic Candor," *BAS*, October 1954, 312–314; Michael Amrine, "Faith, Fear and Fusion," *The Progressive*, October 1953, 6–8.

16. On the state of the peace movement in the 1970s see Lawrence S. Wittner, "The Forgotten Years of the World Nuclear Disarmament Movement, 1975–78," *Journal of Peace Research* 40, no. 4 (July 2003): 435–456. For Day's ideas see Day, *Crossing the Line*, 156. For Day's early activities see pamphlets and information on the Invest in Peace campaign and nuclear-free-zone action kits in Nukewatch file, CDGA Collective box N, SCPC. Information on the truck watch comes from "H-bomb Truck Watch," pamphlet, n.d., Nukewatch file, Nukewatch vertical files, Antioch Community Farm, Luck, Wisconsin (hereafter cited as Nukewatch Archive).

17. The most comprehensive history of the international peace movement is Lawrence Wittner, *Towards Nuclear Abolition: A History of the World Nuclear Disarmament Movement, 1971–Present* (Stanford, CA: Stanford University Press, 2003), 75. There were literally hundreds of antinuclear groups that sprang up during this time—many of them aimed at specific professional groups such as Physicians for Social Responsibility, Lawyers Alliance for Nuclear Arms Control, and the like. On the Freeze see Milton S. Katz, *Ban the Bomb: A History of SANE, the Committee for a Sane Nuclear Policy, 1957–1985* (Westport, CT: Greenwood Press, 1986), 149; Wittner, *Towards Nuclear Abolition*, 176. On church resolutions and involvement see Wittner, *Towards Nuclear Abolition*, 179–182.

18. L. Bruce van Voorst, "The Critical Masses," *Foreign Policy*, no. 48 (Autumn 1982): 82–93. Van Voorst is interested in the question of how to keep these disparate groups together and agitating for a freeze; my interest is in how staying together made them conservative. On individual congressional views see Douglas C. Waller, *Congress and the Nuclear Freeze: An Inside Look at the Politics of a Mass Movement* (Amherst: University of Massachusetts Press, 1987).

19. On public concerns with Reagan's defense policies and how those concerns helped expand the peace movement see John LaForge, interview with Mary Ebling, January 3, 2003, MIMI-NPS; Jay Davis, interview with Mary Ebling, February 6, 2003, MIMI-NPS; Katz, *Ban the Bomb*, 149; and especially Wittner, *Towards Nuclear Abolition*, 74–75. Wittner identifies euromissiles, SALT negotiations, and MX missiles as key to emerging antinuclear activism in the late 1970s. In October 1981, Reagan responded to a reporter's questions about limited nuclear war by saying he thought nuclear war could be confined to Europe. Later Weinberger reaffirmed this point and, in November 1981, Secretary of State Alexander Haig said a nuclear weapon could be used for demonstrative purposes in the event of conflict; Wittner, *Towards Nuclear Abolition*, 121. Defense spending is given in 2005 dollars and comes from Greg Schneider and Renae Merle, "Reagan's Defense Buildup Bridged Military Eras," *Washington Post*, June 9, 2004. On Reagan's strategy see Don Oberdorfer, *From the Cold War to a New Era: The United States and the Soviet Union, 1983–1991* (Baltimore: Johns Hopkins University Press, 1998); Paul Lettow, *Ronald Reagan and His Quest to Abolish Nuclear Weapons* (New York: Random House, 2005); John Lewis Gaddis, *Strategies of Containment: A Critical Appraisal of Postwar American National Security Policy* (New York: Oxford University Press, 1982); Frances Fitzgerald, *Way Out There in the Blue: Reagan, Star Wars and the End of the Cold War* (New York: Simon and Schuster, 2001). "Evil empire" comes from Ronald Reagan, Speech to the National Association of Evangelicals, Orlando, FL, March 8, 1983.

20. On Reagan's abolitionism see Paul Lettow, *Ronald Reagan*, 3–41; Oberdorfer, *From the Cold War to a New Era*, 22–25. For the number of warheads see "Table of US Strategic Offensive Force Loadings, 1976–2012," NRDC Nuclear Program, Index of Nuclear Data, www.nrdc.org. On Kremlin and peace movement ties see Wittner, *Towards Nuclear Abolition*, 258.

21. Quoted in Wittner, *Towards Nuclear Abolition*, 265.

22. Philip M. Boffey, "Contemplating the Heart of the Nuclear Darkness," *NYT*, March 28, 1982, E9; Wittner, *Towards Nuclear Abolition*, 170–173. For specifics see William J. Broad, "Scientists Say TV Film Understates Possible Devastation of Nuclear Attack," *NYT*, November 21, 1983, A19. Jonathan Schell, *The Fate of the Earth* (New York: Avon, 1982).

23. Follow-ons included PBS's *Testament*, NBC's *Special Bulletin*, and the BBC's *Threads* in 1984. Feature films had been dealing with nuclear war for longer, for example, with the *Mad Max* and *Terminator* sagas, the sci-fi film *A Boy and His Dog*, and 1977's *Damnation Alley*. *The Day After*, directed by Nicholas Meyer (ABC Circle Films, 1983).

24. The reality was that even the Freeze was being branded by the administration and some of the mainstream media as a Soviet-led effort to undermine U.S. security, a new form of McCarthyism; see Wittner, *Towards Nuclear Abolition*, 184–190. The administration opposed the movement on the grounds that a freeze would leave the United States in a position inferior to that of the Soviet Union. President Reagan had even argued that the campaign was inspired by people who "want the weakening of America"; quoted in "Freezing Nukes, Banning Bottles," *Time*, November 15, 1982, http://www.time.com/time/magazine/article/0,9171,949625,00.html. Samuel H. Day Jr., "Peace, Politics and Placebos," *The Progressive*, reprinted in the SOS *Newsletter*, March 1984, CDGA collection Box S, SOS. A small section of this article is also reprinted in Day, *Crossing the Line*, 154.

25. J. D. Ames, "Gathering Crowds Boost Local Economy," *Rapid City Journal*, July 27, 1980, 2; Molly Ivins, "An Eclectic Crowd Gathers to Save the Black Hills," *NYT*, July 28, 1980, A12; Charles Ray, "Bucking the Trends," *High Country News*, September 27, 2004, www.hcn.org/issues/283/15021.

26. Davis interview, 6. The sense of community support is important to radical nonviolent action; see Barbara Epstein, *Political Protest and Cultural Revolution* (Berkeley: University of California Press, 1991), 220–222; Stock, *Rural Radicals*, 153–163. Peter Matthiessen, "High Noon in the Black Hills," *NYT*, July 13, 1980, A1; Grossman, "Cowboy and Indian Alliances," 357–379. Race relations in South Dakota deserve a more focused study. Grossman has gone into some detail on the importance of the Lakota/white alliance that grew from uranium protests and that has subsequently become important to the state's social justice network. It would be a gross overstatement, however, to suggest that somehow racial tensions have been alleviated in the state.

27. Howell Raines, "'Sagebrush Rebellion' Had Reagan Backing," *Rapid City Journal*, July 19, 1980, 1. In 1979 many western states passed sagebrush initiatives, led by Nevada but closely followed by Arizona, New Mexico,

Wyoming, and Utah. William L. Graf, *Wilderness Preservation and the Sagebrush Rebellions* (Savage, MD: Rowan and Littlefield, 1990); Cawley, *Federal Land, Western Anger.* Nevada state senator Richard Blakemore and Lazalt are quoted in Raines, "'Sagebrush Rebellion' Had Reagan Backing."

28. Kammerer is quoted in McBride, "Cowboy Populists of Meade County." On the definition of "radical producerism," see Stock, *Rural Radicals,* 16. On the culture of vigilantism that later took over this producerist ideal see Stock, *Rural Radicals,* 143–176; on the rise of interest-group politics and its erasure of true agrarian politics see R. Douglas Hurt, "Agricultural Politics in the Twentieth-Century West," in Jeff Roche, ed., *Political Culture of the New West* (Lawrence: University of Kansas Press, 2008), 57. Producerism is often identified with right-wing politics, but as Stock shows there are distinctions between producerism on the left and producerism on the right. While both strands have espoused nativist and racist ideologies, the emergence of new alliances in the 1980s suggests other outcomes; see Grossman, "Cowboy and Indian Alliances"; William C. Pratt, "Using History to Make History? Progressive Farm Organizing during the Farm Revolt of the 1980s," *Annals of Iowa* 55 (1996): 24–45; and Summers, "From Heartland to Seattle." For a more nuanced reading of populism and agrarian radicalism from an earlier era see Charles Postel, *The Populist Vision* (New York: Oxford University Press, 2007); Elizabeth Saunders, *Roots of Reform: Farmers, Workers and the American State, 1877–1917* (Chicago: University of Chicago Press, 1997). The electoral maps from presidential elections provide ample visual evidence that the missile fields belonged to "red state" America; see the American Presidency Project, University of California, Santa Barbara, www.presidency.ucsb.edu. Since 1968 these states have voted Republican in every election, with the exception of Montana and Colorado in 1992 and Colorado in 2008.

29. On mobilization during the American Agricultural Movement and its ties to a politics of producerism see Summers, "From Heartland to Seattle," 316–318. Summers points out that the radicalism of farmers can also be seen in the antiglobalization protests of the 1990s and 2000s. For these adaptive strategies in South Dakota specifically see Grossman, "Cowboy and Indian Alliances." Jane Adams, ed., *Fighting for the Farm: Rural America Transformed* (Philadelphia: University of Pennsylvania Press, 2002).

30. "Silence One Silo," information brochure, n.d., CDGA collection Box S, SOS. Dick Rebbeck, "Family Farming in Peril," *Rapid City Journal,* July 22, 1980, 2.

31. Dick Rebbeck, "Drought Cycle Taking Its Toll in Area," *Rapid City Journal,* July 31, 1980, 2. Inflation and increased energy costs in the late 1970s certainly exacerbated the problems of American farmers. On the farm crisis in the West see Richard White, *"It's Your Misfortune and None of My Own": A History of the American West* (Norman: University of Oklahoma Press, 1991), 559–561; Dick Rebbeck, "Parts of State Taking on Appearance of Desert Southwest," *Rapid City Journal,* July 29, 1980, 1; Neil E. Harl, *The Farm Debt Crisis of the 1980s* (Ames: Iowa State University Press, 1990); Kathryn Marie Dudley, *Debt and Dispossession: Farm Loss in America's Heartland* (Chicago: University of Chicago Press, 2002).

32. "Rancher Finds Many Soviets Share His Fear of Nuclear War," *Rapid City Journal,* January 2, 1983, Kammerer papers. *SD Peace and Justice Center,* February 1985, SDPJC (emphasis in the original). *SD Peace and Justice Center,* March 1985, SDPJC. "Silence One Silo," information brochure; "Agriculture and the Bomb," Spring 1984, *SOS Newsletter,* SOS. Frazier comment is noted in John LaForge and Barb Katt, "Missile Tour Talk," n.d., Nukewatch Archive.

33. "US to Put 40 MX Missiles in Minuteman Air Base Site," *Chicago Tribune,* January 1, 1982, 5; Kammerer interview, February 2007; Day, "Restless Ranchers," 25; Anti-MX flier, South Dakota Peace and Justice Center folder, CDGA box S, SCPC. "Local Officials React," *NYT,* January 1, 1982, 13. Judith Miller noted before the election that in Montana it was the MX issue that was causing debate, not the freeze; see "Nuclear Freeze Debate Important in a Few Races," *NYT,* October 19, 1982, A18; 57 percent of the voters voted for Proposition 91; see "Montana Citizens to End the Arms Race," information pamphlet, n.d.; "Montana Citizens against the MX," SCPC. Nationally the MX was stymied for some time. In 1982 Congress enacted the Jackson Amendment to the Department of Defense Authorization Act, 1983, Pub. L. No. 97-377, 96 Stat. 1830, 1833, 1846–1849 (1982), requiring the president to submit a detailed technical report discussing alternative basing and weapons systems and conditioned funding of the missile project on explicit congressional approval of

the president's proposals. The result was the Snowcroft Commission, which recommended basing 100 MX missiles in aging Minuteman silos.

34. Tad Bartimus and Scott McCartney, *Trinity's Children: Living along America's Nuclear Highway* (Boston: Harcourt, 1992), 225–226.

35. Ibid., 245–255; Lindi Kirkbride, interview with the author, July 2010; Kammerer interview, August 2006; "Linda Kirkbride: Introduction," information bio in Kirkbride papers, Kirkbride Ranch, Meriden, Wyoming.

36. Kirkbride interview; Samuel H. Day Jr., ed., *Nuclear Heartland: A Guide to 1,000 Missile Silos of the Great Plains* (Madison, WI: Progressive Foundation, 1988), 20; William E. Schmidt, "Farmers Accustomed to Missiles but Leery of MX," *NYT*, November 20, 1982, 9. Mae Kirkbride, letter to the editor, "A Call from the Plains: Where Do We Go from Here?," *NYT*, July 21, 1982, A23.

37. "Called Economic Boon," *Los Angeles Times*, November 23, 1982, B7. Schmidt, "Farmers Accustomed to Missiles"; Tad Bartimus, "A Wyoming Ranch Wife Fights the Bomb, but Resistance Has Its Cost," *Los Angeles Times*, July 3, 1988.

38. Carl Kline, telephone interview with the author, July 2006, 4. On the historiography of religion in U.S. history see Kevin M. Schultz and Paul Harvey, "Everywhere and Nowhere: Recent Trends in American Religious History and Historiography," *Journal of the American Academy of Religion* 78, no. 1 (2010): 129–162. This essay points out that secular academics have tended to erase religious history from the mainstream narrative of the United States, particularly the liberal state-building story of the twentieth century. The exception is the intersection of religion and the civil rights movement and religion and the New Right. For the critical connections between prophetic religion and civil rights activism see David L. Chappell's wonderful *A Stone of Hope: Prophetic Religion and the Death of Jim Crow* (Chapel Hill: University of North Carolina Press, 2004), 3. On religious moral rhetoric, especially in the Protestant churches, see William A. Au, *The Cross, the Flag, and the Bomb: American Catholics Debate War and Peace 1960–1985* (Westport, CT: Greenwood Press, 1985); Jim Castelli, *Bishops and the Bomb: Waging Peace in a Nuclear Age* (Garden City, NY: Image, 1983); Donald L. Davidson, *Nuclear Weapons and the American Churches* (Boulder, CO: Westview Press, 1983); and Glass's gloss on the

subject, *Citizens against the MX*, 40–43. On earlier religious opposition to the bomb, the most useful source remains Paul S. Boyer, *By the Bomb's Early Light: American Thought and Culture at the Dawn of the Atomic Age* (New York: Pantheon, 1985). Samuel H. Day Jr., "The New Resistance," *The Progressive* (April 1983), 24. "Marvin Kammerer: Populist Rancher Is Non-Conformist," *Rapid City Journal*, June 2, 1981, Kammerer papers.

39. On national ignorance of the radical peace movement see Richard Pollack, "Witnessing for Peace," *The Nation*, May 2, 1987, 567–568. Day, "New Resistance," 24. On the Plowshares Movement see Arthur J. Laffin and Anne Montgomery, *Swords into Plowshares: Nonviolent Direct Action for Disarmament* (New York: Harper and Row, 1987). On the Berrigan brothers see Fred Wilcox, *Uncommon Martyrs: The Berrigans, the Catholic Left, and the Plowshares Movement* (Reading, MA: Addison-Wesley, 1991); Statement, n.d., Daniel Berrigan file, Berrigan Box, SCPC. They were convicted of burglary, conspiracy, and criminal mischief; they appealed their sentence and the Pennsylvania Superior Court reversed the conviction in February 1984, though that reversal was then appealed and in 1985 the Supreme Court found in the state's favor—returning the case to the Court of Appeals Panel. For details see Laffin and Montgomery, *Swords into Plowshares*, 33–34. Their appearance on the terrorist list was reported by Paul Mango in "Pentagon Spies on Plowshares 'Terrorists,'" October 5, 1989, and by Anthony Kimery in a 1989 story from the *Washington Post*, both in Minuteman III file, Nukewatch Archive.

40. Information on Plowshares actions comes from Laffin and Montgomery, *Swords into Plowshares*, and the Plowshares Web site, http://www.craf tech.com/~dcpledge/brandywine/plow/Chronology.html. On the Gumps see Barry Bearak, "Parish to Prison: A Nuclear Age Martyr Takes a Leap of Faith," *Los Angeles Times*, December 4, 1988, 1. Ann Morrissett Davidon, "Warheads into Plowshares," *The Progressive*, May 1981, 49–51. Epstein, *Political Protest and Cultural Revolution*, calls the religious sector of nonviolent action one that "espouses the politics of example rather than one primarily of strategic intervention or efficacy" (p. 196).

41. "Subsidizing Certain Silos," *SD Peace and Justice Center*, March 1985, SDPJC.

42. Mark Anderlik, telephone interview with the author, July 20, 2011.

43. Day, "Restless Ranchers," 23; Keith Haugland, "Two Held after Silo Trespass," *Great Falls Tribune*, June 6, 1982, 3B. Quote is from "Nuke Protestors to Be Arraigned Today," *Great Falls Tribune*, June 7, 1982, 6A (from microfilm); Anderlik interview.

44. Anderlik interview.

45. A summary of SOS actions and ideas is found in "History in a Nutshell," *SOS Newsletter*, Spring 1984, 2, SOS. In 1982 three were arrested: Anderlik and Zanzing in June, and Linda Greenwald on November 2 (Election Day); in 1983 four were arrested for crossing the silo: John Worcester on February 16, Jim Wienberg on June 22, and Nigel Cottier and Will Kerling on October 24; five others, including Sam Day, were arrested for getting too close to the silo. In August 1985 Thorton Kimes was arrested for entering the site. References to purchasing land run throughout SOS newsletters; *SOS Newsletter*, Winter 1983–1984, 6, SOS. That newsletter notes that original plans were to purchase the entire ranch, 440 acres, but that it was now considered more realistic to purchase a small parcel near the silo. Day mentions that SOS was trying to raise $500,000 for the purpose; see Day, "Restless Ranchers," 25.

46. Day, *Nuclear Heartland*, 70.

47. Day, *Crossing the Line*, 180, 79.

48. In Missouri the project was coordinated by Roy Pell of the Kansas City Interfaith Peace Alliance. The "Show Me!" map was completed in the fall of 1985, in time for a rally and vigil to be held on the anniversary of the first missile Plowshares action. Nukewatch specifically notes orders from Britain, West Germany, and all of the United States; *Nukewatch Newsletter*, December 1986, Nukewatch file, Nukewatch Archive. In Montana the project was spearheaded by the Last Chance Peace Makers; see *Nukewatch Newsletter*, Spring 1987, Nukewatch file, Nukewatch Archive. Day, *Crossing the Line*, 180–181. "Show Me Missiles," *SOS Newsletter*, Autumn 1985, 10, SOS. Day, *Nuclear Heartland*, 25. The number of silos at which vigils were held comes from "Maps Show 150 Nuclear Missile Sites in ND," *Minneapolis Star and Tribune*, July 24, 1986, 8B, Nuclear Heartland file, Nukewatch Archive. On a tradition being born see Day, *Crossing the Line*, 181. For annual vigils see *Nukewatch Newsletter*, Spring 1987, Nukewatch file, Nukewatch Archive, which notes that a vigil would be held in April in Mis-

souri. Peace vigils were held in Missouri as late as October 1991; see "Missile Silo Site Action," pamphlet for Knob Noster, October 1991, Nukewatch file, Nukewatch Archive.

49. Day, *Nuclear Heartland*, 54.

50. Ibid., 26.

51. Quoted in "Peace Activists Publish Travel Guide for Missile Silos," *Minneapolis Star Tribune*, September 11, 1988, 2G, Nuclear Heartland, Nukewatch Archive. "Nuts and crazies," quoted in Day, *Nuclear Heartland*, 25. The same sentiment was shared by Art Ekblad, president of the Minot, North Dakota, Chamber of Commerce; see Stacy Herron, "'Nukewatch' Maps Our Deadly Flowers," *Bismark Tribune*, May 6, 1988, clip available in Nuclear Heartland, Nukewatch Archive.

52. Day, *Crossing the Line*, 199.

53. Day, *Nuclear Heartland*, 76–77; Day, *Crossing the Line*, 204–205.

54. Wittner, *Towards Nuclear Abolition*, 339–346, 405. FitzGerald, *Way Out There in the Blue*, points out the political motivations involved in Reagan's appropriation of antinuclear ideas, particularly Star Wars.

55. Kline interview; "A Call to Action," Missouri Peace Planters flyer, October 1991, Nukewatch file, Nukewatch Archive.

7. Dismantling the Cold War

1. Carl Kline, telephone interview with the author, July 2006; Lyndy Ireland, interview with the author, Philip, South Dakota, August 28, 2006. Gene S. Williams, telephone interview with Erin Pogany, January 7, 2003; William Bielmaier, interview with Robert Hildebrandt, Wall, South Dakota, August 22, 2005; both MIMI-NPS. The same sentiment was shared by Norman Fauske in his interview with Steven Bucklin, Wall, South Dakota, August 2005, and by William Cissell in his interview with Robert Hilderbrand, Wall Community Center, South Dakota, August 25, 2005, SDSOHP, 3184; both in MIMI-NPS. Kammerer is quoted in "The Peace Dividend—with a Price Tag," *Newsweek*, December 9, 1991, 34.

2. Timothy Pavek, interview with Stephen Bucklin, May 20, 1999, MIMI-NPS; and Pavek, interview with the author, Ellsworth Air Force Base, South Dakota, August 28, 2006.

3. The Atlas and Titan missiles had been deactivated but not before being replaced by Minuteman and MX missiles. The total number of strategic warheads in 1990 was 13,395 (7,816 more stockpiled) for the United States and 11,815 (21,700 more stockpiled) for the Soviet Union; "Figure of US and USSR/Russian Nuclear Stockpile, 1945–2002," Natural Resources Defense Council, November 2002, www.nrdc.org. On nuclear weapons costs and numbers over time see Stephen Schwartz, ed., *Atomic Audit: The Costs and Consequences of U.S. Nuclear Weapons since 1940* (Washington, DC: Brookings Institution Press, 1998). On the sleight of hand of nuclear disarmament discussions see Fred M. Kaplan, "SALT: The End of Arms Control," *The Progressive*, January 1978, 22–27.

4. In the SALT talks, for example, Nixon intended to negotiate limitations while also working toward an antiballistic missile (ABM) system and multiple independently targeted reentry vehicle warheads. Reagan, too, linked arms talks to new weapons systems—namely the Strategic Defense Initiative and to some extent the MX. Nixon and Ford negotiated SALT I and II in the 1970s. The first limited ABMs to two per country and put limits on ICBMs and submarine-launched ballistic missiles. SALT II, never ratified by Congress or the Soviets, placed more limits but did not stop armaments. On the end of the Cold War diplomacy see Don Oberdorfer, *From the Cold War to a New Era: The United States and the Soviet Union, 1983–1991* (Baltimore: Johns Hopkins University Press, 1998); Francis FitzGerald, *Way Out There in the Blue: Reagan, Star Wars and the End of the Cold War* (New York: Simon and Schuster, 2000); Lawrence S. Wittner, *Toward Nuclear Abolition: A History of the World Nuclear Disarmament Movement, 1971–present* (Stanford, CA: Stanford University Press, 2003), 253–484.

5. Richard Hornik, "The Peace Dividend: Myth or Reality?," *Time*, February 12, 1990. For thoughts on spending see especially Seymour Melman, "What to Do with the Cold War Money," *NYT*, December 17, 1989, F3; Michael Oreskes, "Poll Finds US Expects Peace Dividend," *NYT*, January 25, 1990, B9. Oreskes reports that three of four Americans expected that thawed relations would lead to cuts in military spending; John J. Fialka, "'Peace Dividend' from Winding Down Cold War Would Disappear into Sinkhole of U.S. Deficit," *Wall Street Journal*, December 4, 1989, A16. Molly Moore, "Troops, Arms Cut Modestly; Strategic Spending Up," *Washington Post*, January 30, 1990, A1.

6. Pavek, interview with the author.

7. Jeffrey Engel et al., *The Missile Plains: Frontline in America's Cold War* (Historic Resource Study, Minuteman Missile National Historic Site, South Dakota, 2003), 143. This calculation comes from the following figures: the yield of a single W-87 warhead is 300 kilotons; each MX had 10 separate warheads and there were 50 MX missiles deployed for a total of 150 megatons. The Minuteman IIIs, of which there were 500, each carried three separate warheads—some W-62 and some W-78, with yields of 170 and 335 kilotons, respectively. In total, Minuteman IIIs represented some 404 megatons. Nuclear weapons data can be found at www.nrdc.org; "The Summit Goodfellas," *Time*, August 5, 1991.

8. Pavek, interview with Bucklin; Pavek, interview with the author.

9. "Treaty between the United States of America and the Union of Soviet Socialist Republics on the Reduction and Limitation of Strategic Offensive Arms," July 31, 1991, Moscow, www.state.gov.

10. *Record of Decision for the Deactivation of the Minuteman II Missile Wing at Ellsworth Air Force Base, South Dakota* (Ellsworth AFB, November 18, 1991), MIMI-NPS. *Draft Environmental Impact Statement* (Air Force, SAC Headquarters, July 1991).

11. Tim Pavek, "Minuteman II: The End of an Era," Ellsworth Air Force Base, *Deactivation Newsletter*, February 1997, MIMI-NPS.

12. Williams interview; Pavek interview with the author. *Draft Environmental Impact Statement*, 2. For how the Corps of Engineers was going to deal with these concerns see "Deactivation Process Review," which outlines working with South Dakota's Environmental Protection Agency, recovering salvaged storage tanks, testing water and soil at hundreds of places, and monitoring water and soil until 1997. Similar issues arose in Missouri: "Minuteman II Missile Sites, Landowner Information," Missouri Department of Natural Resources, March 24, 2011, www.dnr.mo.gov; Gene Williams, interview with the author, Kadoka, South Dakota, August 31, 2006.

13. Quoted in Peter T. Kilborn, "Ranchers Wary of Plan to Wreck Missiles Silos," NYT, August 17, 1992, A12.

14. Williams, interview with Erin Pogany, 20. As in the 1960s, dues were collected (this time $50) and meetings held; "Williams to Meet SD Delegation," *Rapid City Journal*, March 3, 1993, Correspondence and Reports, 1965–1993, JFP.

15. Quoted in Carson Walker, "Healing the Scars," *Sioux Falls Argus Leader*, October 19, 1992, 1.

16. Senators Daschle and Johnson, Letter to Donald B. Rice, Secretary of the Air Force, July 7, 1992, Correspondence and Reports, 1965–1993, JFP.

17. The number of meeting attendees comes from "Landowners Not Satisfied with Answers of Government on Missile Deactivation," *Pennington County Courant*, August 13, 1992, MIMI-NPS. Paul Jensen, Letter to Daschle, August 17, 1992, "Landowner Impact Statement," MALA file, MIMI-NPS (emphasis added). "Fact Sheet," August 6, 1992, "Congressional Inquiry: Minuteman Deactivation," *BAS*, March 1995, 35.

18. Paul Hoversten, "Treaty's 'Big Risk,'" *USA Today*, September 17, 1992, MIMI-NPS. Paul Jenson, Letter to Daschle, "Minuteman Deactivation Landowner Impact Statement," August 17, 1992, MIMI-NPS. Williams, interview with Erin Pogany, 20.

19. Paul Eakins, "Missile Bases Find New Purpose," *Topeka Capital Journal*, December 3, 2000, www.cjonline.com/indepth/missilesilos/stories/120400_missilebases.shtml. "Subterra Castle: Missile Silo Home," Roadside America, www.roadsideamerica.com; Nathan A. Ferguson, "Bless Our Happy Missile Silo," www.nateferguson.com.

20. Hoversten, "Treaty's 'Big Risk'"; Kilborn, "Ranchers Wary," A12; Engel et al., *Missile Plains*, 145; Williams, interview with Erin Pogany, 20–21.

21. Larry Pressler, Letter to Paul Jensen, October 23, Correspondence and Reports, 1965–1993, JFP. On September 26, Pressler indicated that he would submit an amendment to START during the ratification process, and he introduced the topic on this day. However, it was not until the treaty ratification discussions on September 30 that he formally introduced 3227; *Congressional Record*, 102nd Cong., 2nd sess., September 30, 1992, 28205–28208 and 28880–28884; "Silo Amendment Adopted by Senate," *Rapid City Journal*, October 1, 1992.

22. John Felleman, Jonathan Herz, and Sidney Draggan, "Environmental Impact Assessment," in Cutler J. Cleveland, ed., *Encyclopedia of Earth* (Washington, DC: Environmental Information Coalition, National Council for Science and the Environment, 2010). Eileen Maura McGurty, "From NIMBY to Civil Rights: The Origins of the Environmental Justice Movement," *Environmental History* 2, no. 3 (July 1997): 301–323; Zoltan

Grossman, "Cowboy and Indian Alliances in the Northern Plains," *Agricultural History* (Spring 2003): 355–389; Paul Jensen, interview with the author, Rapid City, South Dakota, August 2008. On land return see 28th Civil Engineer Sqaudron, *Missile Site Deactivation Newsletter*, March 2001, Ellsworth AFB, MIMI-NPS.

23. Williams, interview with Erin Pogany, 19. Kovarik is also noted in Hoversten, "Treaty's 'Big Risk.'" On the rural western response to the environmental movement and environmental legislation see James Morton Turner, "The Specter of Environmentalism: Wilderness, Environmental Politics, and the Evolution of the New Right," *Journal of American History* 96 (June 2009): 123–149; R. McGreggor Cawley, *Federal Land, Western Anger: The Sagebrush Rebellion and Environmental Politics* (Lawrence: University of Kansas Press, 1993); James McCarthy, "The Good, the Bad, and the Ugly: Environmentalism, Wise Use, and the Nature of Accumulation in the Rural West," in Bruce Baun and Noel Castree, eds., *Remaking Reality: Nature at the Millennium* (New York: Routledge, 1998), 126–149; Jacqueline Vaughn Switzer, *Green Backlash: The History and Politics of Environmental Opposition in the U.S.* (Boulder: University of Colorado Press, 1997). Jensen interview. Bielmaier interview, 9.

24. Environmental Protection Agency, "Superfund Clean-Up: Ellsworth Air Force Base," www.epa.gov/region8/superfund/sd/ellsworth/index.html. For a summary of uranium issues see Peter Matthiessen, "High Noon in the Black Hills," *NYT*, July 13, 1980, A1.

25. "Deactivation Process Review" (prepared for the Grand Forks START Meeting, March 18, 1996), 5, MIMI-NPS. For a description of blasts see "Workers Now Dismantling 300 Midwestern Missile Facilities," *AAFM Newsletter*, April 1994, 6. *Draft Environmental Impact Statement*, 2. See Dan Daly, "Explosions at Missile Silos Feared," *Rapid City Journal*, July 8, 1992, MIMI-NPS; and Williams, interview with Erin Pogany, for the sentiment that anything that can go wrong will.

26. "Fact Sheet," August 6, 1992; Colonel Michael R. Emerson, Chief, Programs of Legislation Division, USAF, Letter to Daschle, July 27, 1992; both in Correspondence and Reports, 1965–1993, JFP. The Federal Property Act and Administrative Services Act of 1949 stipulates that other government agencies have right of first refusal; the McKinney Act assures that

the same property is made available for homeless housing. For more on this see 28th Civil Engineer Sqaudron, *Missile Site Deactivation Newsletter*, March 2001. While most landowners would have been granted first refusal, some would have been subject to this more arcane procedure. However, because the Air Force failed to articulate these issues clearly, many people thought all landowners would be unable to repurchase the land. The question in 1992 was really who would have right of first refusal when *more than one* landowner had adjacent lands. *Congressional Record*, 102nd Cong., 2nd sess., October 8, 1992, clipping in Correspondence and Reports, 1965–1993, JFP.

27. *Congressional Record*, 102nd Cong., 2nd sess., October 8, 1992, 34582; S. 3380 would amend U.S. Code 10-9781 and Public Law 100-180. *Congressional Record*, 103 Cong., 1st sess., January 27, 1993, 1417.

28. "Missile Plots Offered to Nearby Landowners," *Rapid City Journal*, September 15, 1993. For final costs see "Deactivation Process Review," 4.

29. The last silo was K-6; Tim Pavek, "Minuteman II Deactivation Program," information sheet, 1 (Rapid City, SD: EAFB, n.d.), MIMI-NPS.

30. John Harris, "Nuclear Missiles Will Be Missed in S.D., Some Say," *Sioux Falls Argus Leader*, April 10, 1994, 5D; see also Pavek, interview with the author, 14; Chuck Raash, "Coming in from the Cold War," *Sioux Falls Argus Leader*, November 12, 1993, 1A; Cara Hetland, "The Last Minuteman," Minnesota Public Radio, September 25, 2005, http://news.minne sota.publicradio.org/features/200109/26_hetlandc_minuteman-m/. Pavek, interview with Bucklin, 20; Ireland interview.

31. Kilborn, "Ranchers Wary."

32. The other two missions were the 99th Strategic Weapons Wing, activated in August 1989, which assumed primary responsibility for B-1B and B-52 advanced aircrew training, and for a brief time the 812th Strategic Support Wing, activated in 1990; "Ellsworth AFB History," http://www .ellsworth.af.mil/library/index.asp. On Ellsworth regaining its footing see "Assessing the Economic Impact of Ellsworth Air Force Base on Local Communities" (Pierre: South Dakota Department of Labor, 2005), 4–9; Richard Muller, host, "What Is Next for Ellsworth Air Force Base?" (2005), radio broadcast, *South Dakota Focus*, South Dakota Public Broadcasting, Brookings, SD. The Missourian is quoted in Eric Schmitt, "In the Shadow

of the Stealth Bomber, a Missouri Hamlet Booms," *NYT,* December 17, 1994, A8.

33. "Deactivation Ceremony: 44th Missile Wing, Ellsworth Air Force Base," brochure, July 4, 1994; Jensen photos, Jensen ranch, August 2006, copies in author's possession. On community involvement in bases see especially Roger Lotchin, ed., *Martial Metropolis: U.S. Cities in War and Peace* (New York: Praeger, 1984).

34. Jensen, Letter to Tom Daschle, July 1999, in Paul Jensen papers, Rapid City, SD, copies in author's possession. Bielmaier interview, 13.

35. Daschle, Letter to William Cohen, May 24, 1999; Daschle, Letter to Jensen, July 15, 1999; both in Paul Jensen papers, Rapid City, SD, copies in author's possession; 28th Civil Engineer Sqaudron, *Missile Site Deactivation Newsletter,* March 2001.

36. Jensen interview; 28th Civil Engineer Sqaudron, *Missile Site Deactivation Newsletter,* March 2001. "Deactivation Process Review," 4, notes that due to PCB findings at launch sites, there would be deed restrictions on resale; among other things, they would "restrict future water wells and other excavations over 2 feet."

37. Jensen interview, 10.

38. Eduardo Lachica, "Expedited Process for Closing Bases Is Passed by House," *Wall Street Journal,* July 13, 1988, 14; Peter Grier, "Panel Urges Putting Bases on the Block," *Christian Science Monitor,* December 30, 1988, 1; Tom Kenworthy, "Bill to Shut Obsolete Bases Passed," *Washington Post,* October 13, 1988, A1.

39. This is out of a total of 500 installations. For figures and the history of BRAC see Global Security, "Report on Base Realignment and Closure," http://www.globalsecurity.org/military/facility/brac.htm. Lachica, "Expedited Process for Closing Bases Is Passed by House"; Kenworthy, "Bill to Shut Obsolete Bases Passed." Procedures of the 2005 round are outlined in Defense Base Closure and Realignment Commission, *Final Report to the President,* September 8, 2005, Arlington, VA, www.brac.gov; see especially the executive summary and chapter 4, "The 2005 BRAC Process"; for total bases closed and savings accrued from 1988 to 1995 see 313–315. For a history of the various rounds see chapter 3, "Previous Experience with Base Closures."

40. Rumsfeld is quoted in "BRAC 2005: Rumsfeld Recommends 5 to 11 Percent Cut in Infrastructure," *American Forces Press Services,* May 12, 2005, www.defenselink.mil/news/newsarticle.aspx?id=31663; on Rumsfeld's goals see Defense Base Closure and Realignment Commission, "Executive Summary," *Final Report to the President,* 1–2. For local response and mobilization to avoid BRAC review see Chris Han, "BRAC's Economic Impact," *Online News Hour,* August 12, 2005, http://www.pbs.org /newshour/bb/military/brac/econ_effects.html; and Lee Bannville, "Politics Surrounding BRAC," *Online NewsHour,* August 12, 2005 http://www .pbs.org/newshour/bb/military/brac/pol_influences.html. Bannville writes that "by March 2005, two months before the Pentagon published its list of proposed closures, states and local communities had already shelled out more than $10 million to promote and defend their local bases." David Axe, "Fighting for Military Money," *Free Times* (Columbia, SC), August 25, 2004, www.globalsecurity.org/org/news/2004/040825-money -bases.htm.

41. For rural areas see Kenneth Matwiczak, project director, *Economic Impact of Rural Military Base Realignment and Closure* (Austin: LBJ School of Public Affairs, University of Texas, 2006); Tadlock Cowan, "Military Base Closures: Socioeconomic Impacts," CRS Report for Congress, May 18, 2005, RS22147, www.fas.org/sgp/crs/natsec/RS22147.pdf, 4. For Governor Rounds's comments see "What Is Next for Ellsworth Air Force Base?" Jim McKeon is quoted in "The Impact of the Recommendation to Close Ellsworth AFB," *Online NewsHour,* August 12, 2005, www.pbs.org/news hour/bb/military/brac/case_studies_ellsworth.html.

42. Allison Crews, "Interacting with Base Realignment and Closure Commission," *Economic Development Review* (Winter 1996): 74. On "military value" see Defense Base Closure and Realignment Commission, *Final Report to the President,* v.

43. Mike Allen, "Thune Delivers on Campaign Vow," *Washington Post,* August 27, 2005, A6.

44. For savings and deliberations about Air Force installations see Defense Base Closure and Realignment Commission, *Final Report to the President,* 111–177. John Hendren and Mark Mazzetti, "Grass-Roots Efforts Helped Save Bases," *Los Angeles Times,* August 28, 2005, A16; Allen,

"Thune Delivers." For BRAC procedures, including the stipulation that two commissioners visit communities near proposed base closures see Defense Base Closure and Realignment Commission, *Final Report to the President*, 326.

45. Chet Brokaw, "Leaders Vow to Fight to Keep Base Open," *Wyoming Tribune*, May 14, 2005; Jesse Hamilton, "Air Base Neighbors Fear a Hard Landing," *Hartford Courant*, June 20, 2005, A1.

46. According to the California Institute for Federal Policy Research, "California Capitol Hill Bulletin," vol. 12, bulletin 12, May 6, 2005, www .calinst.org/bulletins/b1212.htm#_1_2. George McGovern, interview with the author, August 28, 2006.

47. Certainly there was discussion of how to adjust to closure, but it was secondary to the efforts to keep the base around, as is evinced in the amount of media coverage. During the radio broadcast "What Is Next for Ellsworth Air Force Base?," Rounds said that even if it was expensive, it would be good to go after something that put hundreds of millions of dollars back into the economy. As for local development in the event of base closure, Rounds said, "We don't have a grand plan to bring someone in from out of state to fix something."

48. The considerations for BRAC commissioners were those of "military value," including "current mission," "condition of facilities," ability to accommodate future needs, and overall cost. The "other considerations" were cost of realignment, economic impact, existing infrastructure, and, finally, environmental impact; see Defense Base Closure and Realignment Commission, *Final Report to the President*, "Executive Summary," v. "Ellsworth Air Force Base: BRAC in Business," *FedGazette*, November 2005, www.minneapolisfed.org.

49. Marvin Kammerer, "Protect Land Near Ellsworth," *Rapid City Journal*, February 1, 1997, Kammerer papers, Kammerer Ranch, Elk Vale, South Dakota. Others also suggested that keeping the base open for economic reasons would be akin to welfare; see Hamilton, "Air Base Neighbors Fear a Hard Landing."

50. Commissioner Anthony Principi is quoted in "BRAC Commissioners," *Online NewsHour with Jim Lehrer*, August 26, 2005, www.pbs.org /newshour.

51. "South Dakota Ellsworth Development Authority Appointed," http://tsd.sd.gov/images/Ellsworth_Development.pdf; Ellsworth Development Authority, http://ellsworthauthority.org/.

52. "28th Bomb Wing: 2010 Economic Impact Analysis," Ellsworth AFB, www.ellsworth.af.mil.

Conclusion

1. On the creation of the Minuteman Missile National Historic Site see Sue Lamie, former MIMI historian, interview with the author, February 20, 2004. The fuel would have kept the "active" missile upright; when empty, the missiles tend to hunch and collapse on themselves. See "Minuteman Returns to South Dakota," *AAFM Newsletter*, September 2001, 5. For more on this process see Jeffrey Engel et al., *The Missile Plains: Frontline in America's Cold War* (Historic Resource Study, Minuteman Missile National Historic Site, South Dakota, 2003), 142–162. See Gretchen Heefner, "Missiles and Memory: Dismantling South Dakota's Cold War," *Western Historical Quarterly* 38 (Summer 2007): 181–203.

2. Robert Mansfield quoted in "Minuteman Returns to South Dakota," *AAFM Newsletter*, September 2001, 5. Kammerer quoted in "Minuteman Relegated to Monument Status," *Air Force Times*, June 14, 2001. Minuteman *Missile National Historic Site Establishment Act of 1999*, Pub. L. No. 106-115, 106th Cong., 1st sess., November 29, 1999. Five million dollars from the Defense Department was requested because of NPS shortfalls.

3. The process of creating the historic site and thinking about its interpretive materials is covered in NPS, "Special Resource Study for Minuteman Missile Sites: Management Alternatives and Environmental Assessment" (Washington, DC: Department of the Interior, Department of Defense, and the U.S. Air Force Legacy Resource Management Program, 1995), MIMI-NPS; NPS, "Minuteman Missile National Historic Site, General Management Plan and Environmental Impact Statement Newsletter" (NPS, Department of the Interior, March 2002), http://planning.nps.gov/document/miminews2.pdf; and *Long-Range Interpretive Plan, Minuteman Missile National Historic Site, Final Draft* (NPS, Department of Interior, Harpers Ferry Design Center, 2006), http://www.nps.gov/hfc/pdf/ip/mimi

-lrip-2006.pdf. Sue Lamie, e-mail to the author, May 26, 2005; Lamie, interview with the author, February 20, 2004. For thinking about national memory and commemoration, I have drawn on the work of Edward Linenthal, who notes that veneration is "designed to ensure continued allegiance to patriotic orthodoxy" and a "symbolic defense against various forms of ideological defilement"; Linenthal, *Sacred Ground: Americans and Their Battlefields* (Champaign: University of Illinois Press, 1993), 5. See also his *Unfinished Bombing: Oklahoma City and American History* (New York: Oxford University Press, 2003) and *History Wars: The Enola Gay and Other Battles for the American Past* (New York: Henry Holt, 1996); G. Kurt Piehlur, *Remembering War the American Way* (Washington, DC: Smithsonian Institution Press, 2004), 160; John Bodnar, *Remaking America: Public Memory, Commemoration, and Patriotism in the Twentieth Century* (Princeton, NJ: Princeton University Press, 1992). For wording on the plaque see NPS, *Draft General Management Plan/Environmental Impact Statement, 2008* (NPS, Department of the Interior, 2008), ii, http://www.nps.gov/history/history/online_books/mimi/mimi_gmp.pdf.

4. Wendy McNeil, interview with Erin Pogany, Waco, TX, February 3, 2003, MIMI-NPS. Linenthal, *Sacred Ground*, 1–6. Of course, Americans did die in the Cold War during the dozens of limited, proxy wars that were fought around the globe, most notably in Korea and Vietnam. But I am treating these conflicts as separate here because in my research I have found that military personnel seem to do this. For more on the process of creating national memorials for the Korean and Vietnam Wars see Piehlur, *Remembering War*, chapter 5, "From the Korean War to the Vietnam Veterans Memorial." "Minuteman Returns to South Dakota," 6.

5. Bodnar notes that weaving many narratives into a "paradigm of innovation and progress" has long been a way to overcome conflicting interpretations of a historical marker (*Remaking America*, 247).

6. The total cost of the U.S. nuclear weapons program was a minimum of $5.5 trillion, nearly 29 percent of total military spending from 1945 to 1996. Stephen Schwartz, "The Costs of U.S. Nuclear Weapons," Issue Brief, Nuclear Threat Initiative, October 1, 2008, www.nti.org. There were 925 Minuteman I missiles procured, each costing $32.11 million; 668 Minuteman IIs, with a unit cost of $24.55 million; and 840 Minuteman IIIs,

costing $28.14 million each; see Stephen Schwartz, ed., *Atomic Audit: The Costs and Consequences of U.S. Nuclear Weapons since 1940* (Washington, DC: Brookings Institution Press, 1998), 107. These figures do not include construction and maintenance or warhead costs. The total cost of Minuteman III warheads was approximately $48 million per missile. The Department of Defense estimates that it costs $1.6 million per year to maintain each Minuteman missile and that more than $100 billion was spent between 1962 and 1995 on operations; Schwartz, *Atomic Audit*, 108.

7. The Minuteman III's each carry three warheads (ranging from 335 to 475 kilotons). For missile specifications see Duncan Lennox, ed., *Jane's Strategic Weapons Systems*, Issue 50 (Surrey: Jane's Information Group, January 2009), 196–198. For the effects of a 300-kiloton warhead see Report of the International Commission on Nuclear Non-Proliferation and Disarmament, *Eliminating Nuclear Threats: A Practical Agenda for Global Policymakers* (Tokyo, November 2009), http://www.icnnd.org, and Lynn Eden, *Whole World on Fire: Organizations, Knowledge, and Nuclear Weapons Devastation* (Ithaca, NY: Cornell University Press, 2004).

8. David Holley, "Cold War–Era Chills. Tourists Welcome," *Los Angeles Times*, June 24, 2007, www.latimes.com.

9. The film is *Partners for Peace*, Minuteman Missile National Historic Site film, time marker: 40 seconds, http://www.nps.gov/mimi/index.htm. On limiting missiles see Jerome Weisner, "Arms Control: Current Prospects and Problems," *BAS*, May 1970, 6–7. Maxwell D. Taylor, *The Uncertain Trumpet* (New York: Harper, 1960), 148, 158. For corroboration of this see Schwartz, "The Costs of U.S. Nuclear Weapons."

10. *Long-Range Interpretive Plan*, 20.

11. I borrow this term from Andrew Bacevich, *The New American Militarism: How Americans Are Seduced by War* (New York: Oxford University Press, 2006).

Acknowledgments

Without the warmth and openness of the people of western South Dakota, this project would not have been possible. During research trips across that vast stretch of "sameness," dozens of individuals provided food, lodging, information, support, and, in one case, a tow from the side of the road. I found quickly that when Dakotans ask you to stay in their homes, they mean it. Special recognition goes to those who agreed to be interviewed for this project: Lyndy and Shorty Ireland, Paul Jensen, Marvin Kammerer, Carl Kline, Tim Pavek, and Gene S. Williams. Outside of South Dakota, others were also generous with their time. Thank you to Mark Anderlik, Lindi Kirkbride, Sue Lamie, Colonel Charlie Simpson, Jeff Tracy, and Bonnie Urfer. Many others deserve my appreciation for informal conversations. The people working at the Minuteman Missile National Historic Site in Cactus Flats were generous with their time and materials. They have worked hard to put together an educational historic site regarding the missiles and the Cold War. The historians and interpreters at the site have amassed a trove of documents and artifacts that will be invaluable for future historians of the Cold War.

This project germinated far from the plains of western South Dakota, in New Haven, Connecticut. Yale University is a remarkably open and supportive place to study history. I have had the privilege of working with inspiring professors and graduate students who have shaped my thinking and ability to parse the past. I would like to thank, in particular, my advisers for their patience and continual willingness to talk through changes in direction and new discoveries. John Mack Faragher, John Lewis Gaddis, Beverly Gage, and Matthew Frye Jacobson have consistently provided fresh perspective and pushed my work in directions I had not anticipated. Thanks also to Jean-Christophe Agnew, David Blight, Joanne Freeman, Valerie Hansen, Mary Ting Yi Lui, and Jonathan Spence. For all of your unique viewpoints, I am most grateful.

The graduate student community at Yale is truly outstanding. My thinking benefited from informal and formal conversations with countless colleagues. I first began to think about memory and the Cold War during a research seminar. Some of my early ideas about these issues were expressed in "Missiles and Memory: Dismantling South Dakota's Cold War," *Western Historical Quarterly* 38 (Summer 2007): 181–203. Many thanks to the editors and reviewers there for their thoughtful insights. My writing group deserves particular praise: Adam Arenson, Jenifer Van Vleck, Helen Veit, and Erin Wood. Over three years they have read countless derivations of this project. I hope they recognize their own contributions in what appears here. Of course, only I am to blame for any errors. Others have provided invaluable moments of inspiration from the humdrum of writing. Thanks to Gerry Cadava, Blake Gilpin, Martine Jean, Charles Keith, Scott Kleeb, Ben Madley, Ted Melillo, Mike Morgan, Aaron O'Connell, Katie Scharf, George Trumbull, and Susie Woo. Over the years, friends in and out of academia have kept me honest. There are too many to mention here, but my life and thinking have only been enriched by your presence.

The Connecticut College History Department has been a great home while I completed this book. The faculty and students in New London have encouraged me to see things in new ways. Catherine McNicol Stock has been a good friend and mentor, demonstrating to me time and time again that it is possible to be a good historian, teacher, and person at the same time. A special thanks also to Deb Bensko, James Downs, Nancy Lewandowski, Fred Paxton, Sarah Queen, and Lisa Wilson for going out of their way to encourage my work.

History is a collaborate enterprise, and I have been lucky to get feedback on my work at many points along the way. Talks given at meetings of the

Western History Association, the Barnes Club at Temple University, the Society for Environmental Historians, the Boston University Political History seminar, the American Historical Association's annual meeting, Yale's Colloquium on International Security Studies, and the Huntington Library all helped hone my thinking on a number of issues. I am grateful to the organizers, panelists, and audiences at these forums. A special thanks to Jim Campbell, Ron Doel, Ryan Edgington, Monica Gisolfi, Neil Maher, and Bruce Schulman, all of whose paths I will gladly keep crossing. I recently discovered the New England Branch of the Western History Association, which has proven a great place for quiet conversation amidst what usually amounts to a great deal of noise. I have also benefited from generous financial support. A Beveridge Grant from the American Historical Association provided research money. Funds from the Howard Lamar Center, Smith Richardson Foundation, and Yale Graduate School were instrumental.

At Harvard University Press, Kathleen McDermott has been a wonderful editor. She has kept her distance when need be and then swooped in with accurate and thoughtful interventions at the right moment. I could not have asked for better confidence. Many thanks also to Andrew Kinney and John Donohue for their patience and attention to detail.

My family deserves special mention. They have not always known what I am working on, but they have never wavered in their support. My parents, John and Elisabeth Heefner, taught me early on to question almost everything and to find hidden stories in the strangest of places. At various times over the past few years my mother has been my travel companion and research assistant, reminding me to take every story seriously. My sister and brother and their families prod me to see things from new perspectives, rejecting the idea that there is one, academic way to view the world. They have helped care for my children and husband when I have wandered off to the Dakotas in search of missile silos. My in-laws, Barbara Bergstein and Michael Garelick, and Jerry Bergstein have magically seemed to know when to ask questions and when to pretend there is no book being written. Irv and Louise Bergstein have kept me refreshed with their own stories of the past.

My children, Eleanor and Owen, managed to grow up faster than this project. Knowing that someday they will read what I write has always made me work harder. It is my hope that by then, the Minuteman missiles—along with all nuclear weapons—will truly be history.

Finally, to my husband, Brian, whose brilliance and calm have kept me on track. He has been my sharpest critic and best editor, pulling me back from more than one digression. All along he has reminded me that my work is important, and so is our life. He has gamely gone along with schemes to turn research trips into family vacations (Tucson in July? Baltimore in January?). At times he has forced me to turn the computer off. All the while he has been an amazing father, cook, and bartender, keeping my wineglass forever half-full. This has been just one of our many adventures together.

Index

08/31/12